Twisting in the Wind
The Murderess and the English Press

Women accused of murder in nineteenth-century England got bad press. Broadsides, newspapers, and books depicted their stories in gruesome detail, often with illustrations of the crime scene, the courtroom proceedings, and the execution. More than murders committed by men, murders by women were sensationalized. The press – and the public – were fascinated by these acts 'most unnatural' of the fairer sex.

Judith Knelman contends that this portrayal of the murderess was linked to a broader public agenda, set and controlled by men. Women were supposed to be mothers and wives, giving and sustaining life. If a woman killed her baby or husband, she posed a threat to patriarchal authority. Knelman describes the range and incidence of murder by women in England. She analyses case histories of different kinds of murder, and explores how press representations of the murderess contributed to the Victorian construction of femininity.

If readers in the nineteenth century shivered at accounts of murder by women, we should get an equal chill up the spine today reading about how these women were cast out. *Twisting in the Wind* is a book that won't leave any of its readers – true crime fans, sociologists and criminologists, historians, or researchers in women's studies – hanging in doubt.

JUDITH KNELMAN is an associate professor in the Graduate Program in Journalism at the University of Western Ontario.

Twisting in the Wind

The Murderess and the English Press

JUDITH KNELMAN

UNIVERSITY OF TORONTO PRESS
Toronto Buffalo London

© University of Toronto Press Incorporated 1998
Toronto Buffalo London
Printed in Canada

ISBN 0-8020-2915-9 (cloth)
ISBN 0-8020-7420-0 (paper)

Printed on acid-free paper

Canadian Cataloguing in Publication Data

Knelman, Judith, 1939–
    Twisting in the wind : the murderess and the English press

    Includes bibliographical references and index.
    ISBN 0-8020-2915-9 (bound)   ISBN 0-8020-7420-0 (pbk.)

    1. Women murderers – England – History – 19th century.
    2. Murder in mass media – England – History – 19th
    century.   3. Women in the press – England – History –
    19th century.   I. Title.

    HV6046.K53 1998   364.15'23'082094209034   C97-931800-9

University of Toronto Press acknowledges the financial assistance to its publishing program of the Canada Council for the Arts and the Ontario Arts Council.

Let us reform our schools, and we shall find little reform needed in our prisons. – *John Ruskin, 1860*

Contents

viii   Contents

Conclusion   273

Acknowledgments

I would like to express my appreciation to the University of Western Ontario for funding my research trips to England, and to my colleagues, family, and friends for their faith in my project. The generous access and accommodation that I was given at the Weldon Library of the University of Western Ontario, the Robarts Library of the University of Toronto, the British Library, the British Newspaper Library at Colindale, the Bodleian Library, the Public Record Office, the University of Essex Library, Madame Tussaud's archive, the Institute of Historical Research, and the St Bride Printing Library made my task much easier.

In particular I thank Margaret Arnot, John Beattie, Kay Boardman, Howard Book, Undine Concannon, Catherine Crawford, Lelia Driscoll, Beverley Beetham Endersby, Nina Evans, John Fracasso, V.A.C. Gatrell, Phyllis Grosskurth, Kathleen Hartford, Brian Jenkins, Barbara Lew, Margaret MacAulay, Michael Millgate, David Murphy, Alan Noon, Judy Noordermeer, Jean O'Grady, Karen Pollock, Barb Porter, Bruce Robinson, Reuben Rosenblatt, Corinne Salsberg, Rachel Short, and Martin Wiener.

An early version of chapter 1 was presented as a lecture to the University of California Dickens Project conference on Victorian mystery in August 1993. Part of chapter 2 was given as a paper to the Victorians Institute conference on crime and criminality, in September 1994. Part of chapter 3 appears in 'The Amendment of the Sale of Arsenic Bill,' *Victorian Review* 17/2 (Fall 1991), 1–10.

Introduction

I began this study of gender-specific interpretations of nineteenth-century murder in what turned out to be the middle, having stumbled, in an effort to trace the development of sensational reporting in the English press, on a spate of murder trials and executions of women in 1849. This proved to be but one contingent of a steady procession of women to the gallows in the 1840s, which saw the emergence of women as the first serial killers of modern society. How the press responded to this threat is one part of the story; what pushed the women to murder in the first place is another.

Hence this book is divided into three parts. The two chapters in Part I provide a general description of the perception of murder by women. Then the reality of female homicide in the nineteenth century is examined so as to sketch out its causes and extent, and also to provide a context for the analysis of its representation that comes later. In Part II, brief case histories of different kinds of murder, obtained, for the most part, from newspaper coverage, are provided in a roughly chronological progression, with the most significant indicated in a concluding paragraph. Part III shows how the emphasis on sexuality in press representations of murderesses reflected changing popular attitudes and contributed to the Victorian construction of femininity.

Operating on the premise that what constitutes news in any given society defines the limit of 'normal' for that group, I have included all the cases I could find that were of more than routine interest and I have tried to infer why certain circumstances of murder were more or less newsworthy than others. From the perspective of the late twentieth century, the desperation of poor mothers who saw no alternative to killing their children, and the brisk, cheerful industry of baby-farmers seem colossal mistakes, but they were mistakes made largely in good faith in a society where discrepancies between haves and have-nots were perhaps more widely tolerated than they would be today. None the less, these examples tell us much about class, gender, and age bias in nineteenth-century England.

My research shows that expectations about criminal behaviour were different for women and for men, in part because they were based on the fears and insecurities of the dominant social group – men. What most threatened the dominant group – subversive aggression by subordinates – was the most reviled.

TRIAL & EXECUTION,
Of Eliza Ross, aged 38, Years.

>≠><≠><≠>

WHO SUFFERED, this Morning at NEWGATE

On Friday Jan. 6th 1832, the Old Bailey was crowded to hear the Proceedings of the day against EDW. COOKE, Aged 60. ELIZA ROSS, aged 38, was placed at the Bar, arraigned before the Deputy Recorder, upon an Indictment Charging them with the Wilful Murder of Caroline Walsh otherwise Caroline Welsh. On the 19th of August last, the Prisoners appeared not to be effected by their awful situation, they pleaded NOT "GUILTY." in a firm voice.

Mr. Bodkin opened the case for the Prosecution,—Mr. Adolphus, detailed the Particular of the case which he said was one of the most extraordinary that ever occured in the annals of crime. The Learned counsel then went through the whole of the circumstance with great minuteness, in allusion to the evidence of the prisoners' son, he said, he must acknowledge that Boys testimony was the most important in the whole case,

Edward Cook, son of the Prisoner when called, has he passed the dock, the prisoners' turned round to him, and the woman spoke something to him, but we could not here what it was, he was a fine looking boy, — He was Examined by Mr. Bodkin, before August last, Father and Mother, and lived in Red Lion court,

the Old Lady, Elizabeth Walsh, coming to the house 7, Goodman's Yard, Minories, on Friday, August 19th.

In the Evening the old lady, my Mother, and myself had had some Coffee fo Supper, it made me and the old Lady Sleepy, and she shortly afterwards stretched herself on my mother's Bed, placed her Hand under her head, some time after, I saw my Mother go to the bed side, & placed her right hand over her Mouth of the old Lady, and the left over her Body, my Mother continued in this possition for for upwards of half-oour the Old woman did not Struggle but her eyes nearly started from the Sockets, I stood by the Fire, and my Father stood by the Window. all the time, In about halfhour after my mother carrred the body down stairs

Henry REYNOLS Surgeon Examined by Mr. Adolphus he stated the reason for the Prisoner keeping her hand on the old woman's mouth, that was sufficient to produce death by suffocation, And the rolling of the eye was considered the action of death,

At an early hour the front of the goal was crowded to excess, and at the usual hour the unahappy culprit was brot on the platform and after a few moments spent in devotion, the drop fell and she was launched into eternity.

Newgate. January 10th, 1832

My dear Sister,

I now embrace the last oppertunity in writing his my last farewell to you, hoping this will be a warning to you, and all others, at my untimely end. There is no living soul can describe my feelings, since I received the awful sentence, it is a just one. For the eye of the owl see's and hears all things, as the crime of " murder," is of the darkest hue, I do not wish to live, therefore you must forget such a Wretch as I am, pray to the Lord to have mercy on my soul, keep from bad company, for in keeping such has brought me to this dreadful end. fare well for ever, Eliza Ross.

>>>>>>>>>>>>>>>>>>>>>>

A Mournful COPY of VERSES

Written on the above circumstances.

Behold a wretched woman here,
that's on a tree hung high,
Oh ! think off the awful crime,
for which alas she died,

On Friday at the bar she stood
It would make your blood run cold
To see a child against her swear,
a little boy scarce twelve yrs. old,

Before his eyes that cruel deed,
the aged womans life she took,
While he did at the fire stand,
and his father out of the window look'd.

The Judge declared the guilty was
and for her crimes did die,
This morning, to public gaze
appeared upon the gallows high.

A poor, old aged woman dear,
this wretch a Murder did engage,
And on her bed did strangle her,
Full 84 years was her age.

Now Justice did her overtake,
for which at last she did die,
The bolt was drawn, a brow had
her last,
and was launched into eternity,

Carter Printer, Rose Lane Spitalfields.

Broadside issued on the execution of Eliza Ross in 1832 for burking. Bodleian Library: Harding B.9 (121).

Courtroom sketch of Mary Ann Burdock, hanged in 1835 for the murder of her elderly lodger. By permission of The British Library. Bristol *Mirror*, 18 April 1835, p. 3.

Courtroom sketch of Sarah Freeman, serial poisoner, hanged in 1845. By permission of The British Library. Taunton *Courier*, 23 April 1845, p. 7.

LIFE, CONFESSION, AND

EXECUTION

OF

HARRIET PARKER,

For the MURDER of Amina and Robert Blake.

Old Bailey, this morning, 8 o'clock.

At an early hour this morning the sheriffs, with their usual attendants, arrived at the prison, and proceeded to the condemned cell, where they found the reverend ordinary engaged in prayer with the miserable criminal. After the usual formalities had been observed of demanding the delivery of the body of the prisoner into their custody, she was conducted to the press-room, where her hair was cut short. The executioner, with his assistants, then commenced pinioning her arms, which operation they skilfully and quickly despatched. During these awful preparations she sighed deeply, but uttered not a word. At a quarter before 8, the arrangements having been completed, the bell of the prison commenced tolling, and the melancholy procession was formed, the reverend ordinary preceding the culprit on her way to the fatal drop, and reading, in a distinct tone, the burial service for the dead. No sound, if we except the deep sighs of the unhappy woman, interrupted the clergyman, as the procession moved along the subterranean passage. On arriving at the steps leading to the scaffold, she turned round, and tremulously thanked the sheriffs and the worthy governor of the prison, for their kind attention to her during her confinement. Then firmly but with a slow motion she ascended the scaffold, on reaching which she was placed in the necessary position. Whilst the executioner was adjusting the fatal apparatus of death, which was done in an incredibly short space of time, she was deeply absorbed in prayer. The executioner, having drawn the cap over her face, retired from the scaffold; and, on the signal having been given the bolt was withdrawn, and the unhappy woman was launched into eternity. A few convulsive struggles were perceptible, and she ceased to exist. After hanging the usual time, the body was cut down, and conveyed into the prison.

The following is a copy of a letter which she addressed to Mr. Blake, the father of the murdered children, with whom she had been living previous to the fatal occurrence :—

"Newgate, Feb. 7, 1848.

"Dear Robert—This is the last time you will ever receive advice from me. My days are numbered : this day fortnight I shall be silent in the grave. Take therefore these few lines into consideration : never again trifle with a woman as you have with me. Promise to forsake all others, and cling once again to her who ought to hold the only place in your heart—

the wife of your bosom. This, Robert, I sincerely wish. I have deeply injured her, and so have you. Let her then, after this, have your best and purest affections. Oh, Robert, had we parted long since, as I requested, my life, and that of those who were so near and dear to you would have been spared. I deserve my awful fate; and God give me strength to go through all ! And Robert, pray that when the bitter cup has passed, I may be received by him who drank a more bitter one than mine to save us all. God in mercy forgive us ! I freely forgive all your wrongs to me. I have prayed that he will fit you for the heavy trial I have brought upon you; and oh ! may we yet meet in that land in which sorrow and misery will flee away. I only ask that you will sometimes shed the tear of pity and forgiveness over my unfortunate lot. You may yet be happy in this world with Esther. Your innocent children are, I trust, in heaven. This is to me a great comfort, and I pray that it may be to you. Awful as my fate is, I would rather die than live again the wretched life I have done for the last twelvemonths. Be warned, Robert, and remember that those who break the sacred tie pledged at the altar of God will never prosper. More than one within these walls can testify to the truth of this by bitter experience. It has brought us to misery, shame, and sorrow. The heart of man can hardly pity us : only one shed a tear of sorrow on my misery at my trial, and that was Mrs. Moore. I wish you to pay some little debts for me, and I shall die much happier if you will. I owe the milk-woman 8d. Bridget did one half-day's work for me ; and likewise Mrs. Washington a trifle ; and the green-grocer, for coals, I think about 2s. 6d. Be sure and answer directly, and tell me you will comply with my last request. Likewise get my marriage lines from Mrs.

Mears. You can inclose it in the letter : it will be a satisfaction to all. Now, Robert, I must conclude ; and that God in mercy may forgive, bless, and prosper you and yours, is the sincere prayer of the heart that dictates these lines. From the unfortunate

"HARRIET PARKER."

COPY OF VERSES.

In Newgate gaol there does bewail,
  In sorrow, grief, and shame,
A wretched female, doomed to die :
  Harriet Parker is her name.
She's doomed to die a shameful death !
  What a dreadful sight to see,
A woman thus to end her days
  Upon the fatal tree !

CHORUS.

The dreadful bell will sound her knell,
  To warn her death is nigh ;
In grief and pain she does complain,
  And for forgiveness cry.

With Robert Blake from Birmingham,
  This wretched woman came ;
He left his wife, and then in guilt,
  His partner she became.
His children, too he brought with him,
  And gave them to her care ;
One seven years old, one five ; they left
  Their mother in despair.

In Cupid's Court, near Golden Lane,
  They lived not long in peace ;
He slighted her, and she declared
  His happiness should cease.
She cruelly his children killed ;
  How dreadful to unfold !
She pressed her hands upon each mouth,
  And left them dead and cold.

O when their mother heard the news,
  Her feelings who can tell !
She wrung her hands in bitter grief,
  And in despair she fell.
" Oh ! cruelty beyond belief
  My children did endure ;
To gratify a wretch they died,
  Both innocent and pure."

The criminal before the bar
  In agony did stand ;
And there she was convicted by
  The laws of God and man,
To die a death of public shame
  Upon the fatal tree ;
And thousands will assemble there,
  Her wretched end to see.

Printed and Published by   1 & 3, Monmouth Court, Bloomsbury.

Broadside issued on the execution of Harriet Parker in 1848 for the murder of her stepchildren. Bodleian Library: Harding B.9 (201).

Courtroom sketch of Sarah Thomas, a servant, hanged for the murder of her employer. By permission of The British Library. Bristol *Mirror*, 21 April 1849, p. 8.

Courtroom sketch of Maria and Frederick George Manning, hanged for the murder of Maria's lover. By permission of The British Library. *Observer*, 28 October 1849, p. 2.

Courtroom sketch of Christiana Edmunds, convicted of child murder. By permission of The British Library. *Penny Illustrated Paper*, 20 January 1872, p. 1.

EXECUTION
OF MARY COTTON,
At Durham, for the West Auckland Poisonings.

This morning Mary Cotton underwent the extreme penalty of the law, at the county gaol, Durham, for the murder of Charles Edward Cotton, her step-son, at West Auckland, in July 1872.

The prisoner since her condemnation has behaved in a calm and respectful manner to those about her. She has been visited by a distant relative, a sister of her stepfather's, but the visit was of a short duration. The prisoner had up till Saturday retained possession of her infant daughter, born in the prison, but on the taking of the infant from her, she displayed great emotion, and gave way to her feelings in a most remarkable and extraordinary manner. She slept but little last night and appeared very restless. She was the minister early this morning, who remained with her until the arrival of the sheriff and other officers. The operation of

pinioning been gone through; she shook hands with the various persons who had been attending on her, and thanked them for their kindness. The remaining necessary precautions having been taken, and everything being in readiness, the procession was formed, and then moved off in a solemn manner toward the place of execution. Having arrived at the place of the place of execution, the forms preliminaries were gone through and the prisoners was left a few moments with the worthy chaplain. The signal having been given, the bolt was drawn, and the unfortunate creature was launced into eternity. The black flag was then hoisted on top of the prison.

This is the first occasion in which a woman has been executed since the year 1799; the last who suffered was Mary Nicholson, who was also convicted of poisoning.

The trial of Mary Cotton, aged 40, for the murder of her step-son, a child of seven years of age, named Charles Edward Cotton, took place at the Durham assizes.

Mr. Russell, in opening the case, stated prisoner had formerly been a nurse at the Sunderland Infirmary; being at that time Mrs. Mowbray, that she afterwards became Mrs. Robinson, and then married a pitman named Cotton, and lived at West Auckland. The family consisted of Cotton, his wife, his two children by a previous marriage, and prisoner's own son by Cotton. Prisoner subsequently fell into straitened circumstances. She was a widow, with a step-son, whose death she was now charged with having caused; and the household then consisted only of these two persons. No doubt she might have found the care of the child irksome and burdensome, seeing that he prevented her following the employment of a nurse, on doing any other service by which

she might have earned her livelihood. Upon the 5th or 7th of July last year the child became ill, and suffered from purging and vomiting, and shortly died. Strict and accurate analysis of the stomach and viscera has led to the conclusion, clear and undoubted, that the child had died from the administration of arsenic. No one but the prisoner had had the care of the child, and that she had also bought an arsenical preparation.

It was proved in evidence that the child was insured in a club; and that she had tried to get him admitted to the workhouse, and complained of the hardship of having to keep him, and on being refused replied, Perhaps it don't matter, as I shan't be troubled with him long.

The jury after one hour in deliberation, found the prisoner Guilty.

The judge then passed the sentence of death on the prisoner in the usual form.

In Durham gaol, in grief lamenting
A wretched woman now doth lie,
For the horrid crime of murder,
A felon's death is doomed to die,
For slaying of her little step-son,
Charles Edward Cotton was his name
That wretch, by Poison him she slew,
And brought herself to grief & pain

For the murder of poor little Cotton
That wholesale poisoner now must die,
Yet for her crimes she now must suffer,
A felon her slave on the scaffold high,

This wretched woman Mary Cotton,
A widow was, as we are told,
Married a pitman, named Cotton,
Who had a child seven years old,
She allowed that poor little darling,
Her acts were dreadful as we had,
None but a demon could have served
him
Yet she robbed him of his life in time

It seems almost past believing,
That such a monster could be found
At this West Auckland poisoner,
Dwelling upon Christians ground,
Her husband Cotton as we find thee,
Died in a suspicious way,
And many others ent'd to his then,
By deadly poison so they say.

It appears the thoughtfule to get mur-
ries,
It we onward means I'll you true
So she contrived a horrid plan, then
The harmless child for to remove,
She went in haste unto the doctor,
But she'll is ill this wretch did say
But it was the schum of study, coming
That took the darlings life away.

Suspicious they were soon aroused,
That all things, they were not right
So his poor body was taken up,
Which brought
to light

Though other murders were found out
For this one she was tried,
And it was proved that by her hand,
That poor Charley Cotton died.

The jury they have found her guilty
For her crime she was tried & cast:
And upon this guilty woman,
The judge the awful sentence past,
Saying Mary Cotton do your crimes
You are now condemned to die,
No earnest hope for mercy b re,
So I would have you pray to God
on high.

Now one and all I pray forgive,
And take warning by her fate,
Lest the hopster in his snare,
And repentance comes to late.
Let me bide nor yet gold,
Cause, you to be a murderer,
Think of the fate of Mary Cotton,
The West Auckland poisoner.

Broadside issued on the execution of serial poisoner Mary Ann Cotton in 1873.
Bodleian Library: Harding B.9 (217).

Contemporary print of Kate Webster, servant, hanged in 1879 for the murder of her employer. From *Trial of Kate Webster,* ed. Elliot O'Donnell (Edinburgh and London: William Hodge & Co., 1925).

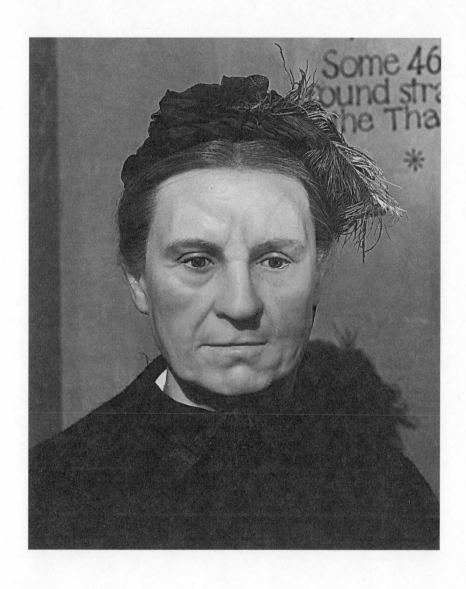

Wax figure of Catherine Flannagan, serial poisoner, hanged in 1884. Madame Tussaud's Archive, London.

Adelaide Bartlett, acquitted in 1886 of poisoning her husband. From *Trial of Adelaide Bartlett*, ed. Sir John Hall (Edinburgh and London: William Hodge & Co., 1927).

Elizabeth Berry, hanged for child murder. By permission of The British Library.
Oldham *Chronicle*, 19 March 1887, p. 3.

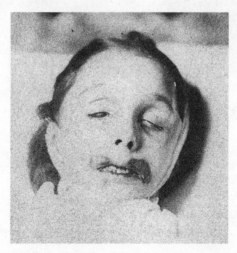

Autopsy photo of Edith Annie Berry, poisoned by her mother in 1887. Public
Record Office, HO144/289/13830.

Penny dreadful, 1889. By permission of The British Library. C. 140.c. 24(6)
Florence Maybrick: A Thrilling Romance.

Florence Maybrick, found guilty in 1889 of poisoning her husband. From *Mrs. Maybrick's Own Story: My Fifteen Lost Years* (New York: Funk & Wagnalls, 1905).

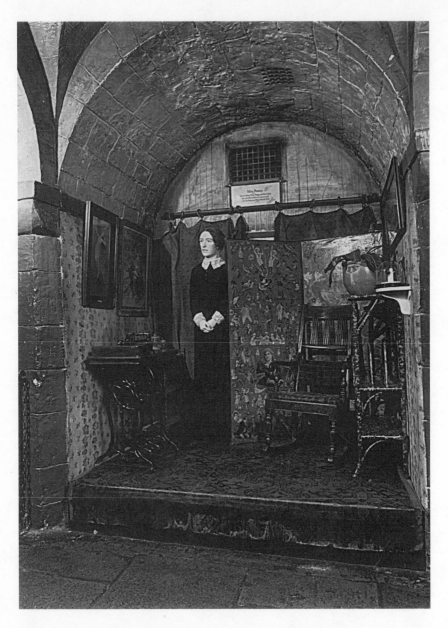

Wax figure of Eleanor Pearcey with her own furnishings. Madame Tussaud's Archive, London.

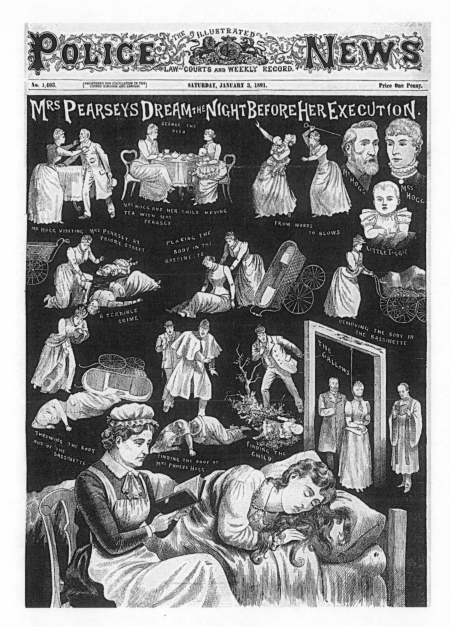

Front-page fantasy on the execution of Mary Eleanor Pearcey, 1890. By permission of The British Library. *Illustrated Police News*, 3 January 1891, p. 1.

Wax figure of Amelia Dyer, serial baby-killer, hanged in 1896. Madame Tussaud's Archive, London.

Part One: Patterns and Perceptions

The Case of the Vanishing Murderess

This book does not attempt to justify murder by women, merely to understand it. Women accused of murder in nineteenth-century England got bad press. It is my contention that women who killed were held in lower regard than men who killed, yet were considered more interesting to contemplate. Were they really as monstrous as they were depicted in broadsides, newspapers, and books?

Until the nineteenth century, murder was thought of as an act that could always be controlled by the will. What set humanity above animals was the restraint of passion by reason. Women's bodies were meant for giving and sustaining life, not for stamping it out. So a woman who killed her baby or flew into a rage and murdered her husband was out of control. She would have to die on the gallows as an example to others. (No matter that others who went temporarily berserk would not remember the moral lesson.)

About the middle of the century, insanity was legally defined, and the law was both more able and more likely to make allowances for madness in murderesses. From there it was a short step to the deduction that women's bodies could betray them, that somehow a state of mind set off by the reproductive function could cause a woman to lose control and kill someone she loved. Thus murder was no longer exclusively an act of free will.

The theory of biological determinism was a mixed blessing for women. While it could save some from the gallows, it could, by the same token, keep them confined to a lunatic asylum for life, irrespective of any improvement in their mental condition. It also

implied links between sexuality and criminality that were not justified. As recently as 1971, Patrick Wilson, in his study of the sixty-
eight women hanged in Britain since 1843, concluded that, because nineteen of them had illegitimate children, women who
committed crimes of violence were often promiscuous.[1] Does an
illegitimate birth prove promiscuity? How many peaceable women
had illegitimate children, and, for that matter, how many men
who were hanged for murder did?

Details about most of the perpetrators of the crimes chronicled
here are sparse, but their life condition is almost always poverty,
be it rural or urban. These are sad stories. The plots are repeti-
tious, most of them beginning and ending with a funeral. The
characterization, where there is any, is contrived, since the press,
by and large, made murderesses seem inhuman.

Though most recorded murders were committed by men, there
was a significantly higher participation rate for women in murder
than in other crimes. But women's murder, as it usually involved
their own unwanted babies or children, was a 'private' crime that
society did not take as seriously as other murder. Relatively few
female perpetrators were implicated in other types of murder.
The rarity and unexpectedness of the murder of adults by women
made exciting news. Taken together, their stories give us a window
into the seething inner life of England at a time of extreme social
upheaval.

DEPRIVATION AND OPPRESSION

By the 'hungry forties,' when murder by women reached an all-
time high, poverty was severe and widespread. Wealth was shifting
from landholders to entrepreneurs, and in the towns that had
sprung up to feed factories, workers were organizing against their
masters. The simple hierarchy of society, in which landowners
owed allegiance to the Crown, servants to their masters, and wives
to their husbands, was falling apart. Trust, custom, fellowship, and
pride of craft gave way to what Carlyle called the 'cash nexus.'

Men were thrown out of farm work into competition for jobs in
urban centres. Working-class women, married or not, were increasingly expected to have paid employment. Families chose to

live crammed together in hunger and squalor rather than disperse to the workhouse, which had its own forms of deprivation. Relations between working-class men and women were tense. Women were less dependent because men were less independent.

As can be expected in a society with a highly visible disparity between the lives of the rich and the poor, there was an alarming – to the rich – amount of criminal activity at the poor end, and a disconcerting – to the poor – tendency on the part of the rich to keep it contained rather than improve conditions so that it would stop. The potential for an explosion was not lost on such contemporary social analysts as Carlyle, Dickens, and Arnold, but warnings of impending anarchy went, for the most part, unheeded. The newspapers tended to cover crime from the comfortable distance that righteousness affords, passing judgment as though criminal tendencies in the deprived were surprising, and turning a blind eye when these apparently operated for the 'good' of society.

There are enough of these stories to set up a pattern. Murder by women in the English underclass was far more prevalent in the 'civilized' nineteenth century than one might think. Thousands of newborn babies were murdered – most of them by their mothers – because their mothers could not provide for them. The pain endured by these women is, in most cases, left to the imagination, but where it has been recorded I reproduce it. Children who got in the way were murdered by their mothers or stepmothers. Families were whittled down by mothers who felt they had to have a little extra money or a little less responsibility. Abusive husbands or employers were attacked by women too angry to be deterred by conscience or consequences. With the exception of new mothers, the women who perpetrated these crimes seem to have been grim, matter-of-fact, and hollow. They were not necessarily, though, antisocial. Indeed, it is highly likely that 'sisterhoods' of female poisoners were a social support in some poor rural areas. Patrick Wilson, in *Murderess*, suggests that a tradition of witchcraft may have been behind clusters of rural poisonings.[2]

It is not necessary to determine the specific conditions in each case that drove a woman to murder: the point is that the misery behind such action was extreme, general, and pervasive, and that the action was a by-product of public apathy to domestic abuse, except when it was an entertainment. Whereas murder by a man frightened the public, murder by a woman, unless it could be explained by insanity, aroused indignation. Until late in the century, very little attempt was made to discover what factors would push women to act against their nature.

In a study of violent criminal behaviour by women in London and Berkshire in the late eighteenth and early nineteenth centuries, Rachel Short remarked on her inability to 'find a fusion of the ideas of the feminine and the criminal to suggest that women have in any way a real and enduring capacity for criminal actions in the same way as do men.'[3] She concluded that society, or at least the press, operated from the premise that women were not in control of their actions while committing crimes. They may have been insane; or under the influence of a man; or overcome by passion, alcohol, or supernatural forces.[4] Women who killed their children or husbands 'were accused of having sunk to the very depths of inhumanity.'[5]

How far do gender roles extend? Can murder be more or less natural for one sex than for the other? Short does not think so, but she offers strong evidence that it was to the advantage of the dominant sex to present women as subordinate in all respects.

By looking at their victims, methods, and motives, we can infer patterns of murder by women, and then look at them in the context of what people believed about such murder. Was there deviant behaviour for murderers or murderesses? If society accepted that some types of murder were to be expected, what was the subtext of these expectations?

According to Martin Daly and Margo Wilson, who have studied murder from the perspective of evolutionary psychology, the predominant variety is that in which unrelated young men destroy each other in competing for females.[6] They argue persuasively that, in humans as in other species, it is natural for a particular male to want to reproduce more than other males in order to perpetuate himself. Most murders, then, are rough, public demonstrations of physical dominance.

This pattern is not evident in reports and statistics of murder in nineteenth-century England. For example, Robyn Anderson's detailed analysis of Old Bailey records between 1856 and 1875 shows that 63 per cent of indictments for murder were for domestic crimes, 44 per cent for child murder, and 19 per cent for spousal murder.[7] Far from struggling to reproduce themselves, the English appear to have been bent on killing off their means of reproduction and their offspring. From the perspective of late-twentieth-century psychology, we can see that, if these people were acting against their own instincts and interests, they must have been driven to it. The Victorians' apparently prosperous and productive middle-class imperialist and industrial society appears to have been built on a rotting foundation of misery and deprivation in the underclass.

MOTIVES AND METHODS

In the cases studied by Anderson, the victims of male murderers (32 per cent) were most commonly their wives, but those of murderesses (91 per cent) were most often babies and children. Perhaps because in England the murder of children, particularly babies, was not unusual in the context of murders generally, it was not unduly publicized. Wife murder, often the unplanned result of a drunken beating, was most of the time fairly casually dismissed as unfortunate by the courts and the newspapers. Husband murder, on the other hand, attracted a great deal of interest, not least because the perpetrator would have had to overcome a handicap of strength and size.

As Mary Beth Wasserlein Emmerichs and others have pointed out, judges and juries in the nineteenth century were reluctant to convict women who had killed their own infants and children. Short found that the label of insanity was often applied to bridge the gap between the expectation of conventional maternal behaviour and the reality of violence. It served as well to explain the particular criminal action under scrutiny 'while sustaining the ideal of women's enduring moral innocence.'[8]

Emmerichs uses the low rate of conviction for women charged with murder to argue further that the courts extended their special treatment for women no matter who the victim,[9] but I would

Figure 1.1
Method of Killing for Fifty Most Notorious Accused Murderesses, 1807–1899

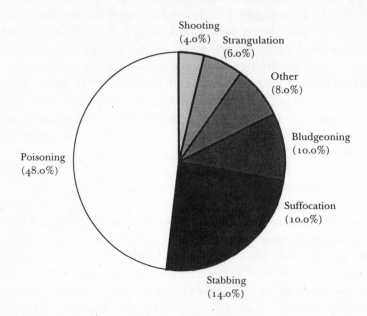

counter that the proportion of murderesses who killed infants and children was so high that any convictions at all would indicate other types of murder. Child murder, especially by women, was tolerated; other, more threatening types of murder were not.

In an analysis of the motives and methods of the fifty most notorious accused murderesses of the nineteenth century (see figure 1.1 and appendix), I discovered that most of them (72 per cent) did not use a visible weapon at all. Of these, 48 per cent used poison, 6 per cent murdered by strangulation, 10 per cent by suffocation, and the other 8 per cent by starvation, neglect, scalding, or drowning. Of those who used a weapon, 10 per cent chose a blunt instrument, 14 per cent a knife or poker, and 4 per cent a gun.

These proportions are consistent with Short's study, which found that 72 per cent of violent crimes by women were accomplished with no weapon, 16 per cent with such domestic weapons as knives or bottles, 12 per cent with other weapons such as brickbats or billhooks, and none with firearms.[10] The crimes ranged from assault and breach of the peace to murder.

Of the accused murderers in Anderson's study, which does not break down figures by gender, 15 per cent beat their victims, fewer than 2 per cent used poison, 41 per cent a sharp instrument, 14 per cent a blunt instrument, and 14 per cent a gun.[11]

Six per cent of the fifty murderesses in my sample were judged insane. At least 70 per cent were guilty of premeditated crimes, and 48 per cent stood to gain financially. Twenty per cent of the women were tried for having murdered their husbands. Only 22 per cent appear to have murdered out of passion – anger, revenge, or jealousy – while another 12 per cent appear to have been motivated by lust.

COMPARISON WITH MALE MURDER

A contemporary analysis of the motives of male murderers tried between 1836 and 1870 shows about one-third to have been driven by greed, another third by passion (revenge, jealousy, anger, or a grudge), and about one-fifth by domestic discord.[12] So it appears that, in comparison with men who killed, women did so more often for money and less often out of passion. Furthermore, as the case descriptions in Part II indicate, a significant proportion of women who killed acted out of an instinct for survival rather than out of greed.

The proneness to notoriety of a murderess was in some sense a reflection of the improbability of her crime. In the first place, as Short has shown, women were often not prosecuted for lesser crimes than murder because, as wives or servants, they were legally in the power of someone who had the authority to discipline them.[13] As a result, the public was not as prepared to accept that women would kill. 'Reflecting popular perceptions, the legal system persistently failed to recognize that women had the same criminal potential as men,' in Short's view.[14] In comparison with her male counterpart, not only was the accusation of murder against a woman unusual, but a conviction was much less likely, as were a death sentence and the possibility that, if rendered, such a sentence would be carried out. Consequently, the farther along this chain she travelled, the greater the likelihood of publicity.

It is clear that women murdered in a different way from men, and that their motives were often different. Women were dominated physically, economically, and politically by men. They could not assert themselves in the way that men could. But it seems unreasonable to argue, as was done throughout the century, that women's murder, because it was subversive, was more vicious than men's. In truth it was simply more frightening to men. In righteously singling out women for particular condemnation, men were perhaps revealing their fear of being sabotaged. It would not be surprising if they wanted to be able to count on continuing their dominance.

There is no suggestion here that murder by women is less reprehensible than murder by men. In fact, there is enough evidence to demonstrate that women are as potentially evil as men, and that men are as potentially out of control as women. As Short has put it, 'beliefs about women's capacity for crime were based upon ideas concerning women's abilities which were far from positive.'[15] The consensus that murder by women was *more* reprehensible was patriarchal. Members of the weaker sex would by definition target weak or unsuspecting victims and use devious methods. A physically inferior specimen is not likely to provoke a confrontation with someone who can crush her.

The disadvantage of women was not merely physical. They were operating on the fringes of society. Women who killed were generally in their twenties or thirties (see figure 1.2) and likely to have babies or young children who were impediments. Few of them went out into the world as men did. The paid employment they worked at was largely centred in the home: servant, nurse, maid, cook, char, laundress, landlady, governess.[16] Therefore the people whom they saw as standing in their way were likely to be related or at least members of the household. The young and the elderly were easy targets because they were weak and defenceless. Husbands would, in ordinary circumstances, be strong antagonists but could be made sick.

Figure 1.2
Age Group of Fifty Most Notorious Accused Murderesses, 1807–1899

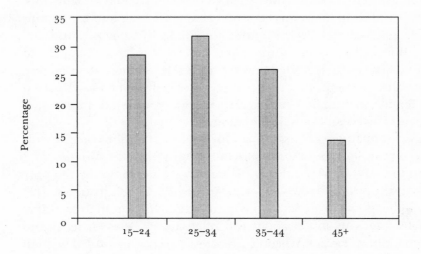

Many careers were ruled out for women in the nineteenth century, but murder was not one of them. In the male value system, however, murdering someone who trusted you was far worse than murdering someone in a confrontation, as would happen between men. Caught by the laws of biology, which decree that it is for women to create and nourish life, murderesses were seen not only to have broken the law of the land, but also to have offended against nature and tradition.

REPRESENTATIONS

To understand the social construction of murder by women, we need to compare the popular culture with the facts. Why did women kill? What were they like, and what did people think they were like? How were they treated? In the nineteenth-century English press can be discerned not only patterns of murders, murder trials, and executions, but also changes in responses to these events.

All murderers were reviled, and women in particular. There was a strong curiosity about how far out of the culture women could venture, that is, about how depraved women could be and how much suffering they could endure. Women's trials and executions were generally very well attended, especially by women. Convicted murderesses who were imprisoned rather than hanged appear to have been more degraded and more closely confined than men in the same position, in part because worse behaviour was expected of female than male prisoners: they were considered 'more emotional, wicked and morally degraded.'[17]

A compilation of sensational murder cases can show us not only the circumstances of ordinary life of working-class women, but also the ways in which deviant women were perceived by the public and the state. How women were treated by the justice system and the press as expectations and rationales for their conduct evolved tells us much about the relationship between legal and social values. Patrick Wilson's *Murderess* describes what led women to the gallows from 1843 on, but not every sensational murder case culminated in an execution. The *Annual Register* is a good source, but less forthcoming about murder trials towards the end of the century than about earlier ones. From the 1830s on, the best place to find this information is Samuel Palmer's index to the *Times*, eccentric though it may be. The more stories recorded under 'Criminal Trials,' the more sensational the case.

The only reliable indicator of sensational murder cases early in the century is the number of broadsides and other printed materials that they occasioned. A few published compilations include such texts, but by far the most useful collections are catalogued at the Bodleian Library under 'Murders and Executions.' The British Library has many murder and execution broadsides as well, some of them catalogued, but most, alas, scattered and uncatalogued and likely to remain so.

The best way to find out about murder trials is to read the newspapers. Trial transcripts are the closest thing to an official record, but they can be more reticent or condensed than newspaper accounts, and, except for the Old Bailey Sessions Papers, they are not easy to find. At the British Newspaper Library at Colindale, one can follow a case in all the papers to get a sense of different agendas, or read a paper through several years of editions to learn what acts were most shocking at the time, or, as I did in the end, read many papers about many cases through a span of a hundred years to be able to spot changing attitudes to crime and to women.

Newspapers are events-driven, but they do not by any stretch of the imagination document all that goes on in a given place on a given day. They are selective and subjective. Newspapers give us what we want to read. If a society wants to read that women who kill are insane or demoniacal, that is how they will be depicted. It is worth considering why the public for so long insisted on this image of murderesses.

Why, now, in an age when gender-neutral language is not only politically correct, but sensible and fair, use the term 'murderess'? 'Murderer' is a convenient generic term, but 'murderess' says so much so simply. It gives us the important information that the killer was a woman, and, furthermore, that there was a distinction made between male and female killers. It connotes glamour, villainy, discrimination, and, above all, nineteenth-century England.

In the early part of the century, broadsides, with their crude sketches and verses, depicted the murderess as a cold, unnatural, ignorant, coarse, defeminized creature. By the 1830s, newspapers were filling her out, enlarging upon details of particular crimes that contributed to this effect. In the 1840s, aversion to the murderess was heightened by a general fear arising from repeated (and justifiable, as it turned out) hints in the newspapers that the incidence of murder by women was much higher than had been thought. By this time, the police were able to conduct reasonably effective investigations, and forensic medicine could sometimes confirm guilt. The sensational press reacted especially strongly to murder by or of a woman of the middle class or to evidence that a woman had murdered more than once.

In one five-year period in England, between 1847 and 1852, thirteen women were executed for murder, and nine more were sentenced to hang but were reprieved. Most of the murders were drab domestic poisonings, but one involved the shooting of her former lover by Maria Manning, a fashionable, exotic, spirited adventuress who, through her position as a lady's maid, had ties to the upper class. She had a strong influence on the popular imagination not only at the time of her trial and execution in 1849, but for many years after that.

From this atypical murderess sprang the stereotypical 'bad' woman of mid-Victorian fiction, a creature who was at the same time charming and repulsive, feminine and animal-like. She was a much more interesting figure than her real-life counterparts. As Virginia Morris suggests in a study of murder by women in Victorian fiction, Victorian readers liked to believe that female killers were oversexed and highly emotional. However, glamorous female criminals – attractive, bold, vengeful, and depraved – did not often surface in real life. Most murders by women were not provoked by passion, and by and large those that were, were sordid and decidedly lower class, of little interest to novelists.[18] Murderesses, apart from their murders, lived ordinary, uneventful lives.

In discussing Victorian women's criminality, I am trying to ignore the middle-class context set up for us originally by the Victorian novel, and more recently by Mary Hartman's classic study, *Victorian Murderesses* (1977). Doubtless there were dark, spirited women like Lizzie Eustace and Lady Dedlock and Lady Audley, but these women, though their conduct was suspicious, immoral, and sometimes illegal, were not dangerous criminals. Nor were Constance Kent, Adelaide Bartlett, Florence Maybrick, and the other 'respectable' women whose cases Hartman describes, though their deviance is fascinating. In truth they were no more typical of Victorian murderesses than they were of Victorian middle-class women.

Murder by women continued to be, for the most part, drab and drawn out, but the image of the murderess acquired and maintained passion, colour, and substance. This was a peculiar symbiosis of fact and fiction validated, not by an actual increase in cases, but by the sensation novel of the 1860s, which portrayed female immorality melodramatically. The garish front page of the *Illustrated Police News* kept this exciting and sex-drenched image going long past the heyday of the sensation novel.

The fictional female criminal had a sexual energy about her that appealed to Victorian readers, whose everyday existence was hemmed in by repressive social mores. The coarseness of this energy was also a factor in her image. She was the embodiment of the classic Victorian conflict between obligation and inclination, a potential angel degraded to whore. Her criminality was evidence of the ultimate wickedness of female sexuality.

The Victorians were eager to flirt with danger in the form of escapist novels or newspaper articles depicting female criminality. They followed these with a prurience fuelled by both admiration and disgust. To this audience, the murderess represented passion unleashed. She had spurned constraints imposed on civilized society, had given in to animal impulses.

NUMBERS AND PROPORTIONS

How rare was murder by women? Between 1855 and 1874, about twice as many men as women were tried for murder, though a much smaller proportion of women was executed;[19] for criminal offences generally, the male–female ratio is usually about six or seven to one.[20] From 1875 to 1879, the proportion is much the same: about 86 per cent of those sentenced to life imprisonment (for all offences) were male, and about 14 per cent female.[21] In 1899, the general criminality of women was estimated at about one-sixth of the total, but 31 per cent of those convicted of murder – nearly twice as many as for crime in general – were women.[22]

The absolute number of murderesses and the proportion of murderers who were female fell after about 1860, but the type of murder committed by women changed as well, so that, by the end of the century, murderesses were killing more adults and fewer of their own children.[23] This trend ensured that at least once every few years a sensational case of murder by a woman would surface in the press. Probably the true murder rate for women was much higher, since it was more easily hidden: women's crime, of necessity, tended to be devious and non-violent. Hartman goes so far as to speculate that there may actually have been more female than male murderers.[24]

Emmerichs contends that, if all the women who were suspected of murder had been brought before the English courts, there would have been more women tried for murder than men. Cer-

tainly baby-farming and infanticide were often ignored by the authorities, and poisoning was difficult to prove. Patrick Wilson suggests that the number of female serial killers was at least equal to
that of their male counterparts.[25] Any student of murderesses has
to come to grips with the chilling probability that the sheer ease of
administering poison and passing off a victim's death as a result of
gastric illness allowed many women to get away with murder.

THE DEATH PENALTY

Martin Wiener reasons that women must have received shorter
sentences on average since they consistently made up a smaller
proportion of average prison populations than of committals.[26]
Short found that, even when convicted of the same crime as men,
women were less likely to be hanged or transported.[27] Anderson's
study of murder trials at the Old Bailey between 1856 and 1875
shows ninety-nine men convicted, and forty-five women. Sixty per
cent of the women were sentenced to one or two years in prison,
while only 17 per cent of the men received sentences this short.
Of the men, 54 per cent were sentenced to death; of the women,
22 per cent.[28] The reprieve rate for women would undoubtedly
have been higher than that for men.

Until the middle of the century, what records there are indicate
that more women were hanged than reprieved, but, though this
pattern continued to hold true for men, it reversed itself for women
(see figure 1.3). As the state grew less and less inclined to hang
women, the situation of the condemned woman provoked less animosity but perhaps more curiosity on the part of the public.[29]

The Home Office files in the Public Record Office at Kew contain fascinating evidence of attempts by the government to adjust
sentences to accommodate changing attitudes towards female criminals. As Roger Chadwick suggests, these memoranda are important not only for the light they shed on decisions in individual
cases, but because they 'constitute a significant debate on the
notion of criminal responsibility and ... provide a rare glimpse of
an emergent establishment morality.'[30]

Figure 1.3

Average Number of Men and Women Executed or Reprieved, 1843–1899

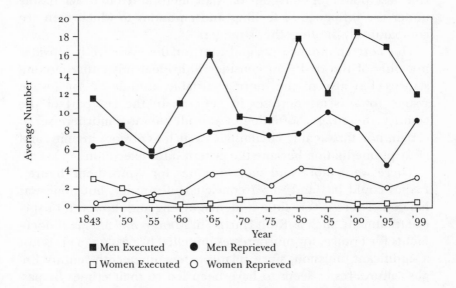

In 1882, Sir William Harcourt, the home secretary, asked his staff for statistics on the number of women actually hanged for murder in the previous twenty years. The answer tells us how endangered the public felt by murderesses as a group, and which type was considered the most dangerous.

Harcourt was informed that ninety-one women had been sentenced to death between 1862 and 1882, of whom seventeen – a little less than one-fifth – had actually been executed. (By contrast, from 1843, when statistics began to differentiate between the sexes, to 1862, only fifty-six women were sentenced to death, but twenty-three, or nearly half of them, were executed.) Most of the convictions were for infanticide and were commuted to imprisonment, usually for life but sometimes for as little as one year. Nine women were convicted of murder by poisoning between 1862 and 1882, with six executed. In other words, poisoners were the most feared. 'In all cases,' says the memorandum to Harcourt, 'the tendency

has been to attach great importance to the element of premeditation in its natural as apart from its legal sense. Women have as a
rule less power of self control than men, and often act hastily
under the influence of feelings and emotions to which men are
comparatively or altogether strangers.'[31]

This correspondence is significant for the evidence it provides
not only of the desire to consider individual mitigating circumstances, but also of the more charitable attitude of the justice
system towards murderesses in general. In the last part of the
century, there was a softening of attitudes towards murderesses in
certain non-threatening circumstances such as obvious insanity, and
clear premeditation became the criterion for execution.

There were more and more respites for sympathetic figures.
Ladies could be (and were) convicted of murder, but none was
hanged. There is very little evidence in England, however, of special treatment, such as Ruth Harris (in *Murders and Madness*) documents for France, for murderesses impelled by passion. This is not
a significant omission, since relatively few nineteenth-century English murderesses seem to have been led to their crimes by passion. Most appear to have known very well what they were about,
and to have been overcome by emotion only on being caught.

There remained in the last third of the century a great interest
in women's murder, but behind this interest often lay a desire to
understand feminine psychology. There was by this time in English society a sophisticated component of the population that was
made uncomfortable rather than angry by the perceived contrast
between villainy and womanhood.

CONCLUSION

A small proportion of working-class women in the patriarchal,
class-bound society of nineteenth-century England who felt themselves locked into intolerable social or economic circumstances
saw murder as a solution. The victims were most often their children, husbands, or elderly parents; the motivation, most often
money or freedom. Because the murders were usually carefully
planned and devious, the perpetrators were especially feared and

cast as monsters. At mid-century, public revulsion at murder by women was palpable but later murderesses were better understood as victims of harsh circumstances, fallen humans but not monsters. Changing popular attitudes to murder by women dovetail with the emancipation of women late in the Victorian period. Until then 'proper' murder, according to male arbiters, was carried out in the heat of passion. It would seem to a modern observer that any woman who took such action against her instincts must have been pressed by extreme misery and deprivation. However, the dominant patriarchal society saw such resistance as a threat and attempted to contain it through harsh punishment that emphasized the offenders' sex.

TWO

The Popular Press

STEREOTYPES

The Victorian murderess presents two faces to readers. One is what E.M. Forster would have called 'flat' – a one-dimensional portrait in a gallery of stereotypes. This is the face sketched in contemporary reports. Broadsides and newspapers depict the murderess as a monster because she has behaved in an extremely unnatural way. She is an outsider who has refused to abide by the rules of society. Literature, because it fleshes out its characters, tends to look into the circumstances that triggered peculiar behaviour. Victorian news reports are black and white in more ways than one.

Literature, more like life, has many shades of grey. So, even when fictional murderesses are presented as bad, they can be attractive, passionate, sympathetic figures – 'round,' in Forster's terms. Such a presentation is much less likely in straight factual reporting.

The press tended to make women who killed ugly, 'masculine,' old-looking, and, in general, inhuman. A murderess had to be presented as other than human so as to preserve the social norm of acquiescent inferiority. For not only had she flouted the human taboo against killing another human being, but she had also challenged the social stereotype of femininity: gentle, submissive, passive, self-sacrificing, delicate. Gentle, submissive, passive, self-sacrificing, delicate creatures do not strangle babies with their bare hands and drop them into the river; they do not bash their mistress's head in for giving one order too many; nor do they poison friends and relatives to obtain a little extra income. Such energy and enterprise were decidedly a perversion of the feminine nature.

Broadsides sold on the streets encouraged the public to, as it were, poke sticks through the cage at women accused of murder, particularly those who were unrepentant. Their crude woodcuts and poetry jeered and gloated. Newspaper reports were more restrained by the facts, but these too cast murderesses in a harsh light, expressing little or no interest in their circumstances.

Even the few papers that agitated for more humanitarian treatment of the poor did not extend their sympathy to desperately poor murderesses. The poor were widely regarded as idle and profligate, poverty being a moral failing that victims brought on themselves. The general reading public found it inconvenient to make the connection between the desperation of poverty and the 'remedy' of murder, as Carlyle suggested in 1843 in *Past and Present*, exclaiming over what excruciating poverty must have been endured by the parents who poisoned a child for the insurance money.[1] More of these crimes were exposed, and several women were hanged for them, each one duly vilified.

The Victorians, reined in by an exacting and repressive social code, were fascinated by deviant behaviour. 'Criminals are public property,' says one of the many books on the subject published in the late nineteenth century. 'The moment one is added to the number already ascertained, he is liable to be exhibited in various ways ... There is a great importance attached to his appearance, and no less to the registration of his deeds, and their penalties.'[2] Or, as *Punch* put it, in a satirical vein:

... upon the apprehension of a criminal, we notoriously spare no pains to furnish the nation with his complete biography; employing literary gentlemen, of elegant education and profound knowledge of human nature, to examine his birthplace and parish register, to visit his parents, brothers, uncles, and aunts, to procure intelligence of his early school days, diseases which he has passed through, infantile (and more mature) traits of character, etc. ... we employ artists of eminence to sketch his likeness as he appears at the police court, or views of the farm-house or back kitchen where he has perpetrated the atrocious deed ... we entertain intelligence within the prison walls with the male and female turnkeys, gaolers, and other authorities, by whose information we are enabled to describe every act and deed of the prisoner, the state of his health, sleep, and digestion, the changes in his appearance, his conversation, his dress and linen, the letters he writes, and the meals he takes ...[3]

The use of the masculine pronoun by no means suggests that female criminals escaped this sort of scrutiny. To the (male) purveyors of information, the female criminal mind was even more fascinating than its male counterpart. How extreme deviants came to act as they did was a question that the Victorians were prepared to spend time and money on.

CURIOSITIES OF CRIMINALITY

Many of them visited Madame Tussaud's Exhibition, a fixture on Baker Street in London since 1835, for its Separate Room, which was dubbed by *Punch* in 1846 the 'Chamber of Horrors' – a name that stuck. This room, separated from the rest of the exhibition so as not to offend the sensibilities of delicate female visitors, featured lifelike wax figures of notorious figures from the world of crime, some of them made from death masks. The price of admission to the exhibition was one shilling, but to get into the Chamber of Horrors one had to pay an additional sixpence.

Among the offerings there were three baby-farmers,[4] four serial poisoners,[5] six other convicted murderesses,[6] and one who was actually acquitted but widely believed to be guilty.[7]

A wax figure of Eleanor Pearcey, hanged on 23 December 1890 for murdering her lover's wife and baby, attracted a record crowd of 31,000 on Boxing Day that year. She was set up in a model of her own kitchen, the scene of the crime, with her piano, pictures, carpets, and chairs arranged as they were when the police came to arrest her. Madame Tussaud's had even purchased some of her blood-stained garments, the actual pram in which the corpses had been transported, and a toffee supposed to have been sucked by the baby just before it died.[8]

The length of a murderess's stay in the Chamber of Horrors is an indication of her prominence in the public mind. By the same token, the greatest overlap suggests the period of strongest interest in murderesses in general. This was from 1884 to 1901. Only four exhibits survived beyond 1970, and the only evidence of any of them today is the toffee and a few other relics from the Pearcey tableau.

A cosy setting for Maria and George Manning, hanged for the murder of her lover in 1849, aroused the ire of *Punch*. An article in that magazine entitled 'The Mannings at Home' observed that 'never did assassination look so amiable – so like a quality to be introduced to the bosom of families.' The exhibition boasted the actual crowbar with which the murder was committed. Both Mannings seem to have been somewhat romanticized. 'When the hangman has done his work, the wax witch takes it up and beautifies it,' *Punch* commented in mock admiration. 'Maria Manning, as done in wax, is really a *chef d'oeuvre* ... A lively rose-blush pervades her full-blown face, and her large, ripe lip seems pouting with the first syllable of "mur-der" ... There she stands in silk attire, a beauteous thing, to be daily rained upon by a shower of sixpences.'[9] Maria Manning, on display until 1971, was an obvious success with the public, the longest-running murderess in the Chamber of Horrors.

Those who would not be satisfied with replicas attended trials, sometimes for an admission fee,[10] or visited prisons. In the fall of 1849, curious Londoners were reported to be applying to Newgate Prison for permission to visit so that they could catch a glimpse of the Mannings; there had been similar attempts a few months before that in Bristol, as Sarah Thomas, a servant who had murdered her mistress, awaited execution.[11] Executions were the biggest draw: as *Punch* bitingly suggested, the build-up in the press made people feel that they would be missing something if they did not attend.

The Manning case, to cite an extreme example, received not only hundreds of columns of coverage on the discovery of the murder, including a description of the premises, on the inquest, on the search for and arrest of the accused, on the hearing in magistrate's court, on the trial at the Old Bailey, and on their appearance and behaviour there and in prison, but also special issues such as the four-page *Observer* supplement published at the conclusion of the trial, a fortnight before the execution. Depositions given by witnesses to the police were published, as were transcripts of the evidence given at inquests, hearings, and trials. At the Old Bailey, shorthand writers took down the proceedings in court for an authorized commercial printer, who then published and sold an abridged version of the transcripts of the testimony as Sessions Papers. As the *Annual Register* pointed out at the time, because the murder had taken place in London, the daily press was

> enabled to record every movement of the officers of justice, and to retail from day to day, with all the skill of practised journalists, the difficulties and mysteries of the case, and the daily progress of discovery and development. There were, besides, ... circumstances which the daily press delighted to set forth in such terms and in such *morceaux* as served at once to gratify and to stimulate the curiosity of the multitude.[12]

Robert Huish's fictionalized biography, *The Progress of Crime: The Authentic Memoirs of Maria Manning,* was put out in penny instalments. A religious tract, *The Track of the Murderer Marked Out by an Invisible Hand: Reflections Suggested by the Case of the Mannings,* was issued by Reverend Erskine Neale.[13]

For the three months between the murder and the execution, London talked of hardly anything else. At the execution, broadsides and ballads were being hawked, with descriptions of the Mannings's lives, last hours, and deaths. One publisher's sales of these reached 2.5 million[14] at a time when England's population was about 20 million. After the execution there was a debate in the *Times,* reported in the other papers, as to whether the public ought to be invited to executions. (Dickens, who sparked the controversy, thought not.)

VARIETIES OF CRIME LITERATURE

Admittedly, the press, primed by a spate of murders by women in the 1840s, was particularly active in the Manning case, but the range of its activities was representative. In the popular literature of crime, there was something for everyone. The nineteenth century had inherited from the eighteenth a tradition of crime-writing broad enough to suit all pocketbooks and degrees of literacy: for the masses, criminal biographies, dying speeches, ballads, and news posters in single sheets (broadsides) on the street; for those who had the time, skills, and money, Sessions Papers or reports of recent crimes in newspapers; for the literate lower classes, fuller reports and chaplains' accounts in pamphlets or chap-books (cheap, miniature books); for the 'respectable' reader, the leisured student of crime, historical compilations in books.[15] All of these genres circulated news of sensational crimes – indeed, made sensationalism possible – in the nineteenth century as literacy increased. It may even be, as Richard Altick suggests, that the tradition of crime-writing motivated the masses to learn to read.[16]

To this array was added in the 1840s the popular Sunday newspaper, and, once the stamp tax was lifted in 1855, the daily penny, and then (from 1868) the halfpenny newspaper. By the 1850s, church schools, dame schools, mechanics' institutes, and various philanthropic associations had spread literacy sufficiently that the middle and working classes between them were able to support an army of new, cheap magazines and newspapers that grew even stronger once the paper duty was abolished in 1861. After the Second Reform Bill engaged the masses politically in 1867, there was no stopping the cheap press. Sensationalism was its staple, with murder by or of women at the top of the list.

Criminal biographies of seventeenth- and eighteenth-century English murderers sketch out the pattern of murder by women: murder of a servant or apprentice, murder of a child, murder of a faithless lover, infanticide, murder of a husband, murder of an elderly parent. These stereotypes recur in the popular literature of crime throughout the nineteenth century, in part because they accurately reflect the tendencies of murderesses and, as well, because these tendencies were fanned into myth. The writers of this material, presumably encouraged by their readers, reconstructed or invented facts into comprehensible and entertaining narratives that explained deviant behaviour and attempted to contain it. This was no mean feat: as Lincoln Faller points out in his study of criminal biography, one might expect that murder, described over and over again, would become tiresome, but 'dressed in the appropriate myth, ... the bludgeonings, stabbings, and poisonings of the popular literature of crime seem not to have palled but rather to have made occasion for special kinds of pleasure ...'[17]

PAMPHLETS

One medium for the exploitation of executions in the early part of the century was the religious tract. 'Scarcely had you got rid of the impudent importunity of the peripatetic vendor of "last dying speeches and confessions,"' complained the chronicler of an execution in 1849, 'ere you were disgusted with some sleek oily faced individual, pertinaciously thrusting into your hands a compound of blasphemy and levity in the shape of tracts, headed by such startling titles as "Hell," etc.'[18]

In a culture that assumed that the potential to commit serious crime was latent in any human being, preaching directly against sinful behaviour was an obvious strategy. An especially opportune time for this was on the Sunday before an execution, when the prisoner was obliged to sit in public view in the condemned's pew of the prison chapel, surrounded by prison officials. Sometimes the coffin to be used after the execution was on display as well. An especially eloquent sermon against crime might be published in pamphlet form and sold.

A twelve-page tract from about 1830 addressed to the spectators at an execution makes the point explicitly that condemned murderers are separated from the rest of the population only by a very thin line: 'The criminal exposed there is your counterpart.'[19] On the first page, below an illustration of the murderer, the hangman, and the chaplain, the spectator is warned: 'What an awful scene is before you! Who that is not sunk into utter brutality can view it unmoved?' This ominous introduction is followed by a description of the miserable villain, 'brought out of a dungeon into the open air ...'

The ritual reunion between God and the penitent criminal on the scaffold was stage-managed by the ordinary or chaplain, who promised salvation in return for a confession.[20] As long as the criminal cooperated, this performance served to remind the community of sinners watching or reading about the execution that they too should repent and reform. Murderesses, perhaps because girls' moral and religious education was comparatively sketchy, or perhaps because they had come to think of themselves as outsiders, tended to resist the offer, thereby reinforcing the theory that they had nothing in them of the human spirit.

There was a brisk trade in chaplains' accounts of a prisoner's last hours, usually with the requisite confession. One of the perks accorded a prison chaplain was the opportunity to supplement his income by publishing the life stories, along with their last thoughts, of those of his flock who were hanged.

COLLECTIONS

The popularity of one chaplain's account of his experiences with prisoners condemned to death (Paul Lorraine, *Numerical Account of All Malefactors* [1812]) encouraged the publication of other compendiums of criminal careers. The best-known of these is *The Newgate Calendar*, which began late in the eighteenth century as a series of chronicles of notorious prisoners confined in one particular prison, but soon expanded to take in a number of other prisons in England and Scotland. The tales cover the period between 1700 and 1825[21] and were published and republished, vividly illustrated, in parts and in bound editions, throughout the nineteenth century under various editors and titles, including *The New Newgate Calendar* and *The Modern Newgate Calendar*. In 1863–4, out of a year's weekly numbers, twelve were devoted to murderesses. The *Calendar*'s purpose was ostensibly to demonstrate that crime would out and justice triumph, but there is no doubt that it had an entertainment component as strong as the moral one. As

Victor E. Neuberg has observed, 'Vice was always a particularly saleable ingredient in mass publishing – particularly when framed by admonitions to virtue.'[22]

As nineteenth-century crimes grew into legend, these, too, were collected and published in book form by various editors. There were numerous collections, some putting recent English cases into a more general historical context. An early example is George Borrow's *Celebrated Trials* (1825), a history that goes from the fifteenth century to 1824. More topical was *Poisoners and Slow Poisoning: A Narrative of the Most Remarkable Cases of Poisoning*, published in 1865 in the wake of several sensational poisoning cases.[23] There were collections of trial transcripts edited by lawyers but aimed at the general public, such as *Reports of Trials for Murder by Poisoning* by G.L. Browne and C.G. Stewart (1883). The *Annual Register* had a special section for notable trials, though these reports were largely digests of the coverage in the *Times*. There were numerous compilations of famous murder cases, some of these presented as memoirs or biographies of the hangman. Several of these were pamphlets (chap-books) sold on the streets in the 1850s, but later in the century came *The Life and Recollections of Calcraft, the Hangman* (1871), *Doom of the Gallows! With the Official Lives and Exploits of Cheshire, Calcraft and Marwood, the Past and Present State Hangmen, and the Horrors of Newgate!* (1879), and *The Groans of the Gallows, in the Past and Present Life of William Calcraft, the Living Hangman of Newgate* (1882). An imitator of *The Newgate Calendar*, *The Calendar of Horrors*, came out in penny numbers from 1836.

FROM FACT TO FANTASY

Throughout the nineteenth century, the most sensational crimes were recorded in individual volumes, some of them chap-books. Two that survive from the Manning case are an early one, *Particulars of the Apprehension of Frederick Manning ... and the Examination of His Wife*, and *Authentic Report of the Trial of the Mannings ... with the Extraordinary Conduct of Mrs. Manning in Court*.[24] The Road Murder, unsolved for five years until Constance Kent confessed in 1865, inspired a sixty-four-page pamphlet published in 1860 that compiled theory, fact, opinion, and newspaper commentary about this puzzling case. In 1865, at the time it was solved, several more pamphlets were circulated, including *Constance Kent and the Confessional*, *The Case of Constance E. Kent*, and *The Case of C.E.K.* The market for contemporary true-crime literature grew even stronger as literacy increased. Mary Ann Cotton, the double-digit poisoner hanged in 1872, was the subject of a book by an anonymous journalist, *The Life and Career of Mrs. Cotton, the West Auckland Poisoner* (Bishop Auckland, 1883), and of a comic melodrama, *Mary Ann Cotton*, which played into the twentieth century.[25] Adelaide Bartlett's murder charge produced a jocular sixteen-page pamphlet, *The Life of the Reverend George Dyson and His Strange Adventures with Mrs. Bartlett* (1886). In 1889, an account of Florence Maybrick's case appeared as a penny dreadful, *Florence Maybrick, a Thrilling Romance*. This was a peculiar blend of fact and fiction, with the heroine given her correct name but her husband and lover given pseudonyms. The Maybrick case also inspired a play, *A Fool's Paradise*, by Sydney Grundy, staged in 1892 and published by Samuel French in 1898. This melodrama stuck to the facts until the end, when the accused poisoner poisons herself on being exposed.

THE MURDERESS IN VICTORIAN FICTION

True crime also inspired the major nineteenth-century novelists. In the 1830s the Newgate novel, which drew on actual cases, was popularized by Bulwer-Lytton, Ainsworth, Dickens, and Thackeray (whose *Catherine*, based on the eighteenth-century husband killer Catherine Hayes, was a parody). By the 1840s crime stories were everywhere. Sunday papers, miscellanies, penny magazines, and weekly numbers capitalized on the broadside tradition. Penny crime fiction, which often picked up themes from *The Newgate Calendar*, became popular as new modes of production facilitated unprecedented speed and complexity in printing at low cost. Each penny part was an unbound booklet of eight pages with prominent illustrations.[26] The sensation novels of the 1860s were sophisticated tales of mistaken identity, murder, and mystery. Altick is certain 'no popular or would-be popular novelist of the sixties and early seventies wholly overlooked the possibilities' of a murder in the plot. By the 1880s such literature was a reference point in actual cases. In 1886, in his charge to the jury trying Adelaide Bartlett for the murder of her husband, Mr Justice Alfred Wills remarked: 'I do not know what you think of the evidence you heard this morning. It is difficult after that to elevate these people into the hero and heroine of an extraordinary sensational romance. It looks much more as if we had two persons to deal with abundantly vulgar and commonplace ... '[27] Three years later, Mr Justice James Fitzjames Stephen, advising the jury to disregard a white lie told by Florence Maybrick, observed:

> No doubt we all know that when a person in a novel is going to commit a crime there are a number of these things which occur to the novelist, and are skilfully arranged, so that one may say afterwards, 'Oh, what a clever fellow you are, how surprisingly well you have written that. You have introduced every kind of precaution that was possible. How much you know of the way of criminals.' But that is one of the distinctions – one of the very many distinctions – between what passes in novels and what passes in real life ... You must take things as they happen in real life, and be on your watch against doing otherwise; for if you do, you are almost certain to attach great importance to things which are probably mere trifles.[28]

After the Maybrick trial, the *St. James's Gazette*, remarking on 'the shameless way in which Fact plagiarizes Fiction,' quoted a passage from *Armadale* by Wilkie Collins, published twenty-three years earlier, in which Bashwood the younger tells his father how Lydia Gwilt had long ago, under another name, been sentenced to death for poisoning her husband, but reprieved after some newspapers took up her case.[29] The same thing happened to Maybrick.

Dickens and Collins heightened the drama of their novels by picking up story lines and characters from recent murder cases. Their sensation novels, in which murder by women became an expression of sexuality, broke the stereotype of the 'angel in the house,' presenting the murderess as attractive, exotic, and passionate.

Dickens modelled the French maid in *Bleak House*, Hortense, on Maria Manning, and Hortense's nemesis, Inspector Bucket, on Inspector Field, a real-life Scotland Yard detective who worked on the Manning case. Collins used details from the Constance Kent case in *The Moonstone* and *Armadale*. *The Moonstone* picks up from the Kent case not only the setting of a large country estate and the hiding of the incriminating nightgown, but the character of Sergeant Cuff, modelled on Inspector Jonathan Whicher of Scotland Yard, and the whole issue of the intrusion of the police into middle-class households and their difficulty in dealing appropriately with genteel young women.[30] In *Armadale*, Gwilt, like Kent, has the sympathy of the public despite her obvious guilt.

Other writers, recognizing their readers' frame of reference, wove historical detail into their narratives. Their attention to the psychology of murderesses is perhaps a criticism of the actual treatment accorded their models. They worked as hard to present these offending women as real people responding to stress as the justice system did to remain blind to that fact. George Eliot based the story of Hetty Sorrel in *Adam Bede* on an actual case[31] described to her by her aunt, Elizabeth Evans, who, like Dinah Morris in the novel, had worked as a travelling preacher. Hardy recalled not only Martha Brown's hanging with the final scene in *Tess*, but also her situation, that of an oppressed 'wife' who finally fights back.[32] Florence Maybrick was in that position as well. It can be inferred that Tess's conviction is largely attributable to her immoral past, as happened in the actual case of Mrs Maybrick.[33] Furthermore, Hardy's portrait of Sue Bridehead in *Jude the Obscure* may be based on Eleanor Pearcey, hanged in 1890 for the murder of her lover's wife and baby. She had a platonic relationship with him before his marriage and had encouraged him to marry someone else.[34]

Dickens, George Eliot, Hardy, and even Trollope gave a human face to female deviancy. Nancy (*Oliver Twist*) is an abused wife. Lizzie Eustace (*The Eustace Diamonds*) is a manipulator and a thief, but one whose charms and anxieties are acknowledged as well.

Hetty's prototype was swiftly executed after her conviction for infanticide in 1802, but her plight was in retrospect so pathetic that Eliot could not kill her in 1859. Hardy's depiction of Tess is so wrenchingly lifelike that its dimension as angry criticism of society's intolerance and callousness is unmistakable.

BROADSIDES

Fiction could provide psychological insights into motives for murder, but broadsides and, later, newspapers were the quickest and cheapest way to the facts. By the 1830s probably between two-thirds and three-quarters of the working classes could read at least a little,[35] well enough to make their way past the huge headlines (e.g., 'Execution!,' 'Horrid Murder,' 'Sorrowful Lamentation,' 'Inhuman Murder,' 'The Last Dying Speech and Confession of ...') through the print under the chilling woodcut illustrations in murder and execution broadsides, the dominant medium of crime news at that time. These were immensely popular and well circulated[36] for the very good reason that they highlighted events on which attention was focused at a particular time: a murder, trial, confession, or execution that people were talking about. The broadsides, fixed indoors in homes,[37] inns, and coffee-houses, and outdoors on posts, gave them more to talk about. There were ballads, reports, confessions, and accounts of trials. 'There's nothing beats a stunning good murder,' a street hawker (running patterer) told Henry Mayhew.[38] News of murders and executions was shouted out on the streets by running patterers or sung in verse by minstrels. The prime business of these men was selling broadsides for a penny or a halfpenny, but some also invented 'sorrowful lamentations,' confessions, letters, and so on for the broadside printers.

There was a reassuring order to murder trials that made them easy to understand. The messages constructed around them were equally simple. A career of sin could tempt one to murder, but murder would be revealed and punished, and a murderer would have to suffer the pangs of repentance in order to avoid eternal damnation. The subtext was that sin at any level was dangerous. Murderers were sinners writ large.

The revelation of murder always shook a community, and broadsides exploited this impact. A 'shocking' murder would be announced. Then, with luck, one member of the community would be identified as the murderer. The deed would be described and explained at the trial, another occasion for a broadside. To save society, the murderer would be cast out – sentenced to death. Before the execution, to speed a condemned but penitent murderer along in the next world, there would be a confession and/ or a dying speech with a moral for others. This, too, occasioned a broadside. To reinforce the message the execution was described, sometimes with a crude illustration of the gallows.

Of course, not every murder case inspired a broadside. But murders by women, because they were rare and particularly threatening, were well publicized. They were often used as excuses for moralizing, as in this account in an early nineteenth-century broadside of a poisoning in Scotland:

> In the dark catalogue of human crimes there are none perhaps of deeper dye, none more important in their consequences, than that for which this unhappy woman forfeited her life. Murder is here exhibited with all its aggravating circumstances. Against the midnight plunderer and assassin we are in some measure guarded by our prudence and ingenuity, and locks, and bolts, and various mechanical instruments, are fabricated for our defence and security: but when a man's enemies are those of his own house – when the wife of his bosom deliberately imagines and compasses his death – no human prudence, ingenuity, or foresight, will be found sufficient to render abortive her diabolical machinations, or avert the direful catastrophe. Whether indeed we consider it as dissolving one of the primary bonds of society, or as a breach of that sacred confidence which ought to subsist between a man and his wife, from which arises all the other relative and social duties of civilized life, the crime will appear of the first magnitude.[39]

Here we have a portrait of the archetypal murderess, a thoroughly bad woman who has committed adultery, who has killed deviously, who has betrayed someone who trusted her, and who in doing these things has flouted her feminine nature. The prospect of such passive aggression haunted husbands as long as wives were oppressed and poison was easy to obtain and hard to detect.

In a society where sudden, unexplained deaths were not uncommon, there was no telling who might next be revealed as guilty of murder. Broadside accounts of exposure and punishment were particularly satisfying because they taught a moral lesson. Many of them are obvious derivatives of the gothic novel, which dates from the mid-eighteenth century. They tell of denied desires, transgression, and supernatural punishments.

As Mayhew discovered by interviewing the men who sold them, fictitious reports – 'cocks' – were used to fill in when actual cases were in short supply, and, even when the basic facts were true, prisoners' last words and descriptions of their executions were often fabricated.[40] There are reports, for example, of various unmarried female servants who slit their babies' throats and then attempted to burn the bodies. The names are invented, but the crime probably did occur once. Most broadsides are undated, so they could be reissued as current long after the actual event had taken place. By the time a broadside was printed, its story might have long since passed into legend.

Though broadsides are obviously less reliable as sources of information than are newspaper reports, they do give us an idea of how the public interest in crime and punishment was manipulated. The executions themselves, of course, which could attract thousands of spectators, served as a primary deterrent. But broadsides could amplify the message both because they reached a much wider public and because they could embellish, and even invent. Colourful biographies and fabricated recriminations by condemned prisoners could be used as moral levers in the social system. The sad stories of good citizens gone wrong did not serve merely to deter crime, but also to keep their fellow citizens within accepted norms of behaviour.

One broadside trope was the wicked stepmother. Children were not infrequently mistreated by their stepmothers, and some were murdered by them. The broadside culture does not dwell on the murder of children by their natural mothers, but seems to have drawn the line at murder by stepmothers. I have seen three versions of a broadside, with two different dates, about the same woman, a Mrs Long, who stabbed two of her three stepchildren.[41]

The issue of whether there actually was such a murder by Mrs Long is unimportant in the larger scheme of broadsides. Some men married two or three times, as wives tended to die in childbirth. Since there was a tradition of wicked stepmothers and there *were* stepmothers who did these things, such stories would be believed, and perhaps serve as deterrents.

NEWSPAPERS

By the time public executions ended in 1868, the broadside was largely supplanted by the popular press. By 1861, the circulation of the *Daily Telegraph* was 142,000, the *Times* 65,000, and the *Standard* 46,000.[42] In addition to this base of daily readers, working people bought Sunday papers for a penny or two a week, and the more expensive daily papers at the time of a royal visit or an execution.[43]

The broadside tradition seems to have fuelled a demand for special-occasion souvenir papers from people who did not otherwise buy them. It may well also have encouraged more extensive and more accurate crime reporting. As Richard Altick has observed, 'The policy [in the 1860s] of the new aggressive, circulation-hungry journalism was to give the broadening public what it wanted; and high on the list of what it wanted was Murder.'[44]

In 1851 a running patterer told Mayhew that the papers were beating the broadside press at its own game, embellishing crimes and criminals with invented detail: '*We* can write the love letters for the fiend in human? That's quite true, and we once had a great pull that way over the newspapers. But Lord love you, there's plenty of 'em gets more and more into our line. They treads in our footsteps, sir; they follows our bright example.'[45] Newspapers did acquire from broadsides the format of illustrating the text with provocative sketches and highlighting it with arresting headlines. Broadsides cribbed their accounts from newspapers. Newspapers did not take the same liberties with the truth, nor did they gloat quite as openly. Their material was, after all, produced by well-educated professional writers, whereas that in broadsides tended to be tossed off by semi-literate street vendors. Newspaper correspondents received a penny a line, patterers a shilling for an entire ballad or confession.

Though the golden age of newspapers did not begin until the 1850s, it was from broadsides that the idea of news as a commodity for the general public came into its own in England. As Leslie Shepherd has observed, without street literature there would have been no medium for the ideas and emotions of the masses.[46] They demanded and got sensational crime news from broadsides to begin with. This appetite was increasingly indulged by newspaper proprietors, who found, despite their propaganda to the contrary, that crime paid. Fortunately there was a good supply of raw material. From the 1840s through the end of the century, in England unusual murders abounded. As detective work became more effective, the stories filled out, and the public was able – and more than willing – to follow a case in many chapters from inquest through execution.

From about 1815 *Bell's Weekly Dispatch* featured what was later called sensational news – seductions, rapes, murders, and so on.[47] By the 1830s weekly newspapers specializing in courts and police reporting had stimulated the public appetite for such news. John Cleave's *Weekly Police Gazette*, for example, founded in 1834, soon had a circulation of more than 20,000.[48] In the 1840s, a flock of lively newcomers – *Lloyd's Weekly Newspaper* and the *Illustrated London News*, founded in 1842, the *News of the World* (1843), the *Daily Express* and the *Daily News* (1846), the *Weekly Times* (1847), and *Reynolds's Newspaper* (1850) – pushed the established papers – the *Times*, the *Observer*, the *Advertiser*, the *Chronicle*, the *Herald*, the *Post*, the *Standard*, the *Globe*, and the *Sun* – to publish more and more about crime. Edward Lloyd, the proprietor of *Lloyd's*, was heavily committed to crime news. Shock and horror were his stock in trade. In the 1840s he also published the *Penny Sunday Times and People's Police Gazette*, which, in order to avoid the stamp tax, ran only fiction and fabricated police reports.[49] His main enterprise at this time, however, was not newspapers but cheap fiction. Between

1836 and 1856, Lloyd published at least 200 penny dreadfuls, most of them tales of murder, rape, or seduction.[50] This connection doubtless motivated him, and, through his newspaper, his competition, to import into newspaper layout and design the lively-looking titles, vivid illustrations, and gruesome subject-matter of crime fiction.

The price of newspapers fell in the 1850s with the substantial reduction of the 'taxes on knowledge,' and, once the masses could afford a daily newspaper, circulation figures rose. Technology allowed the demand to be met: the steam press assisted production; the telegraph, news coverage; and the railway, distribution. In 1855, after the stamp tax was abolished, the *Daily Telegraph* (price: one penny) began publication, building its reputation on crime and war coverage. The *Telegraph* ran the same lengthy verbatim testimony of witnesses used by the *Times*, but prefaced it with penetrating descriptive commentary. The weekly *Illustrated Police News* began in 1864; the *Pall Mall Gazette* in 1865; and the *Echo*, the first halfpenny newspaper, in 1868. The *Illustrated Police News*, its front page covered with sketches of murders, murderers, victims, trials, and executions, was blatantly sensationalist. The *Telegraph*'s crime coverage was broad and full; the *Echo*'s, whimsical, opinionated, and lively. At the other end of the circulation spectrum was the sophisticated *Pall Mall Gazette*, which, in addition to reporting the news, analysed it, created causes, and exposed injustices.

Police-court reporting had, of course, for many years been a staple of the *Times*, which published it as a matter of public record. With more in mind than this, other newspapers arranged for coverage of trials that looked promising. So there was much to summarize every week, and crime news became the backbone of the mass-circulation Sunday papers of the 1840s, '50s, and '60s. As Lucy Brown notes, it was cheap, simple to organize, and popular[51] – and also interesting.

London crime received more space than rural crime, but correspondents were available in all the locations in which criminal trials were held. Women accused of murder, especially in London, were always of interest. Penny-a-liners often wrote the same story for more than one paper, and, being paid by measure, they wrote fully. Though more often than not all they had to go on were official reports, they cast their material in a sensational way so as to be sure to get it published. 'A successful penny-a-liner must be somewhat of an artist,' says a nineteenth-century description of the newspaper business.

> He must contrive, by some means or other, to throw a certain amount of interest around the beginning of his copy ... If not sensational, indeed, he is nothing. He must write with as much seeming earnestness as if his whole mental and moral nature was absorbed in his subject ...
>
> There is another qualification which is indispensable to the character of a true penny-a-liner ... Instead of condensing, it is his duty to lengthen. Words are the things he worships. As he is paid by quantity, he is unfit for his 'profession' unless he possesses the talent of stating a fact, or expressing a sentiment, in the greatest possible number of words of which the statement of the fact, or the expression of the sentiment, will admit.
>
> ... another essential thing is first to arrest and then to keep up the attention of the Sub-Editor ... The way in which this can be done, and it is the only one, is to lug in all the variety of matter which his ingenuity can suggest, in addition to his writing throughout with an earnestness as apparently intense as if his whole soul was absorbed in his subject.[52]

Despite all this effort, routine mid-century newspaper reports on crime look to be all of a piece, with verbatim testimony from all the witnesses.[53] However, from time to time a case would emerge that stirred the public imagination. That case would then hijack the newspaper-reading public until its resolution, usually in an execution. Murder cases in which women were victims greatly excited the public; trials for murder of women, because they were rare, were at least as sensational, though less palatable.

Robert Hariman makes the point that popular trials, through their 'persuasive power and cultural density,' are an important form of public discourse.[54] As we watch and read about trials and weigh the stories told, we are adjusting the shared beliefs that constitute society's value system.

An example is the moral panic over infanticide in the 1860s and '70s. 'Newspapers provided the textual stage upon which multiple melodramas of infanticide were played,' Margaret Arnot has observed. 'It is quite conceivable that vivid and detailed courtroom reporting actively encouraged public participation in trial dramas as they were played out in the courtrooms themselves.' Once the Crimean War was over, she says,

> there were lots of column inches freed for revelations of infanticide. Even the smallest local newspapers in rural areas and metropolis alike carried detailed reporting of trials. In rural areas, the arrival of judges for quarterly Assize hearings was a ceremonial event and scandalous trials a welcome diversion, even a form of entertainment. In more populous London, court sittings were more regular and less ceremonial; nevertheless, the press fed an apparently voracious appetite for crime news with endless, detailed and often melodramatic accounts of trials.[55]

Hariman shows that trials are much more than legal proceedings: they are a means to the social construction of reality.[56] Hence it is not surprising that, once the newspapers began publicizing the arguments and issues in murder trials, their readers responded with rapt and constant attention. The Victorians were quite prepared to plod through masses of peripheral detail on the way to the verdict and the sentence. 'The theory of the *Times*,' said one chronicler of the period, 'was that as every reader knew by experience that every word in the paper was indispensable, he worked his way through the entire solid and black print, from the first page to the last.'[57] Emotions were stirred in the papers of the mid-century, not by typographical appearance – the technology for that did not surface until the 1880s – but by the space allotted, day after day, to a given story. The publication of leading articles and letters to the editor signalled that a story was of especial interest. The established morning papers of the 1880s were later described as 'great heavy-sided blanket sheets full of dull advertisements and duller news announcements' distinguished by 'an utter absence of information that gave the reader any idea of what people throughout the world were doing outside the confines of their various parliament houses.'[58] This tradition was threatened by the *Evening News*, the *Evening Post*, and the *Star*, which, following the style of American newspapers, used typography to emphasize their sensational crime news. Provocative headlines of different sizes and in various styles of type delivered the message that a story was of more than routine interest. Their reporters lured readers with shockingly vivid, graphic descriptions that brought reality closer than newspapers had up to then been able to do. The *Daily Mail*, founded in 1896, and the *Daily Express* (1900) ushered in a new era in sensational reporting. Anthony Trollope observed that 'horrors heaped upon horrors and which are horrors only in themselves, and not as touching any recognised and known person, are not tragic, and soon cease even to horrify.'[59] Although the Victorian press was attempting to bridge the gap between the 'otherness' of remote events and the everyday world of the reader, to expand reality to include what was seen and heard by others, it did not attempt to do this in an objective way. It tended to treat crime as a fiction while presenting it as a fact. Crime reporters titillated their readers with shocking detail, convicted before the courts did, and provided psychological analysis of their own invention. They maintained interest by arousing horror and indignation, and then offering a solution to the mystery and a description of the restoration of order. An entertaining story led to a moral.

As in Victorian fiction, there was a voice of authority behind the narrative. Murders were routinely described as revolting, melancholy, extraordinary, horrible, or dreadful. Despite contempt-of-court laws, which were seldom invoked, English newspapers did not hesitate to take positions on the guilt or innocence of an accused murderer. If they did not agree, following the story became that much more interesting for the reader.

In *Armadale*, Wilkie Collins has Mr Bashwood describe sardonically how the frantic activity of the press saved the neck of a convicted murderess after the verdict was delivered:

On the evening of the Trial, two or three young Buccaniers of Literature went down to two or three newspaper offices, and wrote two or three heartrending leading articles on the subject of the proceedings in court. The next morning the public caught light like tinder; and the prisoner was tried over again, before an amateur court of justice, in the columns of the newspapers. All the people who had no personal experience whatever on the subject, seized their pens, and rushed (by kind permission of the editor) into print ... The general public followed the lead of the barristers and the doctors, and the young Buccaniers who had set the thing going. Here was the Law that they all paid to protect them, actually doing its duty in dreadful earnest! Shocking! Shocking! The British Public rose to protest as one man against the working of its own machinery; and the Home-Secretary, in a state of distraction, went to the Judge. The Judge held firm. He had said it was the right verdict at the time, and he said so still ... The prisoner's death-warrant went into the waste-paper basket; the verdict of the Law was reversed by general acclamation; and the verdict of the newspapers carried the day.[60]

Because it 'reviewed' trials and verdicts, the press saw itself as a judge of the justice system. It was not allowed to comment directly on cases that were being tried, but it could depict prisoners in a sympathetic or unsympathetic light, as it saw fit, and it could praise or malign a verdict. Sometimes a case would be retried if the press was dissatisfied, and sometimes, as in the case of Collins's romantic heroine, public pressure would induce the home secretary to grant a reprieve.

Press interference by no means worked against the interests of justice. As the *Times* claimed in 1845, 'publicity is the best protection against abuse.'[61] Time and again the newspapers alerted the public to what looked like tyranny or privilege. Realizing that the law was an imperfect instrument, they tried, even if they had to go beyond its bounds, to manipulate it to serve society justly.

In 1851, Charles Mitchell, publisher of a directory of newspapers, described the adversarial activity of the press thus:

The press is the corrector of abuses; the redressor of grievances; the modern chivalry, that defends the poor and helpless, and restrains the oppressor's hand in cases where the law is either too weak or too lax to be operative, or where those who suffer have no means of appealing to the tribunals of their country for protection. It is, too, the scourge of vice, where no law could be effective, where the statute law does not extend, where the common law fails, – the law of the press strikes the offender with a salutary terror, causes him to shrink from the exposure that awaits him, and not infrequently arrests him in the career of oppression or guilt.[62]

In 1887, H.R. Fox Bourne ended his history of English newspapers by observing, 'Newspapers are now thrones and pulpits, and journalism assumes to itself the right and power to control and reform the world; and not without some reason.'[63] Occasionally, the more liberal newspapers acted to correct wrongs against women. In general, however, most newspapers, through most of the century, show a bias against women accused of serious crimes. The local paper condemned Martha Brown in 1856, though later in the century Hardy resurrected and retried her. Coverage in the Dorset *County Express and Agricultural Gazette* at the time of her execution included a leading article about the 'ignominious end' and 'well-merited fate' of the 'wretched criminal' for 'the deliberate murder of poor Anthony Brown, by the hand of his own wife.' The description of the execution includes this callous observation: 'While the culprit was hanging, a woman was knocked down by a passing waggon, but not injured, and this is the only casualty which occurred. Considerable inconvenience was experienced by the market people, in consequence of the execution taking place so near the market place, and business was, of course, for a time put a stop to.[64] It is likely that the *County Express* addressed itself to a predominantly male audience, which would take comfort in the condemnation of a husband murderer, however abused. It is also likely that at that time women accepted that husbands had more rights than wives. Later in the century, when women were pressing for equality, the press demonstrated that it could, on occasion, show compassion towards women who killed under extenuating circumstances.

The chapters in Part II, organized by type of crime, explore reports of the century's most sensational criminal trials and executions of women. They provide an indication of the degree to which society's changing expectations of women affected press coverage of murder cases in which women were implicated. By 1870 everyone, poor or rich, female or male, was entitled to an elementary education, one that included moral and spiritual guidance as well as a grounding in the three Rs. This had an impact on the quality of judgment that was passed on accused murderesses by the public. As the proportion of the population that was educated increased, so did the proportion that read and responded to newspapers. The tone of newspaper reports had an effect on the law as well as on public opinion. Newspapers, as the voice of the people, supported the justice system but also alerted the public to perceived inadequacies in the law itself or its application. By the end of the nineteenth century, there was an attempt in the press to understand rather than merely condemn murder by women. Class and gender bias still worked against them, but the barbaric dismissal of any murderess as subhuman was a thing of the past. This had an effect on the administration of the law at the highest level, the Home Office.

Part Two: Murder

THREE

Multiple Murder

**Susannah Holroyd / Jane Scott / Betty Eccles / Sarah Dazely /
Eliza Joyce / Sarah Freeman / Mary Ann Milner / Mary May /
Mary Ann Geering / Sarah Chesham / Mary Emily Cage /
Mary Ann Brough / Catherine Wilson / Mary Ann Cotton /
Ellen Heesom / Margaret Higgins / Catherine Flannagan /
Elizabeth Berry**

The peculiar practice of killing relatives for pin-money appears to have caught on in England by 1840, initially, at least, as a response to the pressure of poverty. A correlation between rates of theft and depressed economic conditions was made at the time;[1] with hindsight, there is no reason to exclude murder for insurance money from such an exercise, and every reason to indict women as the chief perpetrators. Women had the responsibility of putting food on the table. This position not only pressured them into obtaining it, but afforded them the opportunity to doctor it so as to eliminate some of the consumers.

It is no coincidence that 'poisoning' as a category of murder or attempted murder enters Samuel Palmer's *Index to the 'Times'* in 1837. In the last two months of 1838, the silk, cotton, and woollen trades began a decline that worsened in 1839 with a general scarcity of food. In 1840 and 1841, the depression deepened and spread, until its nadir in 1842, when the power to purchase food reached a fifteen-year low, and crime against property soared in

London, the agricultural districts, and the cotton and woollen districts. From 1843 to 1845, conditions improved, but by October 1846 a poor harvest and the high price of cotton, compounded by a downturn in railway shares, precipitated another depression that lasted into 1849.

In the 1840s it became horrifyingly evident that, for some women, serial poisoning was a way of getting along. Because they went about their business quietly, they did not attract much attention until advances in policing, detection, and publicity converged and revealed case after case.

DEFINITION

Multiple murder is generally acknowledged by criminologists as involving three or more victims. It is thought of as a male crime because that is its nature today, but in the nineteenth century there was a strong representation of women in the ranks of multiple murderers. Most of these were serial killers.

Mass murder – the killing of several people at once – is a crime very rarely perpetrated by women. It is possible that power and notoriety simply do not tempt women to a crime so dramatic that it is bound to be found out. Serial murder requires control and patience rather than power and, at its most effective, leaves no trace. It can be used to gain attention, as it probably was by Jack the Ripper, but more often it succeeds because the victims are not missed or are not thought of as having been murdered. Many a career of serial murder has been curtailed because an overconfident murderer neglected to cover up the current crime as carefully as he or she had crimes in the past, or when isolated events suddenly assumed an incriminating pattern. Or, of course, by a confession or an accusation.

It is more usual for prosecutors to attempt to prove multiple murder in court nowadays than it was in the nineteenth century. Today, when capital punishment is rare, and extra convictions are likely to delay or prevent a murderer's release from prison, there is some point to establishing multiple murder. But in the nineteenth century, one murder conviction was sufficient to summon the hangman, particularly in circumstances where other murders were suspected. Some of the women discussed in this chapter were not proved to have committed more than one murder, although there are very strong indications that the crime for which they were executed capped a career of murder. Others with suspicious pasts but less evidence of them are discussed as single-victim murderesses. The serial murder of babies is considered in chapter 6. Only one baby-farmer, Amelia Dyer, was openly accused of more than one murder, but this is a highly suspect group.

A composite profile of the serial murderess in nineteenth-century England would bear no resemblance to what we know of male serial killers, who as a group are irrational, violent, and out of control. The typical nineteenth-century serial murderess, capitalizing on her privileged position as caregiver and purveyor of food and drink, used poison. 'There is a terrible fascination in the knowledge that you hold in your hand the lives of households,' said the *Daily News* in 1847. The serial poisoner was cool, determined, devious, patient, dispassionate, resourceful, quite rational, entirely selfish, and, as she racked up victims, reckless. Her own convenience was her major consideration. Her murders were premeditated. They were a means to an end, which involved either the removal of an encumbrance or the acquisition of money or property. She was dull, poor, unambitious, ignorant, and utterly without scruples, a condition often assisted by a lack of moral training. The increasing incidence of poisoning in the 1840s, said the *Daily News*, could be traced to the national character of the lower class, with its 'coarse and animal brutality, unchecked by religion, uninformed by intelligence, uncontrolled by virtuous activity, unsupported by self-respect ...'[2]

The serial murderess, though very much connected to rural tradition, was an outsider, unconcerned with society and unaffected by its norms. She had nothing to gain by playing by the rules and nothing to lose by ignoring them. This portrait was as true in the 1880s as in the 1840s.

BURIAL CLUBS

It is highly likely that serial murder by women in rural England was a tradition quietly accepted in many communities where poverty and large families were incompatible facts of life. 'What is to be said of a district where cold-blooded murder meets with all the popular favour which is shown to smuggling in Sussex, or agrarian assassinations in Tipperary?' asked a *Times* leading article.[3] In the 1840s, when crop failures threatened many families with the unsavoury alternatives of starvation or the workhouse, there were unsettling references in the press to what seemed to be becoming an epidemic of serial murder for profit. Carlyle conjectured in *Past and Present*, published in 1843, that some parents put their children out of the way one by one in order to keep the rest of the family alive, but no one paid much attention. Judges alluded to the trend when delivering their verdicts. The *Times* referred to 'a large number of women who have adopted the practice of poisoning their husbands and children for the purpose of obtaining the [burial] fees ...'[4] The *News of the World* asked rhetorically: 'Why not place as many impediments in the way of killing the poor, as the impoverished now find in procuring parochial or medical relief?'[5] When a ragged little girl asking at a chemist's shop for twopence-worth of arsenic for her mother to kill rats, *Punch* imagined, an assistant replied: 'Rats, eh? Father belong to a burial club?' She replies, 'Yes, Sir, please, Sir,' but he delivers the arsenic anyway.[6]

Burial clubs were insurance schemes into which the subscriber paid a small amount weekly so that burial fees would be covered if the member died. If death occurred soon after enrolment, the amount paid out by the society would considerably exceed the amount paid in in weekly instalments. It was therefore expedient, in an environment in which many children did not survive to adulthood, to enroll sickly children. Some mothers stretched this strategy to include children who would become sick after they were given poison. In some cases adult family members were also enrolled, always without their knowledge, so that a profit could be made on their disposal.

A report by Edwin Chadwick in 1843[7] on funeral practices established that: (1) working-class funerals cost more than many families could afford; and (2) this expense was often mitigated by burial clubs, which, however, provided an unintended incentive to murder or neglect. The allegation that people were being murdered for their burial insurance was reinforced by further investigations and public commentary, most of it centred on the Lancashire area, where mill employees would have been highly vulnerable to fluctuations in the cotton market.

The so-called death clubs cost about seven pence per quarter, with a possible yield, by the late 1840s, of as much as ten pounds on a death, depending on the number of people enrolled in the club. A more-than-respectable working-class funeral cost no more than half that.[8] A woman could register a family member in more than one club, rid herself of an impediment, and, if there was not too long a stretch between the victim's enrolment and death, make a tidy profit into the bargain.

Requirements for the registration of deaths were so lax that a medical practitioner did not have to certify the cause, and, even if one were called in, it was easy enough to deceive him. In some quarters the apparent epidemic was a scandal; in others it was a joke. 'Burial Club,' a broadside ballad sung in the streets, began:

> My old 'oman one day says to me,
> A thought has popp'd into my head;
> How hard-up our young 'uns vould be
> If suppose as how you vos dead.

The husband goes on to tell the story of how they joined a club, and then he thought of having his wife claim that he was dead so that they could collect. According to the ballad, they were caught and jailed for a year.[9] Women who wanted to be on the safe side did not claim burial insurance for family members who were not actually dead.

In 1850 Parliament approved a trial ban on insurance of more than three pounds on any child under ten. In 1855 the limit was raised to six pounds for a child under five, and ten pounds for a child from five to ten. A death certificate from a medical practitioner was required in order for burial benefits to be released, but this stipulation could be manipulated. Stiffer regulation over the years made insolvency of burial societies less likely, but it did not prevent abuse. Social reformers were no match for the combined opposition of the insurance interests and the working classes.[10]

PROOF OF POISONING

Most serial murderesses in nineteenth-century England used arsenic. Until the Sale of Arsenic Act of 1851, there was no requirement for the purchasers of poison to identify themselves to vendors, nor for vendors to be registered. Arsenic was until 1851 easy to acquire, cheap, colourless, odourless, soluble in hot water, and hard to detect. Since the symptoms it produced were not unlike those of severe diarrhoea or cholera, it was usually not suspected as a cause of death. When it *was* suspected, the Marsh (1836) or Reinsch (1841) tests could sometimes confirm it, but these were often used ineptly, and sometimes produced conflicting results. Though arsenic could betray its presence in the body as long as twelve years after death, the longer the investigation was delayed after death, the harder it was to attribute the cause positively to arsenic.

Poisoning was a time-honoured way for women, who were in charge of a family's food, to do away with people. Until chemical testing became possible, poison was not likely to be discovered. 'The chemical test discovers what the autopsy left hidden,' said the *Daily News*. 'The earth no longer covers the dead.'[11] As the *Lancet* observed, 'The secret poisoning of the Middle Ages was ... only secret because the art of chemical analysis was then very imperfect.'[12] As testing implicated poison in more and more deaths in the 1840s, fears mounted that these were only the tip of the iceberg. 'It can scarcely have escaped the notice of those who are in the habit of reading the public journals,' said the Dorset *County Chronicle* in 1845,

> that nearly one third of the murders that have been brought to light for some years, have been perpetrated by means of poison: and who can tell the number of murders, thus effected, that have escaped detection, or the number of those to whom the deadly drug has, in various ways, been administered, and who, although the wicked design may have failed at the time, have been injured in

constitution, and lingered on in pain and sickness, till death has at last relieved them from suffering?[13]

Poison was (not unreasonably) especially feared by groups that oppressed women, such as the masters and mistresses of servants, and husbands. When a woman was implicated in such a crime, these endangered groups fought back by blackening her name even before guilt was proved. Even when chemistry was able to establish the administration of arsenic, it was not always clear who had administered it. But such terror attached to the female poisoner that she was often branded a monster before being convicted of the crime.

EARLY SERIAL POISONERS

In 1816, a woman living in a village near Lancaster confessed to a mass poisoning and was hanged. She had given arsenic to her husband, Matthew; their eight-year-old son, William; and Ann Newton, the infant daughter of her lodger. The crime that exposed her appears to have been merely the last in a series of successful and attempted poisonings.

Evidently, Susannah Holroyd had a flair for the dramatic. About a month before the poisonings, she told the lodger, Mary Newton, that a fortune-teller had predicted that within six weeks there would be three deaths in a seven-day period at her house. She then purchased some arsenic and fed it, diluted in cereal, to the three victims on the same day. When her husband rejected the cereal for its bitter taste, she said it was the last gruel she would ever prepare for him. She called in a doctor, but refused to administer the remedies he prescribed because she said she was sure that her husband was going to die.

The judge reminded her that the murder of a husband by his wife was called 'petty treason,' second only to 'high treason,' because the obedience owed to a husband by his wife was similar to that owed to a king by his subject.[14] After the verdict she confessed to the murder of her husband, with whom she did not get along, but denied poisoning the children.

Newspapers remarked on the hostility of the large crowd that attended her trial, attributing it to the general belief that, in her career as a minder of infants, she had committed several other murders. A broadside announced in a headline that she was executed for the poisoning of her husband and several children, and added at the end: 'It pleased Providence to cut her short in the midst of her diabolical attempts, for it is a well authenticated fact, that she attempted to poison six women her neighbours, whom she invited to tea, a short time before she was taken up.'[15]

A string of suspicious deaths in the family of Jane Scott, a twenty-one-year-old inhabitant of Preston, Lancashire, aroused suspicions, but when she was tried in September 1827 for the murder of her father, she was acquitted because the witness who could have identified the poison was absent. However, the judge decided to have her tried for the murder of her mother, Mary Scott. She was convicted of petty treason for this crime on 21 March 1828 (petty treason being the violation of allegiance to one's husband, parent, or master), and executed the following day.

This case received wide coverage, at first because it had obviously been a double murder, and then because she confessed to two more murders. There were two stories in the *Times* and three in the *Morning Herald*: one an entire column on the trial, one on the confession, and one on the execution.[16] The last story describes the crowd, which, after the execution, 'dispersed, but with the utmost unconcern imaginable.'

Scott appears to have been rather limited: indeed, the Lancaster *Gazette* called her 'a woman of weak intellect.'[17] She explained that she had poisoned her parents for their furniture, so that she could get married. A broadside suggests that she kept bad company and had been robbing her parents before she killed them. Asked whether she had also poisoned her eighteen-month-old niece in 1826, she admitted that she had, out of revenge, after a quarrel with her sister. She also confessed that she had poisoned her own illegitimate four-year-old son. She had used laudanum on the little girl, and arsenic on the others. The *Gazette* reported that she had to be dragged to the execution.

THE FORTIES POISONERS

If there was serial murder by women in the next decade, they got away with it. It is hard to believe that Esther Hibner, who viciously abused her apprentices, or Eliza Ross, who efficiently smothered an old woman so that she could sell her body to an anatomist, each committed only one murder. The Bristol poisoner Mary Ann Burdock was probably caught well into her career. But their shadowy pasts pale before the industry of a host of known serial poisoners of the 'hungry forties,' all hanged: Betty Eccles (1843), Sarah Dazely (1843), Eliza Joyce (1844), Sarah Freeman (1845), Mary Ann Milner (1847), Mary May (1848), Mary Ann Geering (1849), Rebecca Smith (1849), and Sarah Chesham (1851).

Elizabeth Eccles, the Female Monster!, the title of a pamphlet describing the career of a woman who poisoned her children, gives some idea of how the press characterized murderesses.[18] Eccles, who lived at Bolton, near Liverpool, was hardly an ideal mother, but it is likely that the depression of 1840–3 pushed her to eliminate members of her family. She appears to have been dissolute and ignorant as well as poor.

In the fall of 1842, she poisoned her thirteen-year-old stepson, William, after he threatened to tell his father that she was drunk. She then applied to the mill where he had worked (for three shillings a week, which he handed over to her) for burial money. She received fifty shillings. When she asked at the mill for burial money for a daughter, Nancy Haslam, who had died around the same time but had no connection with the mill, the authorities became suspicious. Arsenic was found in the bodies of these two, and also in the body of another daughter, Alice Haslam, who had died in 1840. In her late thirties, Eccles had had several children, all dead. A coroner's inquest found her guilty of murder of William, Nancy, and Alice, but, once she was convicted of the murder of William, the other charges were dropped.

A broadside sold at her execution on 6 May, observing that she had confessed to her husband that, if she had not been caught she would have poisoned her whole family, warned that 'the love of

money is the root of evil, it led her to crime! and a dreadful end!'
The broadside ballad composed for this occasion tells her story in
thirteen verses, of which this one is typical:

> To the Burial club she did apply
> For burying money they did deny
> For dark suspicion filled their mind,
> That something wrong they soon should find.[19]

On 5 August 1843, Sarah Dazely was hanged at Bedford before
a crowd of 10,000 for the murder of her husband, William, in
October 1842. Spectators were invited to buy a broadside ballad,
'The Lamentation of Sarah Dazely.'[20] She had been married before, to one Simon Mead, who died suddenly in June 1840, and
she was about to marry again in January 1843, when her intended
grew suspicious and called off the wedding. Though only in her
early twenties, she bragged that she had had seven husbands in
ten years. Throughout Bedfordshire she was referred to as 'the
female Bluebeard.'[21]

In March 1843 the last two husbands were disinterred, along
with an infant who had died in February 1840: the decomposition
of Mead's body made it impossible to pin down the cause of death,
but arsenic was found in the other two.

Her motives do not appear to have been pecuniary: she seems
to have killed rather vacantly and automatically, simply to do away
with impediments as they presented themselves. In a rural culture,
where life was cheap, poison widely available, and food in short
supply, this sort of response was immoral and unnatural but not
illogical.

Had Eliza Joyce not exposed her murders, an expert on poisoning said later, medical science would not have been able to establish her guilt.[22] In Boston, in October 1841, Joyce, addicted to
drink, poisoned her stepdaughter, Emma, eighteen months old,
with laudanum; in January 1842, she did the same to her own
three-week-old daughter, Ann. In September of that year, she poisoned her stepson, William. She was tried in Lincoln in July 1843

for the attempted murder of William, but got off. However, her husband and friends believed her guilty and would have nothing to do with her. Forced into a workhouse with yet another infant, she found herself tormented by guilt, and confessed.

On 24 July 1844, Joyce was found guilty of murder and was hanged on 2 August before a rowdy crowd of about 5,000. The local paper observed in the spectators 'rather a fiendish pleasure at the sight than the sad and painful reflection it was designed to produce ... Drunkenness, murder, a hell of mind, and the scaffold! – in these few words, how much of emphatic warning is there for the living.'[23]

There was a warning in this case for the medical establishment as well as the public, and another in the career of Sarah Freeman, a twenty-nine-year-old Somerset woman who buried her mother, her brother, her husband, and her seven-year-old illegitimate son in a thirteen-month period. 'The first thing that should strike every one,' said a local doctor,

> is that so many murders should have been committed on members of the same family without creating suspicion in the minds of the neighbours, and more especially in that of the medical men, if any were called to the assistance of the unfortunate sufferers. As the same means of destruction were employed in every case – namely, the administration of arsenic – a poison which produces well-known and unmistakeable effects, my surprise is still greater that one member after another of the same family should have been attacked with the same violent symptoms, all terminating in death, without leading to immediate and searching investigation into the cause of such fatality.

The doctor, Jonathan Toogood, complained that coroners sometimes, as a matter of economy, did not delve into unexplained deaths, and pointed out that Freeman's two subsequent victims would still be alive if an autopsy had been performed on her son.[24]

Arsenic was found in the bodies of all four, but she swore that she had had nothing to do with the deaths. Her protestations of innocence can safely be ignored, since it was revealed after her execution that she wrote to a former lover and said that her husband and child had died, yielding her twenty pounds in burial-insurance money, asked him to marry her, and threatened him with the same fate as her husband if he didn't. She then attempted to carry out her threat.[25]

Freeman had gone to school for seven years and to Sunday school, but whatever moral training she was given clearly had no impact. Her behaviour was so loose and her temper so vicious that, after her second illegitimate child was born, she was sent away from her parents' house.

She continued to support herself through prostitution, and then married Charles Freeman, a labourer, about 1840. After poisoning her husband and child, she opened a small shop and moved in with her parents and brothers for a few months, but she did not get along with them and they did not want her there. While staying with relatives of her husband, she received a letter from her brother Charles telling her not to come back. She came back none the less, and within a week her mother was dead. Conveniently, she was available to do the housekeeping. However, Charles ordered her out once again. Soon he was dead too. This time, the doctor suspected poisoning and sent Charles's stomach and intestines to a chemist for analysis. They were found to contain arsenic.

Freeman was charged with four murders but tried for only the most recent one. She was found guilty and sentenced to death, whereupon, according to a local paper, 'the atrocious prisoner broke out into furious invectives against the witness, the jury, and the judge, deprecating in coarse terms the sentence pronounced upon her.'[26] Listening to the 'condemned sermon' on the Sunday before the execution, everyone was moved to tears, said the Somerset County *Herald*, but 'no tear dimmed the eye of her, who had the most cause to feel.'[27] She was hanged on 23 April 1845, at Taunton, before a crowd of about 10,000, insisting until the end that she was not guilty. The *Herald* reported that, though the 'exceeding heinousness and atrocity of the wretched creature's crimes put her out of the pale of sympathy or pity,' the spectators did not disturb her last moments.[28] The Taunton *Courier* called her an 'unnatural, remorseless, and unpitied wretch, whose accumulated iniquities must be ranked among the foulest in the criminal annals of this kingdom.'[29] The *Annual Register* rather eloquently observed that she 'exhibited as much composure and firmness as would have lent dignity to martyrdom.'[30]

The *Herald*, deploring the increasing 'tendency to murder by poisoning,' called for a ban on the sale of all poisons to women.[31] Later, in response to male fears of an epidemic of secret murder in the 1840s, Parliament considered just this.

In the late 1840s, serial poisoning by women seemed alarmingly prevalent, perhaps because by this time the police were more suspicious and forensic chemists were more experienced. Newspapers and magazines commented on how ridiculously easy it was to acquire arsenic, and women continued to acquire it, not always for the purpose of killing rats.

In July 1847, Mary Ann Milner was tried in Lincoln for the poisoning of her husband's mother, in whose body arsenic was found. She was acquitted, and then tried for the poisoning of her brother's wife, Hannah Jickels, whose body also contained arsenic. After the jury brought in a verdict of guilty, the judge observed that it was obvious that she had committed other murders as well. A third indictment charging her with the poisoning of her infant niece, Ellen Jickels, was not acted upon. She confessed that she had given her sister-in-law a cake containing arsenic, and the baby a drink containing arsenic. She had not intended to poison her mother-in-law when she gave her father-in-law poisoned rice pudding. He lived, but with brain damage. She explained that she did not get along with her sister-in-law and did not like the way her in-laws treated her.

Milner seems to have been stunted intellectually and emotionally. She could not read well and could barely write. She also seems to have been unable to reason clearly. When her troubles came to a head, she took decisive action to clear her life of obstacles without stopping to consider how obvious, in retrospect, her action would be. In June 1847 she killed three times within a three-week period. She appears to have felt neither concern nor remorse. Newspapers reporting the second trial noted her lack of affect. She betrayed no feeling, even when she was pronounced guilty and sentenced to execution.[32]

The Lincoln, Rutland, and Stanford *Mercury* remarked on the spectators' animosity towards her: 'In the court there seemed to prevail a strong sense of the justice of the sentence; and the horror at such a series of diabolical murders seemed to have subverted that feeling usually betrayed on the sentencing of a wretched fellow-creature.'[33] On 29 July, one day before she was to be hanged, she committed suicide in her cell by hanging herself with her handkerchief.

The *Annual Register* commented that year that poisoning 'appears to have become fearfully prevalent; scarcely an assize passes on any of the circuits without a trial for murder by this means.'[34] Serial poisoning was especially alarming. The serial poisoners exposed up to this point seem to have been acting on their own, but in 1848 rumours of a poisoning ring, in which women advised and assisted one another, surfaced in the newspapers.

That summer, police in Essex began an investigation into a series of poisonings by women in the same district, near Clavering, who knew one another. There were indications that everyone in the neighbourhood was aware of what had been going on. Later the *Times* would say that, in Essex, 'the use of arsenic became a kind of family secret – a weapon in the hands of the weaker vessel by which an ill-favoured husband or a troublesome family might be readily put out of the way.'[35]

In August 1846, police had looked into an accusation that Sarah Chesham, who was then about thirty-five, had attempted to poison an illegitimate neighbourhood baby at the behest of the child's father, Thomas Newport, who was liable for his support. The mother, Lydia Taylor, had been a maid in the service of his mother. Newport farmed his mother's land; his connection with the Cheshams was that their cottage belonged to his mother, and he seems to have employed some of them as casual farm labourers.

Taylor claimed that he had seduced her soon after her arrival, and that, after she was discharged, he gave her money. The child was born 16 December 1845. Chesham inexplicably came to visit her baby when he was two months old, and again a month later, and both times he was sick after she had given him 'sugar.'

Chesham was known as someone who 'could put any expensive or disagreeable object out of the way, and who, as it was understood, had practised her own infamous trade upon her own children.' When she called, people understood that she was on an errand of destruction. 'The village of Clavering seems to have long ago taken it for granted that the prisoner had poisoned her children, and yet they say little more about it than if she had killed her pigs,' said the *Times*. 'It is beyond question that an accepted and reputed murderess walked abroad in a village unchallenged and unaccused, and that all the inhabitants had seen her children buried without remark or outcry, though they were clearly convinced that there had been foul play.'[36]

The child, Solomon Taylor, took sick in June 1846 and died on 27 September. At the inquest on 23 October, the coroner hinted to the jury at a liaison between Chesham and Newport, but the verdict was inconclusive as to whether the death was from natural causes.

Meanwhile, police had been investigating the deaths of two of Chesham's sons, Joseph, ten, and James, eight. (There were four other children.) The boys had died in suspicious circumstances in January 1845 after becoming ill on a day when their father, a farm labourer, was away from home. Both had been enrolled in a burial club. The bodies were exhumed, and a substantial quantity of arsenic was found in each stomach. At the inquest the boys' aunt revealed that, a few days before they took sick, Newport had beaten one of them for stealing two eggs, and their mother had said, 'It would be a good job if it would please God to take them out of the way.'[37] To make matters worse for Chesham, the doctor she called to attend her oldest son told the inquest that, on 15 January, when told he was dead, she declined to order a coffin, remarking that the same coffin would hold two. The second son was ready for a coffin on 17 January.

The local paper, assuming that she was guilty, reported that 'the utmost indignation prevails against the inhuman wretch who thus so secretly destroyed her own unoffending and helpless offspring.'[38]

In due course the coroner's jury concluded that they had been murdered.

In March 1847 she stood trial on three murder charges, but was found not guilty of having murdered either of her sons or the Taylor infant. Her sons had been dosed with arsenic, but it could not be traced to her. In the case of the baby, arsenic poisoning was not proved. The *Times* reported that she 'appeared quite collected, and exhibited almost indifference to the result' of the proceedings.[39] Newport was charged with inciting her to commit murder, but the charge was dropped, presumably because it was not proved that she had committed murder.

Chesham seemed to have been the neighbourhood authority on arsenic poisoning, apparently offering to help make poisoned pies, and even suggesting them as a remedy.[40] She was implicated in another case that surfaced in the same rural area the following year. Among those claiming to have been instigated to murder by Chesham was supposed to have been a woman executed in 1848 for the poisoning of her half-brother. She was strongly suspected of other poisonings as well.[41]

Mary May, who, like Chesham, was in her late thirties, had had sixteen children, fourteen of whom had died over the years. Her first husband had also died unexpectedly. (A few hours before her execution, she told one of her guards that she had given him a bowl of milk three hours before he died, and he did not want another.)[42] In June 1848, her forty-five-year-old half-brother, William Constable, a.k.a. Spratty Watts, died suddenly not long after she had enrolled him in a burial club without his knowledge. She happened to mention to a friend at the time that it would be fortunate for her if her brother died because then she would have enough money to buy a horse and cart and travel from one village to another selling things, a plan that prompted the *News of the World* to comment savagely, after her conviction, 'thus becoming acquainted with the circumstances of each family, and through that acquaintance devising schemes and contriving plots how, by the ready administration of arsenic, she might acquire more money, and by murder add to her wealth.'[43]

Constable, a forty-five-year-old pedlar who lived with May and her husband, became sick on 8 June after drinking a half-pint of porter fortified with arsenic. By 11 June he was dead. Constable's body was exhumed when rumours of May's suspicious career reached the authorities, and on 6 July an inquest found that he had been murdered. She was tried and convicted on 25 July of having poisoned him, and sentenced to be hanged on 14 August. Though she was widely believed to have committed other murders as well, she insisted that she was not guilty.[44] Several papers reported, however, that in a private, eleventh-hour confession she provided the names of a sort of sisterhood of poisoners in her district – as the *Times* later put it, an 'atrocious conspiracy to poison husbands and children.'[45] She was executed, said the *Morning Chronicle*, 'before an immense multitude assembled in front of the gaol, including, as usual on these occasions, a large number of females.'[46]

A broadside ballad marking the occasion was cited by Henry Mayhew as typical for its rush into the subject and its homely reflections:

> The solemn bell for me doth toll,
> And I am doom'd to die
> (For murdering my brother dear,)
> Upon a tree so high,
> For gain I did premeditate
> My brother for to slay, –
> Oh, think upon the dreadful fate
> Of wretched Mary May.
> ...
>
> Good people all, of each degree,
> Before it is too late,
> See me on the fatal tree,
> And pity my sad fate.
> My guilty heart stung with grief,
> With agony and pain, –
> My tender brother I did slay
> That fatal day for gain.[47]

Several bodies were exhumed in the fall of 1848 as a result of revelations by May just before she was hanged, but no proof materialized. After that the coroner reluctantly dropped his investigations.

But that was not the end of poisoning in Essex. In the winter of 1848, Richard Chesham took sick, and his mother later reported that her daughter-in-law, Sarah, had insisted on feeding the invalid herself. At one point the younger Mrs Chesham observed, 'Poor thing, he will not be a trouble to anyone long.'[48] Nor was he: he died in May 1849. Eventually her boasts to neighbours about 'seasoning' mince pies and doing away with people caused the authorities to look into his death, and in March 1851 she was tried and convicted of poisoning him with intent to murder, and sentenced to death. Despite her protestations of innocence, an execution broadside had her confessing:

> My tender, pretty, smiling babes,
> With poison I did slay.
> And after that I did cruel take
> My husband's life away.[49]

The execution attracted about 10,000 spectators, among whom, according to the *Weekly Chronicle*,

> there were hardly any respectable people observable in the crowd, but a most disgusting number of women. Some of these had gay flowers in their bonnets, and evidently set up for rustic belles; others were mothers, giving suck to infants, whom they carried in their arms; others were elderly matrons, presiding at the head of their families, and from the elevation of the domestic spring cart pointing out to their young daughters how they could best see the execution.[50]

A broadside noted that various medical men and an agent for Madame Tussaud's Chamber of Horrors had applied for access to the body (presumably to cast a death mask), but to no avail.[51]

Mary May was described in the newspapers as large and 'repulsive-looking,' Sarah Chesham as masculine-looking. Mary Ann Geering, tried, convicted, and hanged in August 1849 for poisoning her husband at Guestling, near Hastings, in 1848, was 'a woman of masculine and forbidding appearance.'[52] She was strongly suspected of the murder of two of her sons, George and James, and the attempted murder of a third son, Benjamin, as well: all were members of the Guestling Benefit Society. The other charges for the murder of her sons were dropped once she was found guilty of the murder of her husband, but before her execution she confessed to having used arsenic to dispatch all three.

'Such cases have lately become so painfully and horribly frequent,' said the *Daily News*,

> that we cannot but feel surprise that the last session of parliament should have been allowed to pass without some philanthropic and humane legislator feeling that it was his mission to attempt the application of a remedy. That the facility with which every description of poison can be procured in the druggist's shop, and the absence of any inquiry into the causes of death by competent persons, are closely connected with the frequency of these poisonings, there can be little doubt.[53]

Sarah Chesham's execution on 25 March 1851, triggered a stream of indignant newspaper editorials, pamphlets about her well-publicized career as a poisoner, and broadsides describing the manner in which she took her punishment. She adamantly refused to confess to the murder of her husband, though she conceded that she might have poisoned others.[54] She was every man's worst nightmare: a woman who could not be controlled, who had no conscience, and who had the means to kill secretly.

'Sarah Chesham's Lamentation,' a ballad sung to the tune of 'Waggon Train,' explained in basic terms just what code she had broken:

> When she was at the holy altar
> She did a solemn vow then give,
> Her husband dear to love and cherish,

    Whilst God permitted her to live:
    But she the solemn vow has broken,
    Wicked, base, deceitful wife,
    Barbarous and cruel mother,
    Doomed to die in prime of life.[55]

Her village, Clavering, was depicted as equally monstrous in supporting for so long a secret society of poisoners. It was a place, said one weekly newspaper, 'where it would appear, murder by poison is a matter of familiar conversation, among other domestic expediences – where English wives and mothers warm towards this household treachery, and threaten any of the society who should traitorously oppose it.'[56]

English wives and mothers were in danger of being unilaterally branded potential murderesses. By this time there was such great interest in the crime of poisoning, and in the gender of the perpetrators, that the House of Commons had collected statistics for the years 1840–50 on poisonings in all the judicial districts of the United Kingdom. In England and Wales, eighty-seven women and seventy-seven men had been tried for murder or attempted murder by poison; in Scotland, ten women and five men; in Ireland, thirty-one women and twenty-five men.[57] In general, the figures were higher for the last five years of the decade. In the general population of murderers, there were a great many more males than females, but, when only poisoning was considered, the proportion of female murderers to male murderers was slightly higher. So it was clear that poison was used more often as a murder weapon by women than by men. That confirmed for Parliament that poisoning was a women's crime. Something had to be done in response to the newspapers' and the public's demands that the sale of poison be controlled, or at least registered.

On its editorial page of 12 March 1851, the *Times* reprinted from Dickens's magazine, *Household Words*, an article urging the regulation of the sale of poison. 'Two centuries ago poisoning was a science; now, thanks to a sluggish and "never-minding" Legislature, the art may be safely practised by the meanest capacity,' the article sharply pointed out.[58]

Just after the execution, the *Morning Advertiser* observed:

The reader need not be reminded how often, for the last five or six years, we have urged the absolute necessity, forced upon us by the increase of secret poisoning, for rendering the purchase of arsenic in small quantities as difficult as it is possible by legal enactments ... Here the State fails to instruct the depraved in their duty; neglects to prevent them, as far as its means lie, from the perpetration of a particular crime, and, after leaving the instrument within reach, punishes for inability to resist the horrible temptation.[59]

On 24 March 1851, one day before the execution of Sarah Chesham, the House of Lords accepted an amendment to the Earl of Carlisle's Sale of Arsenic Bill, which then passed third reading. The seller of any quantity of this poison in England would be required to keep a record of purchasers' names and addresses and their reasons for buying it. Moreover, no one would be able to get less than ten pounds of uncoloured arsenic without endorsement by a witness and a statement as to why the colouring agent would be harmful. A new clause, quietly inserted, restricted the sale of arsenic to adult males.

In his speech on the bill, the Earl of Carlisle suggested that the less said about the connection with the Essex poisonings the better. In an apparent reference to lower-class rural women, he told the Lords that he 'felt that there was a degree of mysterious horror attached to the use of poison, which seemed to attract and fascinate a certain class of minds.'[60] He added that as it would be unwise to draw up a list of alternatives for potential poisoners, he was restricting the bill to arsenic.

J.S. Mill was outraged at the implicit assumption behind this provision. Were women really more predisposed than men to be murderers, or at least poisoners? The bill reached the House of Commons on 7 April in the same form in which it had left the Lords.[61] It received second reading in that form on 15 April.[62] On 5 May, Mill wrote to Sir George Grey, the home secretary, to complain of the 'gross insult to every woman in the country' contained in the bill.

Mill called the proposal 'monstrous' and warned that such a bill would be a step backward. He pointed out:

One of the characteristics of the improved spirit of the present time is the growing tendency to the elevation of women – towards their relief from disabilities, their increased estimation, the assignment to them of a higher position, both social & domestic. But this clause is a blind step in the reverse direction. It singles out women for the purpose of degrading them. It establishes a special restriction, a peculiar disqualification against them alone. It assumes that women are more addicted than men to committing murder! Does the criminal calendar, or the proceedings of the police courts, shew a preponderance of women among the most atrocious criminals?

He argued that the bill was ill-timed, branding women inferior just when they were beginning to be recognized as the equals of men. It was not the function of the legislature to create laws in response to the latest news. 'If the last two or three murderers had been men with red hair, as well might Parliament have rushed to pass an Act restricting all red haired men from buying or possessing deadly weapons,' said Mill.[63]

The bill, in the end, did not single out women. Given third reading and passed in the House of Commons on 23 May 1851 with no debate,[64] it specified merely that a purchaser must be 'a person of full age' – not, as in the original bill, a male adult.[65]

It is of some significance that nowhere in the newspapers, or in Parliament, was there discussion of the exclusion of women in the bill. There seems to have been a tacit, paternalistic assumption that women needed to be restrained but not consulted. Serial poisoning by women did slow down, but not before the law caught up with Mary Emily Cage, the last of the forties poisoners, in a village near Ipswich. The church bell was tolling and the procession from the cottage to the grave was about to begin when the rector ordered her husband's pallbearers to take the corpse back to the house. An inquest was held the following day, and the victim, her husband, James, was found to have been poisoned.

Six years earlier, five of her fourteen children had died within a fortnight, but nothing could be proved against her. Only four of her children were now living. Though she insisted on her innocence to the end, she was found guilty of murder and hanged on 19 August 1851. Even the *Times* said there was little doubt that she was guilty of other murders.[66]

To judge by press coverage in both broadsides and newspapers, none of these murderesses was, in herself, sensational. However, their chronological proximity had a cumulative effect that was augmented in the forties by isolated poisonings, usually of men by women. We know very little of these women other than that they were typically rural, illiterate, poor, married, oppressed, and fairly young – most were in their twenties or thirties. There were too many of them to dismiss them as psychopaths. They were not outsiders: indeed, many of them, especially the Essex poisoners, seem to have been rather gregarious. Since in poor rural areas policing would have been rudimentary, and sudden death not uncommon, there may have been more murderesses of whom we know nothing: women who 'lost' husbands and children in circumstances that were suspicious but not incriminating. This sort of behaviour may even have been acceptable on the fringes of society. When it threatened to penetrate deeper, the establishment acted to curtail it. Serial poisoning by women did not come to an end, but when it did surface after the forties it was loudly and widely condemned.

MASS MURDER

The one case that I have found of a woman's being tried for mass murder in nineteenth-century England is that of Mary Ann Brough, whose story, as recounted in broadsides, was known as the 'Esher Tragedy.'[67] On 9 June 1854, in the village of Esher, near Guildford, Surrey, she slit the throats of her six children, aged twenty-one months to twelve years, rather than give them up to her husband. She told police at the time that, if there had been forty children there, she would have killed them all. On the night of the murders, she felt a black cloud surround and control her so that, when she thought about the children, she felt compelled to kill them. After the murders, she said, the cloud had lifted.

Brough did not make a sympathetic figure. The only redeeming factor in her story is that she tried, if somewhat half-heartedly, to slit her own throat as well. She seems to have been a thoroughly disreputable woman married to a decent, long-suffering man who finally had her watched and caught her with a lover. She was at this time forty-three years old and had had other children who had died in infancy. Her husband confronted her, and then left her – with the children for the time being, but without any money. Within a week the children were dead.

Brough was tried for the murder of only one of them, two-and-a-half-year-old Harriet. The prosecutor argued that the circumstances appeared to have no parallel in the history of crime. Despite her confession, she was found not guilty by reason of insanity. The most eminent authority in the land, Forbes Winslow, testified that a paralytic stroke in 1852 had affected her mind. Another expert, Alfred Swaine Taylor, thought that this was a case of homicidal monomania provoked by female biology.[68]

There were rumours at the time that because, before her marriage, she had been a wet-nurse to the Prince of Wales in 1841 (a job from which she was discharged for disobedience), there was reluctance at the highest levels to hang her. 'A strange notion appeared to pervade the minds of the vulgar,' says the *Annual Register*,

> that the crimes of this wretched woman would be some stain upon the future of the Prince of Wales, whom she had nursed, and *that she never could be found guilty of murder*, because it would attach an imputation on the Prince for ever. The verdict of the jury caused therefore little surprise, notwithstanding that the evidence of insanity was of the most trivial character.[69]

The *Times* would have none of psychology. A leader after the verdict says nothing of the rumour, but destroys her character, calling her a fiendish wretch and a murderess, and maligns the justice system for its credulousness. It argues that she conducted herself sanely and rationally between the murders and the trial, and, 'indeed, the artistic manner in which the confession is worded would do credit to a romance writer of the Victor Hugo school. It was certainly not the production of a maniac.' Her crime, says the *Times*, was 'the act of a vindictive woman upon the discovery of her enormous guilt.' She was 'a woman of evil life,' and she murdered her six children 'in the most pitiless and cold-blooded manner.'[70]

Roger Smith, who has studied the defence of insanity in Victorian murder trials, believes one reason the jury reached the decision it did was 'widespread benevolence towards mothers who murdered their children.' Another was the assumption in both the medical and the legal professions that women were at the mercy of their bodies, and that therefore medical discourse was appropriate in the courtroom.[71]

CATHERINE WILSON

'Many times recently the dull fear of prevalent secret poisoning has spread through the ranks of the people,' said the *Lancet* in 1862. 'The career of Catherine Wilson gives form and shape to some of the worst of the vague terrors which have been evoked.'[72] The Sale of Arsenic Act did not restrain her, since she did not use arsenic.

Wilson's career as a poisoner was especially threatening because it was not confined to members of her own family and because her criminal activities were not easily traceable. Until she was caught, her life seemed normal and uneventful. The case was well publicized because the murders of which she was accused took place in London – so well publicized that 20,000–30,000 people gathered to watch her die. As a broadside ballad composed for the occasion put it:

> A female die for murder,
> What numbers flock to see,
> Sad and forlorn, exposed to scorn,
> On Newgate's dismal tree.[73]

Catherine (a.k.a. Constance) Wilson was probably the most vicious serial poisoner, though not the most notorious, of nineteenth-century England. A nurse, she supported herself by killing off acquaintances for their money and possessions. Like the other serial poisoners, she murdered for pennies. Unlike them, however, she does not appear to have been either ignorant or weak-minded, but was in fact quick-witted and cunning. She did not live on the fringes of society, nor was she especially poor or oppressed. Indeed, through wholesale poisoning she managed to uphold her position reasonably well in middle-class London society.

What was diabolical about Wilson, as the *Lancet* pointed out, was her perversion of medical assistance. She posed as a nurse, an angel of mercy, while she mercilessly pushed them to death. She would slip them just enough poison to make them sick, and then, ever solicitous, persuade them to take 'medicine' to help them recover. Consequently, the longer she nursed them, the sicker people got. 'Drink it up, dear; it will do you good,' she was reported to have insisted as one friend resisted a glass of sulphuric acid.[74] In other cases she administered overdoses of dangerous medicine. Two victims were thought to have died from the effects of colchicum, used in very small doses for rheumatism and gout.

When these people died, she either inherited or stole from them. The image she consistently maintained was of a concerned friend. 'I would not have her cut up, poor thing!' she advised the credulous husband of another victim, thereby heading off an autopsy.[75]

One broadside called her, accurately enough, a wicked woman motivated by greed. Another, which says she betrayed 'no one knows how many persons' by poisoning them, commented (with more feeling than syntax): 'A vile, a base, a more wicked woman there cannot be upon England's ground.'[76]

After being unaccountably acquitted of attempting to murder Sarah Cornell, who had promised to leave her something in her will, she was immediately rearrested and charged with the murder of her landlady, Maria Soames, a widow who, like the other victims, took sick upon having tea with her. On 27 September 1862, she was convicted. In sentencing her to death, the judge remarked on the singularity of a case 'where the excruciating pain and agony of the victim were watched with so much deliberation by the murderer.' He listed a string of four other deaths dating from 1854 that bore distinct signs of her handiwork: Peter Mawer, a wealthy widower, who took colchicum and employed her as a servant; James Dixon, a common-law husband, who also took colchicum and died in the same manner as Mrs Soames; a Mrs Jackson, who died after exhibiting the same symptoms, and from whom Wilson extracted a large sum of money by forgery; and Ann Atkinson, wife of a tailor, in London with a large sum of money of which she was supposedly robbed before she arrived at Wilson's house. In addition, said the judge, Wilson was clearly guilty of the attempted murder of Cornell and of a common-law husband named Taylor.

The newspapers observed that the murderess heard all this with an air of callous indifference, suppressing any emotion. To the end, she claimed she was innocent. No one believed her, however: there was not one application to the home secretary for remission of her sentence, not even from the Society for the Abolition of Capital Punishment. 'All considerations of sex,' said the *Times*, 'which in some cases of women under capital sentence induce some people to plead for mercy, appear in this instance to have been completely merged in horror at the crime ...'[77] She was hanged on 20 October 1862. 'Her coolness and self-possession were perfectly astounding,' said the *Daily Telegraph*. 'She walked with a firm and resolute step; and it may be truly said that she appeared much less concerned than many of those who were present.'[78]

Public revulsion, the deepest so far at any serial murderess, earned her a place in Madame Tussaud's Chamber of Horrors, where she was remembered until 1894. Clever, cold, and ambitious, she preyed on ordinary people. Her victims were members of the middle class, respectable citizens who trusted her because she appeared to be one of them. Her stock-in-trade was deceit. As the *Annual Register* put it, in the guise of a ministering angel, she performed the work of a destroying demon.[79]

MARY ANN COTTON

Catherine Wilson's hanging would have set an example only to those who heard about it. Mary Ann Cotton, balancing on the

edge of survival in the north of England, did not bother much
with others. In the eight years from 1864 to 1872, this poor,
barely literate, unremarkable-looking one-time Sunday school
teacher and former nurse in her thirties is known to have killed
somewhere between fifteen and twenty people with arsenic extracted from a compound used to kill vermin. Eleven of her own
children, five stepchildren, three husbands, a sister-in-law, a lodger,
and her mother died suddenly with similar symptoms after they
had been in her care. As has since been noted, 'wherever this
woman moved there seemed to be a mild epidemic of gastric fever
around her.'[80] Mary Ann Cotton's last victim, seven-year-old Charles
Edward Cotton, like most of her victims, had burial insurance.
Her first husband, William Mowbray, died mysteriously, as did
seven of their children. Her mother, a Mrs Stott, died after Mary
Ann had come to visit and taken a substantial number of her
household possessions. Her second husband, George Ward, died
suddenly after willing everything he had to her. Her third husband, James Robinson, escaped, but not before three of his children, one of hers and Mowbray's, and one of hers and Robinson's,
had died in her care. When he offended her with an accusation,
not of murder, but of theft – she had been tampering with his
accounts – she left. She went on to marry, bigamously, Frederick
Cotton, and then buried him, his sister Margaret, another of his
sons, an infant of this union, and a lodger, Joseph Nattrass, who
had unwisely made her his beneficiary. Most of her victims exhibited symptoms of arsenic poisoning but were thought at the time
(by authorities in different places) to have died of gastric fever.
Possibly some of them did.

In its way, Cotton's career was more horrifying than Wilson's
because it was more arbitrary. It seems to have been casual and
automatic: when there were too many responsibilities, or when
she had too little money to survive on, she eliminated one of the
responsibilities or poisoned for profit, or both. She was caught
only because she had tried – unsuccessfully – to place her last
victim in the workhouse so that she could marry yet again. When
Nattrass died on 12 July 1872, the master of the workhouse told the
doctor who had attended him of his suspicions, and tests revealed

the presence of arsenic in the body. Nattrass's body was exhumed, and it was discovered that he, too, had died of arsenic poisoning. She was arrested on 18 July, but as she was pregnant the trial did not begin until 5 March. (The baby, a girl, was born on 10 January.)

The curiosity of a wholesale murderess placidly nursing a baby in the Durham prison added to the public interest in this case. She was tried only for the murder of Charles Edward, though she was widely believed to have committed the other murders as well. Once convicted on 7 March, she was promptly hanged – on 24 March 1873. 'A score of homicides is a handsome harvest of death for one woman to reap to her single hand before her operations are discovered,' commented the Durham County *Advertiser*.[81]

A broadside ballad about Cotton summed up the public's fears about the vulnerability of the weak and the sick to trusted caregivers:

> The cursed rimes of the secret poisoner
> We must confess are the worst of all,
> You bless the hand that smooths your pillow,
> But by that hand you surely fall.
> You put your trust in those about you,
> When you lie sick upon your bed,
> While you are blessing they are wishing
> The very next moment would find you dead.[82]

The Newcastle *Daily Journal* put out a special edition on the day of the execution. One story reported the change of feeling against the 'monster murderess' as 'some pictured to themselves the new-born babe that had been torn from the mother's breast, and they argued with themselves that to slay the mother was to cast forth her little one either to premature destruction or to a life of ineffaceable shame.'[83] In fact, as a modern biographer discovered, the baby lived a long and rewarding, though difficult, life.[84] The *Illustrated Police News* of 29 March featured a front-page layout of sketches of the execution, Cotton in jail, Cotton in a room with a mistreated child, and so on, all constructed from the artist's imagination. 'She became a wife but to poison, a mistress but to poison and a mother but to poison,' was this paper's summation.

Despite the rapid accumulation of evidence of her criminal career, Cotton refused to admit that she had poisoned anyone intentionally. She wrote to Robinson on 12 March: 'If you have Won Sarke of Kindness in you Will Try to get my life spard you know your sealfe thare has been A moast dredful to hear tell of the Lyies that has been told a Bout me ...'[85]

'Her path from the altar, thrice visited, to the gaol is strewn with deaths, deaths which it is almost irrational to expect can be explained,' said the Durham *Chronicle*, 'and which it is yet almost equally a tax upon human credulity to believe can have been the work of one wretched human being, however lost.'[86]

The Newcastle *Daily Journal* marvelled that she could have got away with murder for so many years, and pointed out that she seemed to have no difficulty in getting men to marry her. Like its contemporaries, it regarded poisonings as worse than other murders: 'it is strange and terrible that persons capable of committing them can maintain the quiet decencies of ordinary life ... There was no hatred or passion in this case, but a sort of diabolical inhumanity which made the woman absolutely indifferent to everything except the attainment of her own paltry ends.'[87]

Broadsides (unusual as late as 1873), pamphlets, plays, and rhymes marked the execution, and after it there was a place for her in the Chamber of Horrors, where she remained until 1899. Cotton quickly became – and remained for some time – a sort of witch figure, safe to laugh at once she was dead, but frightening all the same. A rhyme used to frighten children into obedience runs:

> Mary Ann Cotton
> She's dead and she's rotten
> She lies in her bed
> With her eyes wide oppen
> Sing, sing, oh what can I sing?
> Mary Ann Cotton is tied up with string
> Where, where? Up in the air
> Sellin' black puddens a penny a pair.[88]

THE DECLINE OF SERIAL POISONING

Very soon, perhaps pushed by the scandal of Mary Ann Cotton's poisoning spree, medical science, point-of-sale record-keeping, and public awareness made it more and more difficult to hide the tracks left by arsenic. In Cheshire in 1878, Ellen Heesom was convicted of the arsenic poisoning of her daughter, Sarah, about eighteen months old, in October 1877, and was thought to have poisoned as well her mother, Lydia Sykes, in November 1877, and another daughter, Lydia Johnson, nine, in March 1876. All were enrolled in burial clubs. The judge remarked that this was a case of unparalleled atrocity.

The Chester *Guardian and Record* also thought it a 'horrible' case, and pointed out that Heesom worked at a glass factory where arsenic was used.[89] At her trial in February 1878, 'she manifested great callousness,' said the *Guardian*.[90] She was found guilty and sentenced to die, but was reprieved when she was discovered to be pregnant. In announcing this the *Guardian* observed that there was not much public interest in saving her.[91] Though the case was sensational locally, it did not inspire London editors to do more than report it calmly and succinctly.

Margaret Higgins and Catherine Flannagan, who subsisted in the slums of Liverpool by insuring relatives and neighbours, and then killing them off, were more conspicuous. By comparison with Mary Ann Cotton, who by any modern definition would be considered insane, or the Essex poisoners, in whom lack of moral training triggered an uncivilized response to the oppression of class and gender in the 'hungry forties,' these women were hardened criminals. They were convicted and executed in 1884.

Like Sarah Chesham and Mary May in Essex, Flannagan and Higgins were probably the ringleaders of a larger poisoning enterprise. The files of the Home Office contain a letter of 22 February 1884 to that effect from Flannagan's solicitor to J.B. Maule, director of public prosecutions, written after her conviction in an apparent effort to stay her execution. Flannagan implicated Margaret Evans, who at one time lived in the same house as Higgins; Mary Carroll, her sister-in-law; Bridget Begley, who held insurance with Flannagan on an alleged victim who lodged with Begley; and a Mrs Stanton, who she alleged assisted Evans in dispatching one victim and held insurance, along with Bridget Pugh, on another.

These stories suggest that Flannagan and Higgins recruited acquaintances who they thought had easy access to intended victims. This appears to have been a sophisticated operation. Though the Liverpool police looked into the allegations, Flannagan was not respited and no further prosecutions materialized.[92]

A local paper called it 'a vulgar tragedy of low life.' In poisoning for petty sums that they could have acquired in any other enterprise, they showed a singular lack of ambition and imagination, said the paper. 'They poisoned for pence, as some poor women make match-boxes, and with no greater desire or hope of profit and advantage.'[93]

Liverpool was England's second-largest city, overcrowded and full of misery and disease. It was, says Behlmer, 'a haven for crime, drunkenness and social disaffection. Perhaps more clearly in Liverpool than in any other English city, slum dwellers seemed to live beyond the reach of law and order.'[94]

Flannagan and Higgins were sisters, Scotswomen married to Irishmen. Flannagan was fifty-five at the time of her trial, Higgins forty-one. Both were illiterate. The older woman kept a rooming-house; the younger was a charwoman. Flannagan was clearly the brains of the operation: in addition to accusing others after her trial, she offered before the trial to give evidence against her sister. After conviction both admitted their guilt, but Higgins insisted that she had been urged on by Flannagan.

The sisters were jointly charged with the murders of Thomas Higgins (Margaret's husband); Margaret Jennings, who, with her father, had lodged with Flannagan; and John Flannagan, her brother-in-law. Higgins was also charged with the murder of Mary Higgins, her stepdaughter. The letter from Flannagan's solicitor named five other people poisoned by the sisters since 1879. However, they were tried only for the murder of Thomas Higgins.

Their weapon was arsenic, obtained through the soaking of fly-papers in cold water. Each fly-paper contained a grain of arsenic, enough to kill someone. The sale of arsenic was regulated, but not the sale of fly-papers. Nor was the insuring of unsuspecting friends and relatives.

Patrick Higgins, brother of Thomas, had heard that Flannagan registered many people in clubs and received money when they died. The dead man 'was ignorant that his life was valued at so little, his death so much,' as the *Lancet* remarked.[95] On finding that Flannagan had insured his brother in several clubs and insurance firms for about a hundred pounds, a very large amount for someone who had lived in extreme poverty, Patrick alerted the doctor who had signed the death certificate. Thomas, a forty-five-year-old coal delivery man, had been in good health until about ten days before his death on 2 October 1883. The doctor notified the coroner of the brother's suspicions and obtained permission to do an autopsy. But the sisters had acted quickly: he had to stop the funeral to do it. Flannagan absconded after instructing her daughter to remove her photograph from a frame in the house and destroy it.

While the police were investigating, the Liverpool *Daily Post* reported that streets where Flannagan had lived seemed to have had a number of untimely deaths while she was there.[96] *Lloyd's Weekly Newspaper* said she had insured neighbours whose subsequent deaths were suspicious.[97] The rapidity with which rumours began circulating suggests that their activities were well known around the neighbourhood.

After arsenic was found in the body of Thomas Higgins, the bodies of Margaret Jennings, Mary Higgins, and John Flannagan were exhumed, and all were found to contain large amounts of arsenic. The sisters were soon located and arrested. They were convicted on 14 February 1884, and hanged on 3 March, Flannagan apparently calm, according to the *Times*, and Higgins obviously terrified.[98] The *Daily Post* called them 'fiends in human shape' and 'wretches' who 'had sent their nearest kith and kin into untimely graves after slow agonies of torture by poisoning ...'[99] Flannagan and Higgins were among the longest-running murderess exhibits in the Chamber of Horrors, remaining there until 1980 and 1979, respectively.

By 1887, when Elizabeth Berry was exposed in Liverpool, burial clubs were more tightly regulated, but there were informal ones in operation that simply did not register. If one wanted higher benefits, it was also possible, as indeed is still the case, to buy life insurance for someone else.

Berry, thirty-one years old, was a workhouse nurse who poisoned her eleven-year-old daughter, Edith Annie, and probably her mother, Mary Ann Finley, for insurance. She was found guilty of the murder of her daughter and sentenced to hang; while she was on trial in Liverpool for the one murder, an inquest, aided by hindsight, found her guilty of the other, though the verdict of guilty in the first trial made a second unnecessary.

The trial took four days in the spring of 1887, longer than most murder trials, and spectators crowded the court. The local newspaper observed that 'the attendance of ladies indicated a morbid curiosity on the part of a portion of the female sex to witness the sad position of this unfortunate prisoner.'[100] The London and Liverpool papers covered it in detail, and the local papers, the weekly Oldham *Chronicle* and the Oldham *Daily Stàndard* and *Weekly Standard,* pulled out all the stops, running interviews with her (through people who had talked to her in prison); pictures of the child dead and alive; anecdotes and descriptions of the murderess's previous life; letters to the editor; and, of course, full details of the inquest, trial, execution, and crimes, from the report of the inquest into Annie's death headed 'Sensational Evidence' to the full page, consisting of seven long, dense broadsheet columns, marking the execution. News stories reported that at the trial the dark, trim, fetchingly attired Berry behaved like 'a cool customer.' After the verdict she was simply 'a cruel and unfeeling woman.'

A representative of her solicitor went to see her in prison, at her request, and told the press that he

> had some minutes to wait before the unlocking of doors and the clanking of keys informed his ears that the notorious murderess was approaching. Another minute and she stood before him. What a change there was from the appearance she presented two days be-

fore! Gone the fashionable dress she wore all through the Coroner's inquiry, the magisterial investigation, and that weary four days' trial at St. George's Hall. It was now replaced by a sombre, shapeless dress of blue serge, relieved only by a white collar. On her head, imprisoning the frisette, which was always a feature of her get-up, and which helped to make her appear attractive, was a prison cap. Her face presented a greater change than her dress. At Oldham it was clear, and her cheeks, for a woman of her age, were ruddy. On Saturday the tints of health were found to have vanished, and were succeeded only by a pallor which showed that mental anguish had made its mark. She was deadly pale, save the faintest tinge of remaining colour. With a wearied step she came forward to the compartment facing that occupied by Mr. Robinson.

The description communicates her suffering and her fall from vanity and power over others. A still more damning description was to come after the execution, when a reporter was taken, with others, to view the body. 'She looked forty, if she looked a day. The face had no colour, and the death hue did not make it pleasant to look upon,' he said.[101]

Lizzie Berry left a trail of profitable bereavement behind her. Her husband, Thomas, had died in 1881; her son, Harold, in 1883; her mother, in 1886; and her daughter, in 1887. She had drawn insurance benefits after each of these deaths. All were sudden deaths, and, at least in the last two, the victim, nursed by Berry, had been recovering when she was struck ill for the last time. Both her mother and her daughter seemed to have been made sicker by the medicine she insisted on administering to them.

Her daughter's death benefit of ten pounds had been a disappointment to her: she thought her insurance agent had insured the girl for a hundred pounds, roughly the amount she had collected on the deaths of her husband and mother. Berry's salary was twenty-five pounds a year, about half of which went for board, room, and schooling for the child, who could not live with her at the workhouse. So it was clear, on examination of her finances, that she could not live on her salary alone, and that the girl's death, if it did not yield as much insurance as expected, did relieve the mother of a substantial financial burden.

The detailed description from witnesses at the trial made the child a particularly pathetic victim and the mother a ruthless, deceitful, calculating villain. Annie was happy, healthy, obliging, undemanding, and well liked. She could not remain, as other murdered children did, a mere statistic, because she had lived apart from her mother for several years and had established an identity of her own. Pictures of her in death, with large blisters on her mouth from the creosote and sulphuric acid that she had been forced to take, which the Oldham *Chronicle* regarded as 'perhaps the most damning piece of evidence against the prisoner in the whole case,'[102] crystallized the public's hatred of the mother, whose insistence until the end that she was innocent of the murder cut away the only possible ground for sympathy, penitence.

Why was this woman an object of such interest? In part, of course, because it looked as though she had murdered her whole family, but also probably because the crime could not be dismissed as an aberration of the underclass. Lizzie Berry was poor, but she had connections with the middle class. She was a fairly young, attractive, determined, upwardly mobile woman who had, it was said, once blackmailed a clergyman who had paid her some attention but decided not to pursue her. She was intelligent and educated: the chaplain remarked after her death on how impressed he had been with her ability, and the newspapers reported that she read sensation novels and other light literature.[103] What is more, she was a trusted caregiver with access to both weapons and victims. She represented a frightening combination of admired and detested feminine qualities.

What explanation can there be of the mentality of women who would do away with friends and relatives for pin-money? Earlier manifestations of the species were dismissed as inhuman, and forgotten – until the next manifestation. At the time of the trial and execution of Mary Ann Cotton, newspapers remarked on her ordinariness. To all appearances she was quite human, though poor:

pleasant, not unattractive, brought up in a God-fearing home. Towards the end of the century, there is evident in the press an effort to understand the workings of the criminal mind. The *Lancet*, for example, analysed the behaviour of Flannagan and Higgins thus:

> It would be an interesting psychological study to trace the state of mind of the convicts from the first-born thought of murder, through the various moods of vacillation and resolution; of hope that the deed would 'trammel up the consequence,' and fear of detection and punishment; and so on, to the stage of action, and this past, the recoil from the contemplation of the deed or callous indifference to it. Success in the first instance emboldened them to further action, and familiarity bred contempt of danger and fear.[104]

There is in this speculation an unspoken acknowledgment of the connection between ordinary human life and extreme criminality, of the murderess as an entrenched insider rather than an easily removable outsider. For it was evident by this time that the most threatening type of female criminal was not a towering, vile monster or an aged crone, but rather an ignorant, emotionally flat, overconfident, unremarkable-looking housewife with no social standing, no means, and no prospects, a woman who could briskly clear her household with no more concern than if she were killing off vermin. Bold, shrewd, insensitive, and deceitful, she operated in the underclass, in which the general rule was that only the fittest survived. She did not expect to be caught. In her circle there may have been a long-standing tradition of murder for convenience.

Newspaper readers had watched with fascination and astonishment as case after case of serial poisoning was revealed in the 1840s. It was only the cumulative effect at mid-century, and the threat that male control of the home could be undermined, that moved Parliament to restrict the sale of poison. Until the last part of the century, the rest of society was not overly inquisitive about unexplained sudden deaths in the underclass. In the 1840s Mary Cotton's career would not have evoked the horrified response that it did when it became known in 1872. Indeed, one of the most remarkable things about her career is that in 1872 she was still able to ignore the humanity of her victims. In the 1840s, to judge by indignant pamphlets, speeches, newspaper articles, and even novels,[105] it was easier for a wife and mother to be callous, and for society to understand that callousness. 'If we had applied our minds with one-half as much vigour to the improvement of our morals, as we have to our machinery,' chided one newspaper, 'or enlightened our people as effectually as our streets, we should not have to lament over the humiliating fact, that there is no country in Christendom so demoralised as our own.'[106]

In the 1870s public priorities were different. A much greater proportion of the population was literate and educated. The second Reform Act and the controversy that preceded it acknowledged that the lower classes were a part of society. Though they did not swiftly and miraculously become privileged and responsible, they could and did demand recognition. It was not quite so easy for the ruling class to sweep their disreputable activities under the rug. And women themselves were interested in the psychology of other women.

Since children were most often the victims of serial murderesses, perhaps the most significant factor affecting attitudes to these women over time was the increasing value that society placed on children. For most of the nineteenth century, however, the murder of babies and children was not considered as serious an offence as the murder of husbands.

CONCLUSION

The first serial killers in modern criminal justice history were women who mixed rat poison into the food of their unsuspecting families. Though the press attempted to make them into witch figures, most appear to have had startlingly ordinary identities. The most reprehensible, and the most written about, were Catherine Wilson, Mary Ann Cotton, and Elizabeth Berry. The popularity of serial poisoning for convenience or pin-money dimmed somewhat with the advance of chemical tests and the Sale of Arsenic Act of 1851, but it continued into the 1880s.

FOUR

Murder of Husbands, Lovers, or Rivals in Love

Martha Alden / Ann Crampton / Sarah Huntingford /
Ann Barber / Sophia Edney / Sarah Westwood /
Catherine Foster / Mary Ball / Sarah Ann French /
Charlotte Harris / Ann Merritt / Hannah Southgate /
Mary Reeder / Maria Manning / Martha Brown / Ellen Cook /
Elizabeth Gibbons / Eleanor Pearcey / Betsey M'Mullan /
Fanny Oliver / Adelaide Bartlett / Florence Maybrick /
Alice Rhodes

Patrick Wilson found that nearly every woman executed after 1843, when Home Office statistics began identifying criminals by gender, was influenced in her crime by a man. 'The husband or lover of a murderess invariably plays a part in causing the murder,' in Wilson's view, 'if only, because, like Everest, he is there. The same cannot be said of male crimes of violence.'[1]

Wilson is not holding men responsible for the murders, but he does point out that the ubiquitous Thomas Newport could well have inspired, and even condoned, Sarah Chesham's poisoning activities, Robert May (who had married Mary after the death of her first husband) probably suspected that she had something to do with the windfall that resulted from her brother's death, and Henry Eccles must have wondered why so many children in his wife's care were dying.[2]

This paternalistic way of considering women's murder must not be seen as an indication that murderesses usually acted out of love or under domination. Some women who killed did so in partner-ship with the men in their lives, but the men in these partnerships were not always the instigators. More murderesses discussed in this chapter were trying to get out of a relationship than were trying to get into one.

Murder is generally thought to be the result of conflict. Martin Daly and Margo Wilson argue that, in spousal murder, regardless of which partner is the perpetrator and which the victim, the principal source of conflict is male sexual proprietariness. 'Marital violence arises out of men's efforts to exert control over women and their reproductive capacities, and women's efforts to retain some independence in the face of male coercion.'[3]

The Church and the law did not always reach down into the living arrangements of the lower classes, but the community did. Neighbours did not hesitate to pass judgment on what they con-sidered scandalous behaviour. They did not make it easy for some-one to walk away from one mate and take up with another. Bigamy was acceptable when desertion had virtually dissolved a marriage, and on occasion the sale of a wife could transfer responsibility for a woman from her husband to her lover.[4] But for most people death was the only respectable way out of a marriage. This may explain why English homicide statistics show spousal murder as a growing proportion of recorded homicides in the nineteenth cen-tury, but it sheds no light on why, within that category, wife-killing increased much faster than husband-killing. Martin Wiener has found that killings of wives by husbands reported in the *Times* between 1820 and 1900 outnumbered reports of killings of hus-bands by wives by about nine to one.[5] A partial explanation for this statistical disparity may be that wife murder tended to be violent, dramatic, and highly visible, whereas husbands could be quietly poisoned so that their murder was never recorded as such.

As the newspapers pointed out whenever a female serial poi-soner was caught, poison was an ideal weapon for women bent on murder because it could be put into food or drink, it did its work slowly, and it was hard to detect. Poison was probably more widely used than we know by women who wanted to escape abuse or replace their husbands. In retrospect it was a practical if immoral and illegal response to oppression: a group kept down by the law simply took the law into their own hands.

Women stirred to rage tended to use violence, which was therapeutic but risky. Unlike poison, it was not reversible, and it was much easier to trace. It was also much less likely to work on someone of at least the same size and strength as the aggressor. But emotional turmoil can overtake common sense and assist the body to tasks and means of which it might otherwise be incapable.

Though in England, as in France, at this time most women who killed a husband, lover, or rival used the traditional means, a significant number made their statements with more direct methods, including cutting, shooting, stabbing, or hitting their victims with a blunt instrument. A favourite implement was the billhook, a long-handled curved blade used for pruning. A frightened or enraged woman could summon the strength to swing an axe hard enough to kill. A sensitive, intelligent young woman could batter and stab her rival with such fury as to drench the premises in blood.

In the nineteenth century, French juries acknowledged that people in the grip of such passion were not criminally responsible. Ruth Harris maintains that, between 1880 and 1910 alone in France, 'hundreds of murderesses committed crimes of passion against erring, irresponsible, or brutal mates and were almost invariably exonerated by the court.'[6] In England the bias worked the other way. English judges and juries, recoiling at the havoc wreaked by furious women, saw to it that they suffered for the indulgence of their passions. Margaret Diblanc was probably saved from hanging because she was French and arrested in France, and the jury knew that a French judge would have taken the extenuating circumstances of verbal provocation into account. (See chapter 6.)

Although infanticide and child murder did not arouse much indignation in England until the last part of the nineteenth century, the murder of an adult male by a woman, in particular of a husband by his wife, was, by contrast, consistently and severely punished. From the mid-fourteenth century until the end of the eighteenth,[7] husband murder called for the wife to be not merely hanged, but burned. If the executioner did not properly strangle the prisoner first, she was (like Catherine Hayes) burned alive. Well into the nineteenth century, women convicted of petty treason were still being dragged to the scaffold in a hurdle, a wooden frame traditionally used for traitors.

The poisoning of a husband or lover was terrifying to the general public because it was subversive. Men were vulnerable to passive aggression by women in charge of their households. An attempt to murder by active aggression was even more alarming because it denied men the automatic protection of their superior physical strength. There was no question of its being excused as a crime of passion. Such action was swiftly dealt with so as to leave no doubt in the public mind that the murder of Englishmen would not be tolerated.

It is clear that in nineteenth-century England more was done to deter women from murdering men than the other way round. From the late 1840s, newspapers registered indignation at the lenient sentences drawn by men who had obviously killed their wives, but the pattern persisted. As the *Examiner* put it, 'It seems to be considered one of the marital rights to kick and beat a wife to death, or to break her neck by flinging her down stairs, without incurring the capital penalty.'[8]

'The law, we cannot but believe,' said the *Daily News*, 'deals too leniently with offences of violence committed against women, even when it asserts itself to the full.'[9] This paper identified in 1846 'the recently-introduced, but very prevalent practice of wife-killing,' which seemed to be considered by juries not murder, but, 'at the best, justifiable homicide; at the worst, manslaughter.' The *News* opposed capital punishment but felt that, if murderers were being hanged, then wife murderers should be hanged as well.[10] As things stood in the justice system, it was much safer to stab one's wife than to defraud one's master.[11]

Even the *Times*, which spoke to the establishment, was shocked at the gender bias in the law. Commenting in 1847 on the incongruity of two recent sentences, transportation for ten years for a man who stole half a guinea from a letter, and nine months at hard labour for a man who killed his wife, the paper observed that there ought indeed to be a strong contrast between the punishments for these offences, but with the severity tilting the other way.[12]

In 1850, a leading article in the *Morning Chronicle* by J.S. Mill and Harriet Taylor demanded: 'Is it because juries are composed of husbands in a low rank of life, that men who kill their wives almost invariably escape – wives who kill their husbands, never? How long will such a state of things be permitted to continue?'[13]

This discourse was still in play in 1872, when J.S. Watson escaped execution, though he admitted having bludgeoned his wife to death in a fit of temper. 'An Englishman's house is his castle; it is also but too often his prison, and a prison from which the gaoler is never absent,' a similarly oppressed husband wrote to the editor of the *Echo* after Watson, a clergyman, was reprieved.[14]

The *Telegraph* was less understanding. 'In a great city like ours,' protested a leader in that paper, 'there must be thousands of homes made miserable by a woman's ill-temper, and by narrow means. It must be a comfort to all respectable elderly gentlemen in Mr. Watson's position – who are tired of their wives and find some difficulty in making both ends meet – to reflect that, if they think fit to murder their wives under circumstances of singular brutality, they cannot ... be sentenced to any worse punishment than imprisonment for life.'[15]

In a similar vein, the *Saturday Review* commented: 'There are, we fear, other aggravating wives ... and they know now what they have to expect.'[16]

Husbands who fell into this category could expect more protection. A sudden fit of aggression by an angry woman against her spouse was highly unlikely to elicit either sympathy or mercy. The rarity of such attacks did not reassure men. The justice system and the press responded in kind by viciously attacking the character of the perpetrator and then doing away with her.

EARLY VIOLENCE

Martha Alden of Norfolk, who appears in *The Newgate Calendar* and in George Borrow's *Celebrated Trials* (1825), was condemned for her audacity. No attempt appears to have been made to find out why she was so angry at her husband, Samuel, on 19 July 1807 that, when he came home drunk and lay down on the bed, she grabbed a billhook with both hands and lunged at him, slicing his throat from ear to ear as well as slashing him across the forehead and down one side of his face. She claimed that he threatened to beat her. Her undoing was that she had had to enlist the help of a neighbour in putting the body in a sack and disposing of it.

After a sensational inquest and trial, she was executed at Norwich on 31 July 1807. An execution broadside, headed 'Treason and Murder,' points out that the judge 'very justly observed, that he had never before met with a case so horrid and atrocious.' At the end of the transcript of the trial, the broadside adds primly, 'the behaviour of the wretched woman during her trial, as well as before it, appeared to be influenced, in a lamentable degree, by that hardened and remorseless spirit which but too surely characterizes the human mind, sunk to the lowest stage of degradation and depravity.'[17]

The Newgate Calendar goes much farther:

> A sleeping man was barbarously murdered in his bed; again and again did the reeking bill-hook fall upon his mangled head. Life had fled; the blood had ceased to throb and flow in his veins; his lips had blanched, his limbs relaxed, and the bedclothes were literally soaked and steamed with the purple fluid that had issued from his gaping wounds – but still did that fiendish woman strike at the mangled remains of her murdered husband with unrelenting cruelty. The more she struck, the more her fury appeared to increase, the fiercer her eyes blazed, and the more murderously diabolical became the expression of her contorted features.

In this version, Mrs Alden has a 'masculine mind.' She has begun to assert her authority over the mild-tempered Samuel a few months after their marriage. He was too frightened of her to contradict her, but she beat him anyway, being 'possessed of one of those peculiarly constituted tempers which require a little contradiction.'[18]

The more outrageous a woman's transgression, the more thrilling it was to read about. Ann Crampton took out her resentment on her unsuspecting lover as he lay stretched across her bed. The nineteenth-century press managed to convey what she had done at first by delicate omission, and finally by calling her 'Mrs. Cut cock.'

On 4 March 1814, in Barnardcastle, Durham, Crampton, a forty-year-old widow of dubious morals gave vent to her jealousy by cutting off her lover's penis as he lay drunk and half asleep. Earlier that evening, as she sat on his lap, he had insisted that she was first in his affections, but she reminded him that 'there was his Nelly.'

The victim, Robert Jordan, survived and testified at her trial for cutting and maiming. He explained that he had not been able to stop her because one of his arms was partially paralysed. It was done in a second, he said, and then he got up and left, bleeding and in great pain.

The Tyne *Mercury*, which described Crampton as ill-looking and sallow-complected, said she cried throughout the trial. The judge chided her for having 'acted from malignancy and disappointed lust.' A woman in her position, with five fatherless children, ought not to have been jealous, he said. Her crime was 'barbarous, wicked, and unnatural.'[19] He instructed the jury to acquit her if they believed she was insane, but otherwise to find her guilty. Convicted, she was hanged on 25 August 1814.

An execution broadside says she was guilty of injuring Jordan 'in a manner too shocking to express,' whereupon it breaks into bawdy verse:

> Mrs. Cut cock's come to gaol,
> Keep her Wolf, and do not fail;
> Of the Jade make an example,
> For it you have reason ample.
> Keep her upon bread and water,
> This audacious Mother's Daughter;
> When the world was first created,

And the living creatures mated,
They were order'd all to breed,
But thinks she, I'll stop your speed;
So determined on her prey,
Swept the whole concern away.
Who the Man is I can't tell
But my Lady bears the Bell;
For crimes among all woman kind
Such another I can't find.

Gentlemen, take care be sure,
Keep you fast the Stable door;
For it seems mischief in common,
Is transacted by the woman;
Turnkey, take a stick and bang her,
Damn her a b——h I would not hang her
Neither, but I'd have an end,
Such as with old shoes they mend;
And I'd take especial care,
How she ever ———.
Any more while in existence,
Shoe makers lend your assistance;
For no excuse can be made,
For the conduct of this Jade;
If she'd really took his life,
With a razor or a knife;
That I freely would forgiven,
But this job I can't by Heaven.[20]

As the ballad suggests, the crime of emasculation was more heinous than murder. This broadside, despite its levity, clearly articulates the attitude of the male establishment to women who threatened their dominance: punish them in such a way as to make an example of them. Underlying this discourse was the uncomfortable awareness of the biological reality that men were reliant on women's honesty as to who had fathered their children. The idea of women's having any more control over men's reproductive capacities than they already had was unconscionable.

When the perpetrators of spousal abuse were women, they were vilified. Sarah Huntingford, sixty years old, of Portsea, near Portsmouth, was by no means an admirable mate, but a man in her position would most likely have escaped hanging. On 24 October 1818, she hit her husband of forty years, Thomas, over the head several times with a billhook.

To support her drinking habit, Mrs Huntingford had pawned his best coat, and he had asked for it that day. The unfortunate man was, added the *Times*, 'of a remarkably quiet inoffensive disposition.'[21] Or, as the *Courier* succinctly put it, 'the deceased bore an excellent character, and the wife a very bad one.'[22] Tried for 'feloniously, traitorously, and wilfully, of malice aforethought' killing and murdering him, she was convicted and executed. A broadside noted that at the trial she 'appeared very indifferent, and did not make any defence.'[23]

The newspapers spared none of the details of the crime. 'We conceive we shall be best doing our duty in noticing this dreadful transaction, by laying before the public the evidence taken before the Coroner's inquest,' said the local paper.[24] According to the *Times*, when the body was discovered, it was 'covered with clotted blood; a great profusion of blood was upon the bed, and blood was also spattered on the wall at the head of the bed, and on the floor ... [F]ive wounds were found in the forehead, four of which had fractured the skull; several other wounds were also found on the head, particularly one on the left temple, where the bond was so depressed, that a finger could reach the brain ...'

EARLY POISONINGS

The most notorious English husband poisoner until the outbreak in the 1840s was Ann Barber, who at the age of forty-five gave her husband, James, arsenic in a roasted apple so that she could marry a younger man. James died on 17 March 1821, a day after consuming the poison.

The couple had lived near Leeds with their two children, who were about nine and ten, and a lodger, William Thompson. In December, Ann and the lodger had run off with some of the furniture and moved into a rented cottage. Their indignant landlords threw them out on discovering that they were not man and wife, and the husband took them both back. About a month before the murder, though, the lodger was driven out by the neighbours. The community had shown her that the only way to continue the liaison was with her husband out of the way.

The week before her trial for murder and petty treason, on being asked the cause of her husband's death, she is supposed to have said: 'How should I know? Can I save the life of a man when the Almighty pleases to take him?' It was alleged at the trial that she had refused to send for a doctor as he lay dying in agony. The press coverage assumes a fascination with the behaviour of one so bold and makes sure that readers know the consequences of such behaviour. The transcript of the trial, reproduced, as was the custom, in a broadside, records that on hearing the verdict – guilty – 'she became sensible of her dreadful situation, trembled exceedingly, shrieked, and fell upon the floor near the bar. She was raised by the jailer; and supported herself by taking hold of the iron bar in front, and leaning backwards and forwards in great agitation.'[25]

A pamphlet records that 'her shrieks and lamentations pierced the hearts of the largest multitude that ever assembled to witness a public execution' in York. As she was being taken in a hurdle from the prison to the scaffold, she looked frantic and prayed 'with dreadful energy.'[26] According to the *Times*,

> throughout this scene, shocking to humanity in its firmest form, she manifested a vigour of motion and a strength of nerve which could not be expected from her appearance and manner at her trial. At the same time her features and the expression of her eyes indicated a distraction and amazement, which showed that she knew not well what she was about. In the most solemn part of the devotional service she gazed wildly around to see the rope by which she was to be suspended.[27]

In 1836, at Cross, not far south of Bristol, as Sophia Edney purchased arsenic, the chemist warned her to be careful. She remarked that many people had been poisoned with it, including 'that poor woman in Bristol.'

'I see you mean the woman that Mrs Burdock poisoned or murdered?' asked the chemist. (See chapter 8.)

'Yes.'

'That was a shocking thing,' the chemist commented. His customer agreed.

Mrs Edney, married at sixteen, was now twenty-three and had a husband of sixty-eight, three children, and a lover whom she wished to marry. She had read about Mrs Burdock's crime and set out to duplicate it. As Mrs Burdock had done, she disguised the poison as best she could in gruel and milk. And she achieved the same result. Her husband, John, died on 5 March 1836.

The Taunton paper reported that at her trial the courtroom was 'uncommonly crowded in every part' all day. In her dark cotton gown and large bonnet, she made an impression as 'a rather goodlooking young woman' with a becoming demeanour.[28] No one speculated on how dreary her marriage must have been.

The summing up took nearly three hours, but the jury agreed on its verdict within fifteen minutes. She was executed on 14 April.

In the spring of 1836, two other women were hanged for poisoning their husbands with arsenic, Elizabeth Rowland at Liverpool and Harriet Tarver at Gloucester. The appeal of this easily obtained, easily administered substance continued despite a forensic test developed the same year. Arsenic poisoning was more often suspected than it had been, especially in the sudden deaths of inconvenient husbands. A witness at Rowland's trial testified that he now realized that she must have poisoned her two previous husbands as well.[29]

MID-CENTURY POISONINGS

Such an alarming number of husbands subsequently succumbed to poison that a bill was drafted to prevent women from purchasing arsenic. (See chapter 3.) The victims of multiple poisoners

Sarah Dazely, Mary Ann Geering, Sarah Chesham, almost certainly Sarah Freeman, and probably Mary May, included their husbands. In addition many others were hanged in the 1840s and early 1850s for poisoning their husbands. In 1843 Sarah Westwood, forty-two, of Staffordshire, because she had a lover, put arsenic in her husband's gruel. (Two days before her execution, she was allowed a visit from her sister and brother-in-law, but her lover took the place of her brother-in-law!) In 1847 in West Suffolk, Catherine Foster, a seventeen-year-old bride who regretted her marriage, gave her husband of three weeks a dumpling made with arsenic. Mary Ball's husband, Thomas, beat her when he spied her with her lover through a chink in the wall of their house in Warwickshire. The couple quarrelled frequently. She threatened to poison him, and eventually did, on 18 May 1849. In rural Sussex in 1852, Sarah Ann French, twenty-seven, poisoned her husband, William, because she had a promise from a younger man that he'd like her better if she weren't married.

Though she must have heard of Sophia Edney's misery, Charlotte Harris poisoned her husband, at Bath, in April 1849 in order to marry an old man with money. She was sentenced to hang, but reprieved because she was pregnant. The following year, Ann Merritt was found guilty of having poisoned her husband in Hackney, east London, but because there was some doubt as to whether she actually did, her sentence was commuted to life imprisonment.

The press reported on the trials of accused husband poisoners with increasing fascination as they became almost commonplace. The story of Catherine Foster was particularly disturbing.

> Catherine Foster is my name,
> Overwhelmed with grief and shame,

ran the chorus of a ballad that detailed her career as a murderess.[30]

Catherine Morley had been happy as a servant until John Foster talked her into marriage. He was a kind, intelligent, devoted fellow, but she did not love him. Within her limited experience, the obvious way out was to become a widow. That way, perhaps she could be reunited with the lover whom she had abandoned to marry the better-off Foster.[31] Only later did she come to terms with what she had done. Her letter of confession was pathetically illiterate, as is illustrated by the apology at the end that it was 'riten veary bad.' A letter to her mother found after the execution said that she was not sorry to have died, since she was going to a better place, where she hoped to be reunited with 'that dear creature,' her husband, to be with him for 'the years that I might have spent in pleasure with him on earth.'[32]

The following year, the possibility of a conspiracy of Essex poisoners surfaced, and several deceased husbands were exhumed after Mary May's execution. Hannah Southgate's first husband, Thomas Ham, had died conveniently in 1847 once she announced that she would like to replace him with her new lover. The Hams had lived at Tendring in Essex, not far from Clavering, where Sarah Chesham lived, or Wix, the home of Mary May. Indeed, the day after Ham's funeral, May came for dinner.

According to a servant in the house, Hannah Ham had told her husband more than once: 'I like Johnny's little finger better than your whole body.' To which he had replied: 'You must stop, madam, and get rid of me first.' She promised: 'If you don't die soon, I'll kill you.'

In the view of an inquest jury, that was just what she did. He was found to have enough arsenic in his stomach to poison five people. She was found guilty of wilful murder and bound over for trial in the spring of 1849. Meanwhile, a London paper reported, the police had

communicated to the coroner's jury very important facts relative to other suspected cases of poisoning which, in order that the ends of justice may not be defeated, we decline publishing for the present. We may state that the particulars, if true, develop a most diabolical system. The disinterment of the bodies will no doubt be immediately ordered.[33]

At Southgate's trial, the Crown prosecutor reminded the jury that a charge against a wife for the murder of her husband was 'the highest in guilt ... in English law' and alluded darkly to the implications of such treachery. 'It was a case ... deeply involving also the interests of society at large,' said the local paper in summarizing the prosecutor's argument, 'because if crimes of this sort were to be accomplished by means which no human care, caution, or prudence, could prevent or defeat, no human being was safe, and all the comforts of life would be at an end.'[34]

Despite the verdict of the inquest, she was acquitted at the trial, largely because her claim that her husband had taken the poison on his own could not be disproved.

Nathaniel Button of Ramsey had died in September 1846, 'a few days after Mary May's first husband, about whom some suspicion also exists,' said Bell's.[35] 'There were strong reasons to believe [he] had been poisoned by his wife, from the levity which she exhibited, as well as from other circumstances,' this paper later added.[36] His body was exhumed along with that of a man named Palmer, also of Ramsey, who had died around the same time. Shortly after his death, Mrs Palmer had left Ramsey with another man. Poison was not, however, found in either body, probably because coroners in smaller centres did not have the skill required to trace its presence long after death.

If public suspicions – and Mary May's allegations – were correct, women were indeed poisoning their husbands in order to be able to replace them. It is entirely possible that publicity about this activity in Essex suggested it to other women who might not otherwise have thought of it.

In 1849 a leader in the *Times* complained of two years of 'outrageous wickedness far beyond any of those crimes which have hitherto found a place in the formal records of history.' This was to put in context the case of Charlotte Harris, who, replacing her husband, had committed 'a specimen of murder, which, in its sublimated atrocity, transcends anything we have yet recorded.'

The *Times* was horrified because neither jealousy nor revenge motivated her. She simply saw a chance to marry up and took it.

It appears as if the motives acting on this class of criminals were not such as would impel them to any deeds of actual violence, but that the quiet and noiseless despatch insured by a few grains of white powder irresistibly lures them to crime. It seems almost clear that a woman who would not lift her hand against a man or child will unhesitatingly drop arsenic into their food. Violent assassination presumes either sudden provocation or long-harboured intent, and it would demand both the exertion of bodily force and the occurrence of rare opportunity. But, as long as a pennyworth of poison can be procured in the next street, and the minds of the people are familiarised with its properties and action, there can be no security against deeds which, while they involve the most hideous wickedness, require none of the hardihood, and, as it appears, scarcely any of the motives of violent crime.[37]

In 1849 Henry and Charlotte Marchant had been married for several years and had two children. She was thirty-two, he thirty-eight. He made good wages as a stonemason; she sold oranges in the Bath market. He died suddenly on 7 April, and on 16 April his widow married a seventy-year-old widower. On 19 April an item in the Bath *Chronicle* headed 'Strange Story' told of the rumour that a man had been poisoned. Once the body was exhumed and an inquest established that he had died of arsenic poisoning, Charlotte Harris was charged with murder. She escaped hanging because she was pregnant, but was transported for life.

The guilt of Ann Merritt of Hackney, on the other hand, appeared to some to be in question. The jury found her guilty of poisoning her husband on circumstantial evidence only. An eminent professor of chemistry testified at the Old Bailey that James Merritt had ingested arsenic in gruel the evening before he died on 25 January 1850. He had belonged to a burial society, but the benefit would have been nearly one-third higher had he died a week later. His wife claimed that, depressed over his unfaithfulness, she had bought the arsenic to use on herself, and put it away. She insisted that he must have taken it by mistake. If this had been true, however, he would have to have taken it in the morning, not the evening.

Ann Merritt was found guilty and sentenced to die, but the execution was delayed while the home secretary investigated the possibility that the scientific testimony was wrong, and ultimately the chemistry professor admitted that she could be telling the truth. When her sentence was commuted, the *News of the World* complained, with some logic, that if she was innocent she should not be punished at all.[38]

Publicity about one of these husband poisoners inspired a wife poisoning.

'Do you think there is any harm, Elias, in poisoning for love, as Catherine Foster did?' asked Mary Reeder of her brother-in-law.

'No,' replied Elias Lucas, a farm labourer.

'How much arsenic would poison a person?' she asked.

'As much as will lie on a shilling.'

During the winter of 1849–50, Elias Lucas had become embroiled in an affair with his wife's younger sister in Castle Camps, Cambridgeshire, which is not far from Bury St Edmunds, where Catherine Foster was executed. Elias, twenty-four, was muscular, and cheerful; Mary, at nineteen, was young and innocent-looking.

He gave her some arsenic, and on 21 February, 1850, she put an appropriate amount into a mixture of bread and water and gave it to her sister Susan. When Susan complained of the peculiar taste, her husband said, 'I would eat mine if it killed me.'

It did kill her, and the guilty couple was immediately suspected. When arsenic was found in Susan's stomach, they were charged with murder, found guilty despite their denials, and sentenced to hang. Both confessed before the double execution on 13 April, an event that drew a vast crowd to Cambridge. Magdalen St and Castle End were filled with vendors of gallows literature: one group had two singers and a fiddler.[39]

'For an account of the agony the poor creature [Susan Lucas] suffered the reader is referred to the report of the trial which follows,' said an execution broadside, 'and their blood will curdle with horror as they read from those who witnessed the poor wife's death, and the cold-blooded atrocity with which the crime was perpetrated.'

Among the verses being chanted, supposed to have been written by the pair the night before the execution, was this cheerful confession:

> A deadly poison we confess,
> We put into our sister's mess,
> Hoping when quiet in her grave
> More guilty intercourse to have.[40]

In an editorial entitled 'Cordials for Criminals,' the *News of the World* deplored the bargain that Lucas appeared to have made with the prison chaplain. Confessing an outrageous crime should not automatically entitle a murderer to salvation, the leader insisted. 'As for penitence in cases of the class we have in view, not a trace of its real nature is to be found. On the contrary, the criminal rejoices that he committed the crime, as through its consequences and chastisements his career of sin is cut short, and he is sped to the joys of Heaven.'[41] There was no suggestion that his paramour was granted the same dispensation.

MORE VIOLENCE

Five months before this had occurred, another double execution, the most sensational one of the century, to judge by contemporary news reports and the recollections of street sellers to Henry Mayhew. Maria Manning was not, like Mary Reeder, fragile and easily led; she was a Lady Macbeth who turned to her husband for the physical strength needed to accomplish the murder of a man.[42] The newspapers therefore called her 'masculine.' Much was made of her boldness and ruthlessness.

She was also young (twenty-seven), exotic (Swiss, with an accent), attractive (though not beautiful, the newspapers insisted), ambitious, passionate, and vain. Though she was hardly a role model, the middle class could identify with her. She was not, as were most criminals of her time, 'other.' She was poor, but she had connections to the upper class through her position as maid to Lady Blantyre, daughter of the Duchess of Sutherland. She knew how to dress and what to say and how to make men notice her.

Maria Manning was a performer, aware that each appearance was being reviewed by the press. When she first appeared in police court, said the *Observer*, 'she was very neatly dressed, and from her easy and graceful manners, she is evidently a person who has mixed a good deal in society.'[43] On the first day of the trial, said the *Morning Post*, she looked worn but 'had not ... neglected to pay great attention to her toilet.'[44] On the way back to the jail, she congratulated herself: 'I showed them resolution, did I not?' she said to her guard. On hearing the death sentence at the end of the trial, she threw down some pieces of rue that had been lying in front of the dock and shouted in disgust: 'Base, shameful England!' She was widely admired for having died 'game,' unlike her obviously chastened husband.

The murder of the relatively well-to-do Patrick O'Connor, a customs officer, was committed out of anger. A former suitor of Maria, who, with the approval of her husband, had continued his attentions after her marriage, O'Connor had agreed to enter a *ménage à trois* with the couple, and then changed his mind. They had in anticipation taken larger lodgings in London's east end. When he reneged she decided to kill him in order to rob him.

With meticulous attention to detail, Maria arranged for him to come to dinner; with her husband, purchased a crowbar, a shovel, and some lime; and dug a grave under the floor of the basement kitchen. The guest arrived and was coaxed down to the kitchen from the upstairs parlour, ostensibly to wash his hands. As he approached the sink, standing on the flagstones that had been replaced over the grave, she shot him with a pistol from behind. George came along, heard him moaning, and finished him off with the crowbar. The couple then lifted the stones, threw the body into the grave with lime to dissolve it, and replaced the stones.

The Mannings were suspected when their friend's disappearance was eventually investigated by the police, but by that time they had abandoned their lodgings and escaped in different directions, the wily Maria apparently intending to leave her husband holding the bag. 'There seems to be little doubt that Maria Manning was as treacherous to her husband as she was to O'Connor,' said the *Observer*.[45]

Had a suspicious policeman not noticed that part of the kitchen floor appeared to have recently been replaced, the body would not have been discovered. Once it was, the papers declared the Mannings murderers, and the hunt was on. In the words of the *Observer*,

> They decamped immediately after police had made the first inquiries ...; they disposed of their furniture at a loss; they left no trace behind them as is usual in ordinary cases of removal, however rapidly made; and above all, Mrs. Manning not only called at the lodgings of the murdered man ..., but she actually opened his drawers and swept away all their valuable contents. That this frightful crime was meditated for some time is quite clear.

Readers were further told that O'Connor had been a usurer and a womanizer – a man of sordid habits who was not liked by his colleagues. His connection with Maria, 'altogether of a criminal nature,' had been countenanced by George for gain.[46]

He was last seen alive on 9 August, but it was not until 17 August that the body was discovered. The papers reported regularly on the piecemeal clues to the murder, then on Maria's arrest – she was retrieved from Edinburgh – and finally on her husband's arrest. For three months London talked of little else. Between the first report on 18 August and the end of September, the *Times* ran more than thirty stories, seventeen more (some of these substantial, as reports of the trial were practically verbatim) in October, and twenty-five in November before and after the execution. The dense, detailed testimony and examination were dramatic enough to have been as faithfully read as they were reported, for, since there was no denying that at least one of the Mannings was guilty, each lawyer set out to prove that the other's client had committed the murder.

The *Globe* remarked on 'the extraordinary nerve of the Mannings, particularly the female.'[47] The fascinated *Observer* noted that, on her arrest, she 'did not appear to be in the least perplexed by the unusual interrogatories addressed to her, or alarmed at the dreadful position in which she stood.'[48] The *Standard* related that she had prepared a roasted goose for Sunday dinner over the spot where the body lay.[49]

Maria did not falter in her insistence that her husband was entirely responsible; he was ready to admit his part but threw the bulk of the blame onto her. On 29 October he wrote urging her to confess and asking to see her. His letter began, 'I address you as a fellow sinner and sufferer, and not as my wife.' Her response began, pointedly: 'I address you as a husband.' She said she would see him only if he told the authorities that it was their lodger, not she, who had shot him. She was furious at his lack of chivalry and, for that matter, at the lack of chivalry demonstrated by the justice system.

Despite their condemnation of the crime, the papers admired Maria's 'masculine' daring and determination as much as they deplored her husband's 'feminine' limpness and passivity. The incongruity of the vileness of the murder and the dignity with which she endured her punishment was not lost on them. 'The annals of crime have seldom furnished such an instance of a female doomed to die by the hands of the common hangman who exhibited such a ferocity of disposition, such a determination of purpose, and such an obduracy of heart, as Maria Manning,' said the *Standard*.[50]

The barbaric behaviour of the crowd at the execution, on 13 November 1849, provoked Dickens to write an indignant letter to the editor of the *Times*, deploring 'the atrocious bearing, looks and language, of the assembled spectators' and urging that executions thenceforth be carried out in private.[51] 'Strange it is,' mused the *Advertiser*, a consistent foe of public hangings, 'that the morbid thoughts and feelings of the people to witness a public strangulation are so great, that remaining throughout the night in the streets and the probability of being seriously injured or robbed, are not thought too great risks to encounter ...'[52] The *Times* defended the spectacle. 'When deeds have been committed that would seem to pollute the earth,' it said in a leader, 'then we purge the land, and hang up the guilty authors before the Sun in the sight of God and the people.'[53]

The final public appearance, on 9 August 1856, of Elizabeth Martha Brown, replayed in *Tess*, took up three columns (nearly half a large broadsheet page of small, dense type) of the Dorset County *Express and Agricultural Gazette*, an amount of space warranted by the first execution of a woman in Dorchester in twenty-three years. No mention was made of the fact that the victim had been a violently abusive husband.

The coverage included a leading article about the 'ignominious end' and 'well-merited fate' of the 'wretched criminal' for 'the deliberate murder of poor Anthony Brown, by the hand of his own wife.' Reproduced in their entirety were her confession and the sermon preached to her on the Sunday before the execution and recounted efforts to grant her a reprieve. There was also what amounted to a review of the performances of the executioner, his victim, and the audience.

Martha Brown was a good-looking woman in her forties who kept a shop. Anthony, a carter, eighteen years younger than his wife, had probably married her for her money. They lived in relative harmony except when he was drunk, when he would beat her with a whalebone whip.

Anthony had been seen in the company of another woman, Mary Davies, and, one night when he was out late, Martha saw them together through the other woman's window. When he arrived home early on the morning of 6 July and she accused him of having been with Davies, he responded by kicking the bottom out of the chair on which she had been sitting. After more words, he struck her on the side of the head with his hand and laced her across the shoulders three times with the whip. Then he kicked her and bent over to unlace his boots, whereupon she grabbed an axe used to break up coals for the fire and hit him over the head several times.

'I had never struck him before, after all his ill treatment,' she said, 'but when he hit me so hard at this time I was almost out of my senses, and hardly knew what I was doing.' She did not call for help until three hours later, when she said she found him dying at the door from kicks from his horse. She made the mistake of sticking to this story until two days before her execution.

Reporting the murder, the *Express* said, 'There is a very severe blow over one eye, quite driving in the skull, and the left side of the head is beaten in. The violence of the blows must have been very great.'[54] Another report on the same page insisted that 'it was utterly impossible for him to get home from the field as the wife pretends that he did ... The woman's tale about being held fast by the dying man is quite out of the question.'

On 21 July, Brown was convicted of wilful murder and sentenced to die, but in several towns her cause was taken up and petitions were circulated to be sent to the home secretary. The Dorset County *Chronicle* endorsed this activity, arguing that she acted 'under the fell influence of a foul, but irrepressible, passion,' and was therefore guilty only of manslaughter;[55] the *Express*, calling her a 'blood-stained creature,' maintained that her lies and unconcern made it impossible to believe that the murder was not premeditated.[56]

On 7 August the chaplain of Dorchester jail obtained the truth from the condemned prisoner about the manner of her husband's death. He hurried up to London to inform Sir George Grey, the home secretary, of the extenuating circumstances. Sir George, however, was away in Ireland and could not be contacted in time. No one else had the power to grant a reprieve, and Martha Brown died on 9 August, apparently with great fortitude.[57] The *Express* reported:

> After remaining the usual time, one hour, the body was taken down by the executioner and placed in an elm shell, on the lid of which were the initials 'M.B.' Her bonnet and cap were also put in with her body, and in this state she was buried according to the sentence, 'within the precincts of the gaol,' shortly after one o'clock the same day, without any funeral service. We understand from parties who saw the corpse, that the features were not at all contorted, and that her appearance was as nearly as possible the same as before she was executed.[58]

Thus was a friendless, poor, ageing abused wife disposed of by the justice system. According to local legend, the bloodstain left by her husband could not be removed: it stayed there until the house fell down.[59]

After the execution there was a correspondence in the *Times* as to whether Brown should have been hanged, a child-murderess having recently been reprieved in London. A resident of Bridport, near Dorchester, asked readers to contrast her 'defenceless child with the drunken, adulterous husband, who cruelly thrashes his wife because she remonstrates with him for his deviations from the path of chastity.' The letter claimed that the general feeling in the county was that Brown should not have been hanged.[60] A reply from Dorchester denied that the feeling was general and charged that she probably lied about the abuse.[61] The local vicar wrote to reassure readers of the *Times* that the death penalty was appropriate for her crime.

In 1869, an aggrieved wife confirmed men's worst fears about the capacity of a volatile woman to challenge their control and destroy their identity. This was castration anxiety in its most literal sense. Ellen Cook, 'a tall, powerful Irishwoman,' to quote the *Times*, kept a coffee-house in London's east end with her husband, James. One morning, tired of his habit of taking prostitutes to not only her house, but her bed, she invited him upstairs to bed herself. She then told him he must do penance, tied him by the arms and legs to the bedstead, and began sharpening a knife.

James Cook thought that his wife was merely being playful, the *Times* reported, but 'she stooped over him and he felt himself cut about in a frightful manner.' Then, in another highly symbolic gesture, she tried to gouge out his eyes. He grabbed the knife, extricated himself, and rushed to an apothecary's shop, but the 'inhuman and barbarous deed' left him 'fearfully maimed,' said the *Times*. She was tried at the Old Bailey for having feloniously wounded her husband with intent to murder him, found guilty of wounding with intent to do grievous bodily harm, and sentenced to fifteen years: execution was no longer an option, as it had been in the case of Ann Crampton. Spectators began to applaud as the sentence was passed.[62]

Nearly twenty years after the Dorchester hanging so long remembered by Hardy, a middle-aged woman was found guilty of the murder of her husband in London under considerably less provocation. She was sentenced to die, but reprieved and released after five years precisely because the home secretary considered that the death penalty was not appropriate for her crime.

Elizabeth Gibbons, a respectable middle-class woman of fifty-four, shot and killed her husband at their home in Hayes, on the western edge of London, in a jealous rage. The press deferred to her, and the public sprang to her support, though one wonders whether she would have been spared had she been, like Brown, a nonentity.

She had been married to James Gibbons, a sixty-three-year-old railway contractor, with whom she got on tolerably well – on 'middling' terms, according to a friend of his – for thirty-seven years. He was a prosperous and a good provider, and he saw to it that she had household help.

For more than two years this help had been Lucy Venn, the fifteen-year-old daughter of his cousin Mary. Though he wanted her to stay, he had asked Lucy to leave his house in September 1884, because his wife wanted her out. However, he took an interest in the girl, and he would not stop seeing her. The Gibbonses were childless.

It is worth considering here that, although the Divorce Act of 1857 made secular divorce possible and accessible for a couple in the Gibbonses' financial circumstances, only the husband could seek a divorce on the ground of adultery. A wife wishing to be rid of an adulterous husband had to prove not merely adultery, but some related offence such as cruelty or desertion. These grounds Eliza Gibbons did not have. At some level she must have realized that, for her, there was only one way out of the marriage.

On 15 November, the day of the murder, James had quietly arranged to go alone to Taunton to visit his relatives and return the same day. His wife, fearful, according to Mary Venn, that he was going to change his will in their favour, let him know on his return that she was not pleased that he had made the trip. In the bedroom, they had an argument about it. She had been drinking, and the prosecution alleged that she snatched up the revolver he kept by the bed and fired.

The widow maintained that his death was suicide, but the direction of one of the shots, which entered from the back, under the shoulder, was said by two doctors to have made that impossible for a right-handed man. She stuck to her story, but her explanations of what had excited him and where she had been when the first shot was fired were not consistent. On 19 December she was found guilty and condemned to die.

Coverage of the trial had been subdued, but after the verdict the papers argued that the medical evidence was given too much weight. The *Observer* felt that she should be given the benefit of the doubt.[63] The *Echo* reprinted the expert opinions of the *Lancet* and the *Medical Times*, both of which argued that he might have shot himself if the gun had gone off accidentally during a struggle. Several hundred people signed petitions asking for a reprieve, which was granted on 30 December.

After her sentence was commuted to life imprisonment, the *Observer* ran another leader on the case, arguing now that she was entitled to a pardon since it was obvious that there was doubt that she had committed any crime at all.[64] A few days later the *Echo* reported that Gibbons had confessed to 'a high official' that the revolver had gone off in a struggle between them resulting from a declaration by her husband that he was in love with the girl.[65] Up to this point the *Echo* had been reticent to mention this, and the *Times*'s reports had omitted to include evidence from the Venns at all, but a careful reader could have gathered that, whether he was or was not in love with the girl, his wife thought he was. This is confirmed by a statement by Gibbons dated 15 December 1884, claiming that, although her solicitor had advised her not to say so, her husband had told her he was madly in love with Lucy and that, if she couldn't come back to live with them, he would have to leave home.[66]

After her respite Gibbons was by no means forgotten. Madame Tussaud's enshrined her immediately in the Chamber of Horrors, where she remained until 1889. In 1900 her punishment was adjusted to modern practice, and she was set free even though she had not completed the normal requirement of twenty years. By that time, says a Home Office memorandum of 19 March 1900, she had practically admitted her guilt and asked for mercy.[67] She was by then seventy years old.

At the end of the century, society was more interested in restraining born criminals than in punishing people who had acted uncharacteristically in a moment of mental irresponsibility and were unlikely to offend again. In the intervening fifteen years, English law, under the influence of Cesare Lombroso's theory of determinism, had tended more and more to take into account the individual circumstances of a criminal rather than automatically fitting the punishment to the crime. Criminality was regarded by the new science of criminology as outside a person's control, determined by heredity and environment and impulses in the brain. If violent passions overcame reason, it was not a matter of moral choice, but rather of involuntary motor responses.

In France, it would have been routine for a murderess in Gibbons's situation to declare herself a *criminelle passionelle* and walk away free. In England, men were being excused for crimes of passion, but not women. 'Jealousy has been held to extenuate the crime of murder when committed by men under great provocation, without premeditation,' says the Home Office memorandum, 'and if the prisoner's story is in the main true, which there does not seem much reason to doubt, I suggest that it may well be considered in this case to justify letting this woman out ...'

Le crime passionel was mostly thought of as an irrational but understandable response to betrayal by someone whom one had loved. Though there was a psychological orientation, an attempt to get at the instinct that led to the trial of Eleanor Pearcey, it would have been too much to ask an English jury in 1890 to spare her because a criminal passion had led her to murder not her lover, but his wife and child. Like Gibbons and Brown, she insisted on her innocence, though a mass of circumstantial evidence pointed to her involvement, and, like them, she was convicted of murder and sentenced to hang. Her lawyer then asked for a reprieve on the ground that she was not responsible for her actions when she committed the murders, but it was denied, and she was executed at Newgate on 23 December.

Pearcey, an attractive and stylish young woman, lived in a flat in Kentish Town, north London, 'supported by the gifts of a gentleman,' as the *Times* put it.[68] In the fall of 1888, when she was twenty-two, she learned that Frank Hogg, with whom she had an intense but at the time platonic relationship, felt under pressure to marry someone whom he had made pregnant. Pearcey encouraged him to marry the woman. The relationship between Pearcey and Hogg then deepened.

A year after the marriage, the two women met and became friends. On the afternoon of 24 October 1890, Phoebe Hogg arrived in Pearcey's kitchen with her eighteen-month-old daughter, also Phoebe, nicknamed Tiggie, in response to a written invitation. In the evening she was wheeled out in Tiggie's pram, dead.

The body was so destroyed that the murder was at first feared to be the work of Jack the Ripper. The most likely scenario is that Pearcey flew into a rage at something her guest said, then bludgeoned her several times with a poker, and finally cut her throat with a carving knife. 'The cut was of a terrific character,' said the *Pall Mall Gazette*, 'severing the large sinews of the neck and the vertebrae of the spine, and leaving the head attached to the body only by two or three sinews and the skin at the back.'[69] In her death-struggle the victim smashed a window, and broken glass was scattered about the room.

It was never established whether the little girl died of suffocation or exposure. The mother was found in a Hampstead field, the child in a field near Finchley Road, and the pram in St John's Wood. Blood and broken glass all over the kitchen established Pearcey's guilt, but Frank could not be linked to the murder. It is more than possible, however, that in the evening he helped dispose of the bodies.[70]

Coverage of this case was dramatic as well as extensive, advances in typography and production having made possible subheads and lively four-layer headlines, and advances in literacy having expanded the popular press. Interest was therefore widespread and intense. Pearcey was arrested on 25 October; before the end of the month, a broadside ballad titled 'The Terrible Murder of a Woman and Child,' sung to the tune of 'Shelter Your Mother and Me,' had hit the streets, according to the *Echo*, and the undertaker in charge of the victims' funerals was mobbed by people offering to pay for a view of the bodies.[71] The *Standard* devoted four of its seven long, dense columns on page 2 to coverage of the first day of the trial, and more than two columns on each of the next two days. Madame Tussaud's bought Pearcey's furniture even before her conviction, and later (by offering to shave them off) acquired Frank's long beard and moustache for its tableau of the Hogg family at home.[72] *Lloyd's* devoted two pages (with several sketches) to Pearcey right after the trial, and one page on each of the next two Sundays, including a gossipy interview with her mother.[73] All of London was trying to find out what made her tick.

The fascination of the case lay in her intelligence and strength of character. She is an example of a type identified by Elisabeth Bronfen in a discussion of destructive femininity as the woman who will 'break conventions or commit a crime punished with death, such as adultery, infanticide or murder, as an expression of liberating subjectivity, of assuming authorship and responsibility for her destiny.'[74] Her action can be explained only as an irrational attempt to escape from a situation in which she felt she could not continue – an attempt to take control.

Pearcey would implicate no one else, would give no explanations, would make no admissions. The *World* suggested rather uncharitably that she was encouraged to kill by the respite of Florence Maybrick the year before.[75] After she issued final instructions for a cryptic advertisement in a Madrid paper,[76] the *Telegraph* ventured that perhaps she was seeking attention.[77] Neither of these theories fits with what we know of her.

More intelligently, a leader in the *Standard*, commenting on her 'criminal passion of the most violent and unreasonable description' for Hogg, found 'something touching in the devotion expressed by this otherwise worthless woman for a man still more worthless, in the ordinary sense, than herself.'[78]

Though all this scrutiny revealed her as a human being rather than a monster, the justice system made no concessions, and the public demanded none. 'In Mary Eleanor Pearcey,' said the *Pall Mall Gazette* after the verdict,

> the law has sentenced, with an assurance of justice which could scarcely be much surer, a murderess of rarely brutal ferocity. For her at any rate no one can feel, and we trust no one will attempt to inflame, any pity other than that which humanity does not deny to the worst criminal standing midway between a ghastly infamy and its imminent and hardly less ghastly penalty. Any whim of public sympathy for jealous women who kill, not the sharer of a disgraceful liaison, but some innocent persons in some way connected with him, would be a further calamity ...[79]

It was no accident that Hardy was interested in this case.[80] Like Martha Brown and his own Tess, she submitted to what Bronfen calls 'the embrace of death.' Bronfen sees Tess as 'translating necessity and destiny into choice, acknowledging death by choosing it.'[81]

MORE POISONINGS

Not long after Martha Brown's execution at Dorset, Betsey M'Mullan, thirty-eight years old, was tried in Liverpool for the murder of her husband, Daniel, at Bolton, Lancashire, on 2 July. She had been seen by a servant giving him antimony, the poison used by the notorious William Palmer. Palmer was hanged at Stafford in June 1856, around the time antimony surfaced in the M'Mullan household.

It is hard to know whether Betsey was an abused wife. Daniel did go on benders every couple of months, but, according to the servant, drinking and physical fighting in the M'Mullan household were not unusual. Yet she seems to have been well thought of in the community, and according to the *Telegraph* her father was 'a highly respectable tradesman, whose family are thrown into the deepest distress by this melancholy event.'

The question was whether Betsey had intended to kill her husband. The powder she gave him, tartar emetic, was sometimes furtively used by women to break their husbands of the drinking habit because, when taken in alcohol, it induced nausea. In Bolton it was called 'quietness.'

The judge was incensed to hear of this practice. Betsey was found guilty of manslaughter rather than murder, but reprimanded for her deviousness. He expressed horror at 'the notion that a woman lying in a man's bosom, and almost breathing his breath, should be administering to him, unknown to him, a medicinal drug for the purpose of sickening him, with whatever object ...'

The sentence, transportation for life, was to be an example to others, he said, sternly admonishing her for 'a gross breach of social duty in the most important aspect – the duty of a wife to her husband ...' He warned that a chemist who sold poison to women to give to their husbands without their knowledge could be charged with manslaughter if death resulted.[82]

Fanny Oliver, tried at Worcester in July 1869, was found guilty of the murder of her husband, Joseph, the previous May, despite a lack of evidence. As it did Ann Merritt, the justice system punished her just to be on the safe side. Though it was established that she had purchased arsenic under a false name, the poison was not definitively implicated in his death. Two Reinsch tests failed to pinpoint arsenic in the body, though a Marsh test detected a small amount. Despite her insistence that she was innocent, she was sentenced to hang.

There was much controversy over the justice of the sentence. The Birmingham *Post* published a letter, reprinted in the *Times*, in which Fanny asked her parents to believe that she was innocent.[83] After she was reprieved, the *Medical Times and Gazette* ran an editorial, also reprinted in the *Times*, cautioning that she should not be freed: 'A married woman who dictates love-letters to a former lover, purchases arsenic, giving the lover's as her own name, who nurses her husband through an illness, and in whose husband's body arsenic is found after death, cannot be surprised if society considers her a dangerous person, and disposes of her accordingly.'[84] Despite obvious doubts as to her guilt, she was sentenced to life imprisonment but released on licence in 1886.

Sexual impropriety continued to be accepted by some as evidence of criminal tendencies in women. After Fanny Oliver's there were three major trials in the press of suspected husband poisoners, all of them women of some social standing but dubious sexual conduct. It is much more likely that Adelaide Bartlett did poison her husband, but she was given the benefit of the doubt. Florence Maybrick was not given the benefit of the doubt but should have been. Innuendo about Florence Bravo did not get past the inquest on her husband in the summer of 1876; the case will not be dealt with here as the courts never picked it up.

The circumstantial evidence against Adelaide Bartlett in the chloroform death of her husband, Edwin, in Pimlico, London, was so strong that, after she was acquitted in April 1886, the eminent surgeon Sir James Paget was supposed to have remarked that in the interests of science she should now explain how she accomplished it.[85]

Adelaide's life story won her the sympathy of many a New Woman. She had been married off at the age of seventeen to a kind but very serious, much older man who was a successful grocer. He sent her to school abroad so that she could acquire a proper education before settling down with him three years later. There were no physical relations. The marriage was eventually consummated, at her request, she claimed, because she wanted a child. She did become pregnant, but the baby was stillborn.

Her story was that her eccentric husband thought that a man needed two wives, one to keep house and one for sex and companionship: and Adelaide was to be the housekeeper. There was never any suggestion, though, that he had someone else for sex. In 1885, when he was thirty-nine and Adelaide twenty-nine, he provided her with a highly compatible suitor in the form of a young Wesleyan minister, George Dyson, whom he wanted Adelaide to marry should he, Edwin, die. This arrangement worked nicely until December 1885, when, according to Adelaide, Edwin began to demand sex. She was unenthusiastic, presumably on account of her attachment to Dyson. After his death she told his doctor that she had thought she would be able to repel him by waving a handkerchief dipped in liquid chloroform in front of him whenever he came too close.[86]

Late in December, without giving him this reason, Adelaide had asked Dyson to buy some for her, and he did. Although the sale of chloroform was not regulated under the Pharmacy Act of 1868, since it was not considered a 'secret' poison, that is, one that could be administered without the knowledge of the patient, it was obvious from his having purchased it in three lots that he knew he was doing something suspicious.

On 1 January 1886, Edwin was found dead. Shortly after that, Adelaide disposed of the chloroform bottle. The cause of death was chloroform taken by mouth. Both of them were charged with murder, but the case against Dyson was dropped, and Adelaide's lawyer, Edward Clarke, in what the *Times* called 'a long, eloquent, and forcible speech' of nearly six hours, was able to persuade the jury that perhaps Edwin had committed suicide.[87]

As the *Standard* remarked after the trial, the case combined all the dramatic elements necessary to attract attention.[88] The mystery posed at the inquest in January, the preliminary hearing in February, and then the trial attracted an enormous amount of attention, but no solution. On the front page of the 27 February *Illustrated Police News* was a series of sketches about the case, including one of the crowd pushing to get into the court. Written before the trial, so that it could be sold (for a penny) when interest was highest, was a curious sixteen-page pamphlet that told the story in a jocular style.[89] For a solid week in April the *Times* ran a story of substantial length every day. The day the trial started, 12 April, the *Evening News* carried four full columns of coverage in its final edition. The Birmingham *Daily Times* reported that at first Adelaide had been receiving letters of abuse, and then, as the trial went on, letters of sympathy, with seventeen offers of marriage conditional on her acquittal.[90] On Saturday, 17 April, the *Penny Illustrated Paper and Illustrated Times* ran a full-page illustration on page 1 of the three major figures; in the same location of the following week's issue, there was a large sketch of the story's heroes: Adelaide, her lawyer, and the judge at the Old Bailey.

In making a judgment, hindsight gives us a benefit that Adelaide's supporters did not have. After the trial she went to live in Boston, supporting herself by teaching voice and piano. Eventually she returned to England, where, at the beginning of the Great War, she raised money for the Red Cross. She soon left England, however, because she was suspected of siphoning off some of the funds she had raised. She escaped to France, and then returned to Boston in 1915.[91]

The Bartlett jury went so far as to point out before delivering the verdict of not guilty that, although Adelaide might have administered the chloroform, there was no proof that she had. The problem in poisoning cases was that the evidence tended to be entirely circumstantial unless the suspect confessed. A jury might err on the side of caution, as this one appears to have done; equally, it might make the leap from suspicion to certainty and convict someone who was actually innocent.

Character assassination could propel the leap. Adelaide was able to maintain her pose of purity despite evidence that she and Dyson had been seen, even by Edwin, kissing and caressing each other. According to them, he wanted it that way. She was thus able to project onto the dead man the taint that should by rights have attached to her. Her story was that she had had sexual intercourse but once in her life, for the purpose of procreation. There was no admission – or even suggestion – that she and Dyson had had a sexual relationship.

But they obviously did have, and, as it seems to have been with Edwin's approval, there was no chance of a divorce. Adelaide would have had the strongest of motives for doing away with her husband. She was otherwise condemned by the law to live with and submit to a man whom she found repulsive, and to be deprived of a domestic arrangement with the man she loved. It is ironic that such motives implicated Florence Maybrick, who had much more reason (in the form of two children) to stay with her husband and much less (as her lover does not seem to have been a serious rival to her husband) to want to replace him.

As prosecutor in the Bartlett case, and then defence lawyer in the Maybrick case, Sir Charles Russell got scraped on both edges of this sword. The judge and jury seemed as hostile to the defendant in the second case as they had been sympathetic in the first.

The reason is that Florence Maybrick admitted that she had committed adultery. The judge was prepared to believe, and to persuade the jury, that the sort of woman who would deceive her husband might also kill him. The jury, supposedly of her peers, consisted of three plumbers, two farmers, a grocer, an ironmonger, a milliner, a painter, a butcher, a baker, and a candlestick-maker.

The story behind the trial is a complex one.[92] In 1881, Florence, an American, was married at eighteen to an apparently prosperous Liverpool cotton merchant nearly twenty-four years her senior. She used arsenic for her complexion, soaking it out of fly-papers. James used arsenic as a tonic – it was considered a sexual stimulant – as well as strychnine and many patent medicines: indeed, as a letter-writer to the *Times* put it, his stomach had functioned as 'a druggists' waste-pipe' for several days before his death in May 1889 at the age of fifty.[93] She admitted having put a white powder that turned out to be arsenic into his bottled meat juice. However, she contended that he had asked her to do so.

The cause of his death was given as gastric inflammation, and arsenic was implicated as a possible irritant. However, two doctors said in court that he died, not of arsenic poisoning, but of disease of the bowel. It was never established that James died of arsenic poisoning, and, even if he had, it was never proved that Florence had deliberately poisoned him. None the less, on 7 August she was found guilty of murder and sentenced to hang.

The verdict was an unpleasant surprise to many people. The outspoken judge and the jury were hissed at after Florence walked out of the courtroom to return to jail. The *Times*, which expressed grave reservations about the outcome though it was reluctant to retry the case in the press, maintained that 'the large majority' of 'the hundreds of thousands of persons who ... followed the case with eager interest and attention' were expecting the jury to give her the benefit of the doubt and bring in some equivalent of the Scottish 'not proven.'[94]

The case *was* retried in the press, as the newspapers were by no means united against the verdict. The *St. James' Gazette* argued in its favour that, though there was not absolute proof of her guilt, 'there is a cumulative weight of damning probabilities against her.'[95]

The Liverpool *Daily Post*, the Manchester *Guardian*, the *Standard*, and the *Telegraph* all thought the verdict fair.[96] The *Evening News & Post* and the *Star* vigorously opposed it. 'Holborn Radical' complained in a letter to the editor: 'Home Rule for Ireland has hitherto been the raison d'etre of the *Star* newspaper. Now, sir, take it down, and replace it by the legend, "Home-poisoning of husbands for ever!"'[97] Both papers published a mass of public opinion supporting the condemned woman. 'SHOULD SHE BE HANGED? PUBLIC OPINION CONTINUES TO PROTEST AGAINST THE SENTENCE,' the *Evening News* announced in an introduction to a selection of letters to the editor.[98] The *Star* gave letters against her such ironic headlines as 'Hang her because she is young' and 'Hang her because she is not poor.'[99] In the same vein, in an apparent allusion to the jury's misguided faith in the judge, 'Henpecked Husband' wrote: 'I am a married man, and have got two children. My wife has carefully studied this case from the beginning, and she thinks the verdict a very just one. And as I am never allowed to contradict I have come to the conclusion that the capital sentence should be carried out.'[100]

While Florence awaited her execution and heard the gallows being erected, her wax effigy stood in an ante-room of Madame Tussaud's Chamber of Horrors, in readiness for the larger room once she was dead. For two weeks her supporters flocked to rallies and meetings and collected signatures on petitions. The pressure of public opinion won her a reprieve on 22 August, and the furore subsided.

None the less, she was going to have to serve a life sentence. There were murmurs of protest that, if she was being spared because it had not been established that there had been a murder at all, then she should be set free. However, the rationale of the Home Office for retaining her in custody was that administering poison was a felony punishable by life imprisonment. Added to that was the firm conviction of Queen Victoria, from whom all pardons flowed, that Florence was a wicked woman who must be punished.[101]

A few people remained active in efforts for her release, among them her lawyer, Russell. In 1891 Alexander MacDougall, a London barrister, published a 600-page document of the case. He asked for volunteers for a committee 'to consider what steps should be taken to Right Wrong, ere this woman succumbs either to death or madness in Woking Prison.'[102] In 1892, in response to a change of government, a petition with 3,000 signatures demanded an inquiry, but to no avail. Gail Hamilton, an American author, published an open letter to the Queen in the September 1892 issue of the *North American Review* asking for a pardon in deference to the wishes of Americans. Helen Densmore, who published a book on the case in 1893 and tried to organize a lecture tour of Britain to focus on Florence's innocence, said she found the press closed to a discussion of the case. Densmore felt that most people believed she was guilty, though they had not wanted her to hang.[103]

There was a glimmer of hope in October 1892, when W.T. Stead, founder and editor of the *Review of Reviews*, published a forceful article alleging a miscarriage of justice. 'This American woman was sentenced to be hanged by a judge on the verge of dotage,' said Stead, 'after the counsel for the prosecution had remarked it was impossible to find a verdict of guilty in the face of the medical evidence.'[104]

Finally, in 1904, Florence was released from prison, and the wax model of her was removed from Madame Tussaud's. She settled in the United States and died a penniless recluse in rural Connecticut in 1941.

NEGLECT

In 1877 a case of wife murder in which two women were implicated drew attention to class and gender bias in the justice system.

Louis Staunton, his brother, Patrick, his sister-in-law, Elizabeth Staunton, and her sister, Alice Rhodes, hid away and starved Louis's wife, Harriet, to clear the way for Alice to take her place. Harriet, who at thirty-four was ten years older than her husband, was mentally impaired but rich: she brought a fortune of £1,600 when she married Louis. By the time her mother finally found her in April 1877 in Penge, south of London, she was filthy, emaciated, and dead.

Two books on the case that came out immediately after the trial, *Harriet Staunton, or, Married and Starved for Money* and *Life and*

Trial of the Four Prisoners Connected with the Penge Murder, as well as extensive coverage in the papers, confirm that most people believed the four guilty of murder. Whether they actually killed her by starving her or merely neglected her so that she succumbed to disease is a moot point. Whether the women, especially Rhodes, actively caused her death was another troubling question.

An effort by the defence to represent her death as resulting from apoplexy at the trial on 19 September was unsuccessful. After the verdict – all four were found guilty and sentenced to death – the *British Medical Journal* ran a leader asserting that death was due to exhaustion from starvation and neglect,[105] while the *Lancet* said it was not sure of the exact cause but the verdict was correct because 'evidence of criminal neglect was overwhelming.'[106] The *Medical Times* was sure that starvation was not the cause of death.[107]

The *Telegraph*, which described Elizabeth Staunton as Harriet's jailer, felt that the 'jury in the street' had decided the trial.[108] However, a citizens' group demanded that the verdict be set aside.[109] Inexplicably, the three Stauntons had their sentences commuted to life imprisonment, while Rhodes, who was only twenty, was given a free pardon. Elizabeth was released in 1883.

'The feeling that the female convicts should be spared their miserable lives was a feeling born of British dislike to hand women over to the hangman,' said the *Illustrated Police News.* 'There was no doubt as to their guilt, or as to their deserts.'

In a perverse, patriarchal way, the system thus announced that, as Rachel Short has shown in another context, it did not take women as seriously as men either as victims or as perpetrators of crime.[110] Ordinary women – 'attractive, respectable-looking people,' in the words of Carolyn Conley – could not have starved a rich young woman to get her out of the way. 'It was, and is, more comforting to believe that murderers are monsters, who neither think nor behave as the rest of us do.'[111]

CONCLUSION

The most sensational murderesses were spirited women who were a threat to the social order. Men and women alike were fascinated by the audacity and aggressiveness of Maria Manning, a woman scorned, who shot her lover; Eleanor Pearcey, who stabbed her lover's wife; Adelaide Bartlett, who probably poisoned her husband; and Florence Maybrick, who probably didn't. All of these were attractive and rather loose young women whose femininity was made much of in the press. Catherine Foster, by contrast, was of interest because she was fragile, penitent, and terrified. Martha Brown was a scapegoat, an abused wife who had to be punished as an example to others in the same position. Eliza Gibbons was luckier, perhaps as much because she had social standing as because her crime occurred at a time when women's rights were being strongly asserted.

FIVE

Child Murder

**Ann Sandys / Ann Arnold / Celestina Somner / Selina Wadge /
Louise Massett / Elizabeth Warriner / Frances Kidder /
Ann Barry / Jane Crosby / Harriet Parker / Frances Stewart /
Ann Lawrence / Christiana Edmunds / Constance Kent**

Though nowadays twice as many victims of female killers are husbands as are children, in nineteenth-century England babies and
children were the most common murder victims of women. In
Victorian Kent, for example, only one woman killed her husband,
but 71 per cent of the victims of murderesses were children. There
was an even higher rate (more than 90 per cent) of females indicted for murder at the Old Bailey between 1856 and 1875 who
were thought to have murdered their children. Carolyn Conley,
author of the Kent study, speculates that husbands were protected
at the expense of children because 'male dominance had been
accepted and internalized.'[1]

'The high proportion of women indicted for murder [at the
Old Bailey] highlights the burden of child care placed on them
and the tensions experienced in their role as mothers,' says Robyn
Anderson. 'The immediate power that women could exercise over
young children was in stark contrast to their powerlessness within
the family and in society as a whole – and which sometimes found
a violent and despairing outlet.'[2]

Some children were murdered out of brutality by women used
to abuse from their husbands. Just as wives were considered to be

the property of husbands, who could do with them as they liked, so children were the property of their parents – particularly, in the lower classes, of their mothers, since many fathers deserted their families or were away from home most of the time.

The state assumed that parents who had children in their care cared for them. Of course, especially in the underclass, where drink, extreme poverty, or a lack of moral education pushed impulse into action, this assumption was not always valid. Many children needed protection against their own parents, but the state was loath to interfere. 'To patrol industry on behalf of the young was England's Christian duty,' George Behlmer has observed. 'To patrol the home was a sacrilege.'[3]

Looking at recorded homicides is only one way to determine the extent of child murder in Victorian England. The unofficial toll must be considered as well. The disappearance of children does not seem to have been of particular interest among the poor, whose rate of reproduction was perhaps greater than was felt necessary by the rest of society.

As Margaret Arnot has observed, many bereaved parents experienced real sorrow, but 'overall, when compared with our own experience, nineteenth-century parents could face the deaths of their children with an extraordinary degree of equanimity' because the statistical probability of losing a child was high.[4]

Deaths from overbeating, or even deliberate poisoning, could be easily explained away as accidental or the will of God if the victims were seen as insignificant in the larger scheme of things. In addition, large numbers of poor children died of deliberate neglect, which was effectively, if not statistically, murder. The motive in many of these cases would have been burial insurance.

PROFIT

In 1848 the *Weekly Times*, in a story headlined 'The Murder Clubs,' noted a coroner's observation that, in all burial-club cases, whatever the cause of death, he suspected murder. He mentioned one over which he himself had presided in which the death of a child from exposure in bad weather had brought the family thirty to forty pounds from different clubs. The case that occasioned the observation was the inquest of two children of the same family, one of whom had been left alone with an older child and burned to death; the mother then allowed a younger child to be taken to stay where there was scarlet fever, and that child died a few days later. Both children were in burial clubs.[5]

Though the Friendly Society Act of 1847 barred children under the age of six from membership in burial societies, it appears that societies already in existence at that time did not regard this regulation as applicable to them. Even new clubs sometimes ignored the age requirement. A letter to the *Times* from the social activist John Clay, the prison chaplain at Preston, made this point in 1849 in arguing that press reports of murders for burial insurance were just the tip of the iceberg.

'No one can guess how many more victims – infants especially – have been poisoned or otherwise destroyed for the sake of the coveted burial money,' said Clay, who elsewhere in the letter defined 'infants' as children between the ages of two months and five years,

> though neither inquiry nor suspicion may have been excited; nor how many children, entered by their parents in burial clubs, are, when attacked by sickness, suffered to die, without any effort being made to save their lives. But that the predominant feeling in the mind of a parent whose sick child is in a club is too often fixed on the money which can only be obtained by that child's death, no one can doubt who has seen the working of these societies.

To bolster his argument that parents were not trying very hard to save their children's lives once they became sick, Clay's letter provided figures showing that in 1847, in one town where half the deaths were of children, only one-eighth of the patients at a local charitable hospital were under five. Furthermore, these children as a group were much sicker than the other patients. Their mortality rate was one in six, while for older patients it was nearly one in twenty.

In 1846, one town of 61,000, says the letter, had at least eleven burial clubs with memberships amounting to nearly 52,000. Since infants under two months old and all persons known to be sickly were inadmissible as members, and since some in the working class and everyone in more prosperous circumstances would not have wanted to belong to a burial club, it can be assumed that some people had multiple memberships. According to an officer of one of the clubs, three-quarters of the names on the lists in this town were children's.[6]

The first that the public heard of this stratagem was in August 1840. Robert and Anne Sandys, a couple from Stockport, near Manchester, were investigated when it was revealed that two of their children had died not long after being enrolled in a club. If anyone suspected foul play when six-month-old Elizabeth died, nothing was said. At the time of her death, her father had been asking when she would be considered a full member. However, when her older sisters, Jane and Marianne, exhibited the same symptoms about three weeks later, and Marianne died, an inquest was held. Marianne's death yielded another £3 8s 6d. Arsenic was found in her stomach but not in Jane's. The body of Elizabeth was exhumed, and arsenic was found in her stomach as well.

At the same time, suspicion was thrown on Robert Sandys's brother George and his wife, Honor, whose daughter, Catherine, had been enrolled in a club in May 1838 and died in July 1840.

The inquest found that Elizabeth, Marianne, and Catherine had all been murdered. In an apparent attempt to contain the scandal, the parents were labelled 'Irish and Catholic' – safely 'other.' A letter to the editor of the Stockport *Chronicle* corrected the impression that the four were Catholic. (The coroner had implied that they might have thought that they could get absolution by confessing to a priest.) Only the women were Catholic, said the correspondent, and they had been excommunicated for immoral behaviour.[7] The *Chronicle* had earlier noted that Ann, who had 'anything but a creditable reputation,' had another husband living in her native Ireland.[8]

The inquest, exceeding its mandate, implicated the parents, going so far as to find Ann guilty of murdering Elizabeth and Marianne, and Honor guilty of murdering Catherine, and the husbands guilty of aiding and abetting them. The four were arrested, but the case appears never to have come to trial.

The *Times* ran three stories on the case, and the other London papers also picked it up. The case was referred to later in the 1840s, when child poisoning acquired a higher press profile as the serial killers Betty Eccles, Eliza Joyce, Sarah Freeman, and Sarah Chesham were successively implicated. Attempting to explain the phenomenon whereby healthy insured children died faster than uninsured children at Preston, the *News of the World* blamed industry. Factory owners employed young people and made them economically able to marry before they were otherwise ready, it said, and when children came they were seen as an expense until they were old enough to work – or dead, if they had been enrolled in a club.[9]

The issue surfaced again in the 1880s, when Catherine Flannagan and Margaret Higgins, and then Elizabeth Berry, were hanged at Liverpool for murder for burial-insurance money.

FINANCIAL BURDENS

Some children were murdered, not for profit, but as a sort of economy measure. They were perceived as encumbrances by either stepmothers or prospective stepfathers. This rather simple-minded but effective response, judging by the stereotype of the wicked stepmother preserved in broadsides, must sometimes have worked.

It is not unusual, in the annals of child murder in nineteenth-century England, to find women resorting to the murder of their children in order to satisfy men who they feared did not want the burden of other men's children. In a time when illegitimacy was common in the lower classes, women lived to regret mistakes that constrained them. A father might be willing to support both his child and its mother, but it was too much to ask him to undertake the support of children who were not his.

As early as 1813, the exposure of Ann Arnold as a murderess caused a sensation. Reports keep readers a comfortable distance away, dismissing her as 'other.' Arnold, a servant unable to keep the child with her, had a four-year-old son being raised elsewhere. She drowned him in a pond in a field in Suffolk because she had a chance to marry the father of her younger child if she could persuade the father of the older one to take him off her hands. She could not. A shepherd discovered the drowning three weeks later, and the child was identified as hers.

The Bury and Norwich *Post* reported that she had taken the boy out of care, stopped at a nearby pond, and stripped him. Twice she tried to throw him in; on the third, successful, try, the child struggled to the other side and got out, 'when he in vain implored the succour of his merciless parent, who had the further inhumanity to cast him again into the pond, and accomplished the vile purpose of drowning her offspring.'[10]

She was tried at Bury on 26 March, found guilty, and executed on 29 March. The *Post* branded her an 'inhuman mother.' A chap-book sold for sixpence in Suffolk, Norfolk, and Essex announces: '*Murder!!! The Trial at Large of Ann Arnold for the Wilful Murder of Her Infant Child*' and provides a transcript of the trial, the address to the jury by the Crown, and the testimony of witnesses.

Despite the rhetoric, the desperation that moved Arnold to her extreme action must have gained her at least a measure of sympathy. Her situation as an unmarried and unmarriageable mother would not have been uncommon. Celestina Somner, on the other hand, convicted of murdering her ten-year-old daughter in London in February 1856 and sentenced to hang, was widely and justly hated for her gratuitous brutality. Her trial was well reported,[11] so that the public understood the callousness of her crime. One broadside ballad, which alleges that the child's father was her mother's brother, has the mother saying:

> A wretch distressed I must confess
> I am as all the world may see,
> Before me stands the fatal tree,
> And my darling's spirit haunting me.
> Oh! I am almost wild.[12]

She was respited, and a few months later, when another woman was hanged who seemed by comparison a victim of circumstance, there was a public outcry at the injustice. One correspondent of the *Times* called her 'the cold-blooded German murderess'; another asserted that 'a more cold-blooded, atrocious murder was never perpetrated than by her on that helpless child.'[13]

Somner was fourteen when her child, Celestina Christmas, was born. She put her out to nurse and continued to pay for her keep elsewhere. At the time of the murder, Somner was living with an abusive husband and a servant-girl in Islington and had just removed the child from care. The servant, pretending to be asleep, heard the mother summon the child and take her down to the cellar. Realizing that her mother was about to cut her throat, the child cried out that she was being murdered. Somner finished the deed, muttering fiercely, 'I will kill you, I will kill you. I will teach you to tell any more lies about me.' The next morning, the servant managed to alert a visitor to what had happened, and police found the body.

'The slaughter of her child by Celestina Sommer [*sic*] ranks as one of the most deliberate and cruel murders ever recorded,' said the *Annual Register*.[14]

The Somner trial at the Old Bailey followed by one day the pathetic case of Elizabeth Harris, twenty-five years old, who had taken her three illegitimate children out of the workhouse with the intention of going to live with the father of the youngest. Fearing that he would not be able to support them all, she threw the two older children into a canal. She was found guilty of the murder of the eldest, Ellen, five, and sentenced to death. After the conviction, the *Telegraph* protested in an editorial that she was clearly out of her senses at the time of the crime and demanded a reprieve. The judge, it said, was 'iron-hearted.'[15]

In neither case had the jury recommended mercy. To the surprise of the public, however, both these young mothers had their sentences commuted, possibly because the execution of two young women at the same time would have been particularly offensive. Somner was certified by mad-doctors, but the public was not satisfied that she belonged in a lunatic asylum. 'The medical discourse prevailed,' says Roger Smith, 'but it did not coincide with the commonsense view that there had been criminal intent.'[16] A contemporary report said:

These unexpected reprieves excited much private and public comment, and were repeatedly mentioned in Parliament. The dissatisfaction long felt by the public at the uncertainty of the sentences of the courts of justice, and the still greater uncertainty whether the sentences passed would be really inflicted, was greatly raised. It was felt that this indecision had reduced our judicial punishments to a lottery, in which the criminal who drew a bad ticket was very unlucky indeed.[17]

After the execution of Martha Brown in Dorchester in August 1856 for the murder of her husband, the *Times* published a letter arguing persuasively that if as vicious a murderess as Somner had just been reprieved, then the hapless Brown should not have been hanged.

No cries of compassion could touch the hard heart of that woman [Somner]; no maternal feelings would arrest her hand ... [T]hat girl whom nature would bind her to protect was inhumanly sent to her last account ... Contrast this defenceless child with the drunken, adulterous husband, who cruelly thrashes his wife because she remonstrates with him for his deviations from the path of chastity.[18]

The truth was, however, that the reprieve of a child murderer sent a less threatening message than the reprieve of a husband murderer. Excuses could be accepted for the murder of a child, but the murder of a husband under any circumstances was not to be condoned. Somner was released in 1876.

In Cornwall in 1878, Selina Wadge, a single woman of twenty-eight, was promised marriage if she could dispose of one of her two children. By all reports she had been a kind mother, but the offer prompted her to drop her two-year-old son down a well. She was promptly convicted of murder and hanged in August, less than two months after the murder. Newspaper reports were factual and dispassionate: no one questioned what sort of prospects would lead an ordinary woman to a desperate measure of this sort.

The hardness of Louise Massett, a thirty-six-year-old French governess working in London, shocked the public. Travelling to Brighton to meet her lover, she hit her three-year-old son over the head on 27 October 1899, and then smothered him. The body was later found in a lavatory at a junction en route; a bag of his clothes turned up at the Brighton station. She collected the lover at the station on the Saturday, spent the weekend with him, and then returned to her duties, but, on discovering that the body had been found and identified, she became highly agitated, though she denied any prior knowledge of the murder. She was found guilty and executed despite a plea for mercy from the French government.

A *Times* leading article speculated on her motives: did she fear that he would be too heavy a financial burden, or did she regard him as an obstacle to marriage? The writer mused, 'It is next to impossible to follow the workings of a feminine mind of the criminal type ... In the first agony of shame and apprehension women frequently kill a newborn infant, and probably persuade themselves that killing a thing barely alive is no murder.' The *Times* felt that she deserved her fate: 'It was a very deliberate, callous, and cold-blooded murder.'[19] Massett had a brief sojourn in the Chamber of Horrors, but her notoriety waned quickly despite some spirited objections to her execution raised by, among others, the *Daily Chronicle*, and she was removed in 1902.

STEPCHILDREN

The wicked stepmother did not live only in fairy tales. Widowers with children were motivated to remarry so that there would be someone to run the household, but some of the women who married them found this no easy task. Even stepchildren who were cooperative resented competition and comparison, and those who were insubordinate were seen as formidable obstacles to contentment between the parents. It seems reasonable to surmise from the broadside trope of the 'mother-in-law' – literally, the woman who on her marriage became a 'mother in law' to someone else's children – that suspicions cropped up from time to time in many communities that the 'solution' of murder had been applied to a stepmother's problems.

Such a crime was reported to the press in 1817, and a broadside must have been issued then, for a copy of a reissue, dated April 1822, is held by the Bodleian Library.[20] Elizabeth Warriner, the second wife of a Lincolnshire farmer, was hanged in August for the murder the previous November of her stepson, John, who was about eleven years old. Since their marriage the couple had had three more children, one born after the murder. The woman had given the boy poison with his morning cereal, and then laid him under a halter in the barn so as to give the impression that he had hanged himself. He had no marks around his neck, however, and arsenic was found in his stomach.

According to the testimony of a neighbour who guessed before he finally died that the boy had been poisoned, Warriner defended herself by citing two other child murders in the community by 'one woman [who] had burnt, and another had [over]slept her child to death, and what was she to be hanged for any more than they?'[21]

The judge did not agree, calling her a cruel and unnatural murderer who had bound herself by marrying the father to be the protector and second mother of his child. 'However her misery might be commiserated, there did not seem to be an individual in court who was not fully impressed with the certainty of her guilt,' the *Courier* reported.[22]

An account of the trial in the *Star* ends, 'The moment that she heard that her life was to be forfeited, she jumped up from the floor in greatest agony, wringing her hands, and exhibited other symptoms of distraction.' The broadside lifts this, adding, after 'forfeited,' 'for the barbarous murder and cruel treatment to her step-son.' The interpolation illustrates the tendency of broadside writers to underscore the suffering and punishment of the criminal as a warning to others.

This was a classic case that was referred to later in the century in other cases of child poisoning, especially that of Eliza Joyce, who poisoned two stepchildren in Lincolnshire in the early 1840s.[23] (See chapter 3.)

A similar case caused much less stir in 1868. Frances Kidder, twenty-five, on marrying the father of her bastard child, had unwittingly acquired another of her husband's bastards, twelve-year-old Louisa Staples. She had not been aware until after the marriage that the child existed.

The murder took place on 25 August 1867, at New Romney, Kent. Kidder forced Louisa to remove her holiday finery and put on rags before she drowned her in a ditch. Because the ditch held only a foot of water, the woman held her stepdaughter down until she suffocated.

Despite these grisly touches, newspaper accounts encouraged public sympathy for Kidder. Her husband, said *Lloyd's Weekly Newspaper*, treated her cruelly and had exposed her as the murderer of his child. 'Some idea may be formed of the character of the man with whom the poor woman became connected,' *Lloyd's* added, 'from the fact that he is actually at present cohabiting with the sister of the culprit, a girl seventeen years of age!' The paper then noted that Kidder was ignorant and illiterate, 'unacquainted with anything like religious notions.'[24]

The *Times* devoted two full columns to a report of the trial,[25] but only a handful of spectators turned up at Maidstone to see her executed on 2 April. Her husband was burned in effigy on that day. She was the last woman in England to be publicly hanged.

In January 1874, Ann Barry, thirty-two, was hanged at Bristol with her lover, Edwin Bailey, for helping him kill his one-year-old illegitimate daughter. The child, Sarah, was being raised by her mother, an eighteen-year-old servant, but the couple apparently feared that the child might become a financial drain on them.

REVENGE

Children were sometimes the target of women who felt powerless to express their anger against their peers. Wife abuse was tolerated, and for the most part accepted, among the lower classes as a remedy for extreme rage. For the weaker sex, children – or at least those who were weaker still – sometimes absorbed women's anger. A woman wanting to take out her frustrations on a man could not hurt him physically, but she could attack him indirectly by depriving him of his child.

The most brutal child murder in these pages went unpunished. The victim, Sarah Ann Crosby, was seven years old and lived with her family near Penrith, Cumberland. In January 1845 the child mentioned to her father that her mother had been drinking. This accusation would not have been untrue: Jane Crosby was known to be addicted to spirits and laudanum. She was also known for her bad temper.[26] To punish the child for calling attention to her drunkenness, the mother held her by the arms and legs and roasted her in the kitchen fire, in the presence of an older sister, until she had burned to death.

The public, alerted by reports of the inquest, was out for blood. A leading article in the *Times* began: 'A most barbarous and revolting murder was committed ...' and ended with a wish 'that sufficient evidence will be elicited to warrant the coroner in committing the wretched woman for trial for the cruel and unnatural murder ...'[27] When she was, the evidence of the only witness, a child, was not considered adequate, and the woman was ultimately acquitted.

Harriet Parker, a much more sympathetic figure, was not so lucky. She and her common-law husband had a violent relationship: after he boasted to her that he had other lovers, she followed him, swinging a tile tied in her handkerchief, and he punched her in the mouth.[28] A few hours before she struck, on New Year's Day 1848, the landlord of a London public-house heard her say, 'I will have my revenge on the children if I can't on him ... I have had it on my mind for some time past.'

She then killed Robert Blake's two children, six and four, to punish him for spending the night with another woman, by pressing her hands over their noses and mouths until they were suffocated. 'I felt as if I could have killed a thousand children,' she told the court.

The press was initially unanimous in its condemnation of not only her crime, but her person. Parker, thirty-eight, 'kept a low-looking house'; was 'a repulsive, downcast-looking woman'; a 'wretched woman' who 'walked boldly into the dock' and had a sordid past.[29] As one broadside ballad put it,

> In Birmingham I long did dwell,
> In wickedness, how sad to tell.

> To live in sin, was my delight,
> I proved a sad unfaithful wife,
> From my lawful husband I did part,
> And my ill usage broke his heart.[30]

Another, though acknowledging that she had asked for forgiveness, did not mince words over what she had done:

> She cruelly his children killed;
> How dreadful to unfold!
> She pressed her hands upon each mouth,
> And left them dead and cold.[31]

At first glance, Parker was a threat to the establishment, a reminder that middle-class social values did not control all members of a society. Clearly respectability was of no concern to a woman who had left her husband, taken up with a man who had a wife and children, and lured him away. This was a scarlet woman if ever there was one. The jury found her guilty but recommended mercy on account of the provocation by Blake. None the less, she was sentenced to hang, and there was no reprieve.

This was as she would have had it. A model penitent, she had given herself up and admitted to the crime, refused to plead not guilty,[32] and, according to the chaplain who attended her, when she first arrived in prison 'folded her dress tightly round her lest any one should come in contact with one so polluted, saying, "Don't touch me, I am a murderess!"'[33] Though she had had only the skimpiest education up to the time she committed the murders, once she reached Newgate, a chaplain, assisted by pious lady prison visitors, taught her to read the Bible and explained the concepts of sin and redemption.

While in prison, she sent a letter to Blake that was reproduced, with her original underlining, in the *Weekly Chronicle* – and, minus the underlining and semicolons, in the execution broadsides. Given that, according to the *Chronicle*, Blake never answered the letter, this appears to have been a public-relations exercise for the church, with the letter edited by the chaplain. Dated 7 February 1848, it melodramatically records Parker's repentance and urges him to repent as well by going back to his wife:

> This is the last time you will ever receive advice from me. My days are numbered. This day fortnight I shall be <u>silent</u> in the <u>grave</u>. Take, therefore, these few lines into consideration; never again <u>trifle</u> with a woman as you have <u>with me</u>. Promise to <u>forsake all others</u>, and cling <u>once</u> again to her who ought to hold the <u>only place</u> in your heart – the <u>wife</u> of your <u>bosom</u>. This, Robert, is what I sincerely wish. I have <u>deeply injured her</u> and <u>so have you</u>. Let her, then, after this, have your best and purest affections ... I <u>deserve</u> my awful fate, and God give me strength to go through <u>all</u> ... I freely forgive <u>you</u> for all your <u>wrongs</u> to me ... Be warned, Robert, and remember that those who <u>break</u> the <u>sacred tie</u> pledged at the altar of God will never prosper; more than one within these walls can testify to the truth of this by <u>bitter experience</u> ...[34]

The chaplain reported after her death that she had been talked out of inscribing to Blake the bible that she had been given in prison and 'soon saw the impropriety of polluting even the cover of God's holy Word with a record of a connexion which had been one of crime, and had led only to crime.'[35]

Most of the newspapers were by this time sympathetic, but the public quest for redemption did not dampen the enthusiasm of the rabble anticipating the spectacle of her suffering. 'The miserable woman has ever since her sentence shown great penitence for the horrid offence which she committed, and fully acknowledged the justice of her sentence,' said the *Standard*'s report of the execution. None the less, the 'dense mass of human beings' yelled, hooted, and whistled.

The public a generation later was much less interested in Frances Stewart, who also killed a child to punish the father. Stewart was a respectable forty-three-year-old widow living in London with her daughter and son-in-law. In April 1874 she had an argument with him over his accusation that she had broken the door of the chicken-house. He told her that either she or he must move. On 27 April, two weeks after the argument, she did leave, taking along her year-old grandson, Henry Ernest Scrivener. She sent her son-in-law a note saying she and the child were both going to die so that the father would never forget what he had done to her. 'It is the only thing I can do to make your heart ache, as you have made mine for so long.'

At her trial on 10 June the jury recommended mercy, and the judge said he thought she 'had committed the act under some perversity of mind,'[36] but she was executed on 29 June. According to the *Echo*, Marwood, the executioner recently appointed to succeed Calcraft, who had resigned a few weeks earlier, bungled the job by making the knot too loose, so that she had to struggle for several minutes.[37] Even this detail was given in the straight, matter-of-fact way that the newspapers had by this time adopted for reporting murder trials and executions.

INSANITY

There is a fine line dividing murderous rage from insanity. If the Victorians were more conscious of this line than we are, it must be said that there is far more social control, through public opinion as well as police measures, over domestic violence today. The legal system was quite willing to accept that virtually all infanticide was attributable to insanity, but they balked at extending this legal leniency to child murder. Still, some child murderesses were clearly insane, even by stringent Victorian definition – that is, if, as dictated by the McNaughten Rules of 1843, they could not distinguish between right and wrong – and were therefore not executed.

Amy George, for example, a religious fanatic of nineteen, was let off in Bath in 1824 despite having hanged her little brother. The verdict was not guilty by reason of insanity. The girl had intended to secure his eternal happiness. The *Times* evidently thought the less said, the better; the *Morning Herald*, though, devoted nearly half a page to its report.[38] (The Constance Kent affair revived interest in this case, described in *The Newgate Calendar* for October 1864.)

Ann Lawrence was executed in January 1867 for the murder of her four-year-old son, Jeremiah, in Tunbridge Wells. She had apparently also intended to kill her lover, Walter Highams, who had another mistress with several children by him. Lawrence was perhaps motivated by an insane jealousy. At any rate, the methods that she used suggest that she was highly overwrought: she cut the child's throat, and then attacked Highams with an axe after unsuccessfully trying to pin the murder on him. A broadside ballad explains:

> They lived unhappy, often quarrelled,
> Faults on both sides we may see;
> Ann Lawrence in a fit of frenzy,
> Overpowered with jealousy.
>
> Determined was to kill her offspring
> Revengeful, shocking to unfold,
> To aggravate her own paramour,
> Her little boy but four years old;
> At Tunbridge Wells she basely murder'd.
> Wickedness ran in her mind,
> When her child she'd slain, said with disdain,
> The innocent child was killed by Highams.[39]

SENSATIONAL CHILD MURDER

Christiana Edmunds, the genteel daughter of a declining family, was so obviously insane that, although she did not qualify under the McNaughten Rules, the home secretary intervened after the trial and sent her to a lunatic asylum instead of the gallows.

Edmunds was tried in January 1872 for the bizarre random murder of a four-year-old child at Brighton. She went to a great deal of trouble to cover her tracks, thus demonstrating an awareness that what she was doing was wrong.

The public was fascinated by the psychology of this quiet, middle-aged spinster in love with her doctor. It was a classic case of what today would be called 'erotomania.' As the details emerged, it became clear that she was unbalanced. Because the trial took place in London, it received a great deal of press coverage, including artists' sketches of the main figures in the case. By and large, the newspapers were horrified but sympathetic. However, the citizens of Brighton were not inclined to be charitable. Many of them had been endangered by her activities.

Though Charles Beard had not paid her any undue attention, Edmunds fantasized that, with his wife out of the way, he would declare his love. She therefore bought some strychnine, which she proceeded to inject into a box of chocolates. In April 1871 she sent some to the Beards, along with a card signed simply from a friend. The handwriting on the card later proved to be hers.

The doctor's wife bit into one of the chocolates, and then spit it out. She deduced that it was poisoned and that it had come from Edmunds. The Beards thereupon put an end to the friendship. Distressed by this turn of events, Edmunds concocted a plan to show that she was not to blame for the poisoned candy. She bought more chocolates, injected them, and placed them in shops so that others with whom she had no connection would be poisoned. This course of action caused illness in several people, and death in the case of Sidney Barker, who was on a seaside outing with his uncle.

Edmunds wrote anonymously to the father of the dead child, urging him to implicate the owner of the shop from which the candy had been purchased. However, the poison and chocolates were eventually traced to her, and she was charged with murder and attempted murder. As the Brighton *Herald* put it, she was caught in her own web. 'She had been building a Palace of Sin on a foundation of crime, when at a touch it sank beneath her and overwhelmed her.'[40]

In jail she continued to be self-absorbed and unaware of what was going on around her. The *Pall Mall Gazette* (written by a corps of intellectuals for an élite audience) reported with some amusement that she objected to sharing a cell with a woman charged with bigamy (in the *Pall Mall*'s opinion, it was the accused bigamist who had grounds for complaint) and objected to a ruling that she would not be able to wear her bonnet and sealskin jacket in the prison chapel.[41]

Newspaper coverage of the trial dealt with her appearance in detail: dignified, not unattractive, subdued. The *Times* described her as ladylike in appearance, with a becoming manner. The *Stan-*

dard and the *Times* thought her appropriately yet fashionably dressed.[42] The *Telegraph*, which, as was its custom, provided not only verbatim transcripts of the testimony, but extensive and vivid commentary, remarked: 'Somehow, grey hairs, old age, and deep rugged wrinkles strike an observer as less discordant with sin, sorrow, and suffering, than do soft fair hair, a smooth unwrinkled face, and bright clear eyes ... [A]part from the hypothesis of insanity, it seemed difficult to connect the quiet, lady-like, almost girlish woman in the dock with a murder ...'[43] She was clearly unbalanced: the chaplain of Lewes Gaol is said to have remarked on her 'unnatural calmness and exceeding levity' and on her tendency to laugh though she had just been crying.[44]

She made a sympathetic figure, but, as the *Daily News* said, 'We cannot wonder that human sympathy turns away from a woman so reckless and abandoned ...' This paper judged her 'one of the worst criminals who have in recent times come before the public for judgment.' She was 'one of those hideous malformations which society is sometimes doomed to produce, and which it is naturally anxious to hide away from sight and forget for ever.'[45]

Local coverage was even harsher. The Brighton *Herald* depicted her as callous and indifferent when exposed, interested only in the effect her story had on Beard and the general public. It pointed out that she had continued trying to poison Mrs Beard after the child's death, sending cakes laced with arsenic to several households, including the Beards'. She then aroused suspicion by complaining to police that *she* had received a poisoned cake.[46] Despite its indignation, the *Herald* was glad when she was respited, 'as there is something ... revolting to the human mind in the hanging of a woman.'[47]

Edmunds was, logically enough, found guilty, though it had been argued on her behalf that insanity ran in her family. Her mother testified that the father had gone mad in the prime of life and died a raving lunatic, a brother had been born an idiot, and an older sister had attempted suicide and died of hysteria. Still, mad though she may have been, Christiana had known what she was doing. Sentenced to death, she attempted, pathetically, to invoke the loophole of pregnancy, but of course she was not pregnant.

In an irregular move, the home secretary, rejecting the verdict, stepped in and had her examined, and pronounced her insane, thereby promoting her, in the view of the *Spectator*, to an 'aristocracy' of respectable criminals not suited to execution.[48] She would not hang, but would be confined for life to Broadmoor.

The idea that a person could escape execution by being deemed insane undermined the assumption of individual responsibility on which the criminal law had up to then been based.[49] The *Lancet* thought it entirely fitting that Edmunds not be considered responsible. In her circumstances, and with her heredity, it argued, it would have been remarkable if she reached the age of forty-three without going mad. However, the *Spectator* argued that the home secretary's intervention liberated descendants of the insane from fear of legal retribution for crime, and thus destroyed respect for the law. It charged that the respite was a response to pressure from the newspapers, particularly the *Telegraph*, against capital punishment.

It was true that by this time the newspapers did have a distaste for capital punishment, particularly for women. Most of the papers expressed relief at the respite but dismay at the manner in which it came about. The *Spectator*, however, thought it 'cruelty towards an unhappy but most wicked convict' who would be trading 'two minutes of suffering for years of the torture of life among the insane.'[50]

Constance Kent could have claimed insanity but apparently chose to risk being hanged rather than face a lifetime in a madhouse. She would have realized that commitment to Broadmoor, an asylum for criminal lunatics, was merely a death sentence of another sort. As Alfred Swaine Taylor put it, it was a place where 'those who have been acquitted of murder on the ground of insanity, after having once entered this establishment, are as dead to the world as if the earth had closed over them. Beyond the walls, whether sane or insane, the murderers once committed to Broadmoor never pass, either in life or after death.'[51]

Constance was a sixteen-year-old schoolgirl in June 1860, when the mangled body of her four-year-old stepbrother, Francis Savile Kent, was found outside on the substantial family estate at Road,

Wiltshire.[52] The child had been strangled in his bed, and then nearly decapitated as his body was stuffed into a privy. The prime suspects were Constance; his nursemaid, Elizabeth Gough; and his father, Samuel.

After Constance was held for questioning and then let go, she became something of a folk heroine, receiving proposals of marriage and invitations to visit various parts of the country.[53] Later it was rumoured that police had deliberately bungled the case by not following up on a clue that incriminated her, a bloody nightdress. A year or so after the murder, police became aware that she had confessed to a relative (presumably her father) that she was the perpetrator, but their second investigation was dropped as well.

The crime would never have been solved had she not come forward in 1865 with a confession. She said many years later that she had committed the murder on her dead mother's behalf out of resentment at her stepmother, a former governess in the household and the mistress of Constance's father during the lifetime of the first Mrs Kent, who her husband claimed was mad.[54]

This macabre crime, set in a sprawling country house whose inhabitants seemed to roam around at night, investigated by bumbling police officers who were trapped for hours in the kitchen when they were supposed to be searching the premises, dominated by a master of the house who clearly had something to hide, and climaxed by a dramatic confession from a black-clad, veiled young woman under the influence of a priest, was a sensation novel come to life.

The newspapers took it up immediately: the *Times*, usually conservative in the extreme, convicted Constance without trial by publishing news of her confession as soon as she surrendered herself to the police.[55] Most of the papers were sympathetic, suggesting that she was insane, and they registered relief when it was announced that she would not hang, but the *Times* aggressively condemned her in several leading articles run in April and May, though she was not tried until 21 July.[56] Enterprising publishers rushed pamphlets into print right after the trial, and a broadside summarizing the case and containing a ballad about her impending death on the gallows was said to have sold 150,000 copies.[57]

Many contemporary analysts of the case thought Constance Kent insane. Taylor had just published a textbook on medical jurisprudence identifying suppressed menstruation in girls, especially those with a hereditary predisposition to insanity, as a cause of homicidal mania, a condition that it was believed could delude people into murdering their loved ones.[58] Had she claimed such a condition, it probably would have been accepted, but she did not.

Commenting on her confession, the *Morning Post* noted that her behaviour had been 'altogether out of the course of nature, and there can be few who do not hope that its eccentricity may be accounted for by hereditary disease.'[59] The *Times* felt that adolescence was anyway a time when 'the tide of natural affections runs the lowest,' and 'it is the softer sex especially which is said to go through a period of almost utter heartlessness.' Boys were 'bad enough'; girls, 'harder and more selfish still.'[60]

Five years after the murder of her stepbrother, Constance was clearly not a danger to anyone else. The Kent case marks the first time that the individual circumstances of a murderess were taken into account by the English justice system.

Though sentenced to death, she was reprieved and given a sentence of penal servitude for life. This, in practice, meant twenty years, and before that time was up she had gradually faded from the public eye. The surest indicator of her increasing obscurity is that Madame Tussaud's, which had installed a wax effigy of her in the Chamber of Horrors in 1865, withdrew it in 1877. She was released in 1885, whereupon she went to Tasmania, and then to the mainland of Australia. She appears to have used the rest of her long life – she lived to be 100[61] – to serve others, training and then working as a nurse.

It is not surprising that the two most notorious child murderesses of nineteenth-century England were not hanged. Child murder was not a crime that incited public vengeance. Their crimes were bizarre but were peculiar to their own unhappy situations. They were not perceived as threats to the general public. Still, other women were hanged for child murder who were probably insane. These two, however, belonged to respectable society.

The murder of children was in many ways a natural extension of the underground culture that permitted the murder of unwanted babies. Most murdered babies and children, unlike adult victims, left no one to press their case with the authorities.[62] If they were not missed by their own parents, the public was unlikely to take much notice.

As the *Pall Mall Gazette* observed in 1865, a large part of one's repugnance at murder derives from the fear of being put in the same situation. An adult contemplating a case of child murder would not identify with the victim, would not feel similarly threatened. Repugnance was grafted on to humanity, as it were, as children became more valued by society. In response to this movement, press coverage of child murder increased as time went on.

CONCLUSION

All the victims of these crimes were sympathetic figures, but not all the perpetrators were seen as villains. Much was made of the personal lives and appearance of Christiana Edmunds and Constance Kent, who were of special interest not only because their motives and methods of murder were bizarre, but also because they were from the middle rather than the working class. Celestina Somner achieved notoriety for escaping the hangman's noose despite the barbarity of her crime. Harriet Parker was immortalized for her melodramatic penitence.

SIX

Baby-Farming and Infanticide

Mary Lockham / Hannah Halley / Rachel Bradley /
Catherine Welch / Ann Harwood / Rebecca Smith / Jane Taylor /
Ellen Lanigan / Amy Gregory / Ann Barnes / Charlotte Winsor /
Margaret Waters / Amelia Dyer / Ada Chard Williams

Infanticide was the most common type of murder by women. It
was also by far the easiest type to hide and, in its traditional form,
the least threatening to the general public. But in the second half
of the nineteenth century, the child-care industry developed to
the point where it was obvious that women were professionally
murdering babies for money. People tend to react to crime according to how threatened they feel, and these hired murderesses
aroused strong antagonism in the public mind.

Many murderesses were no more than teenagers who had killed
their illegitimate babies out of a sense of shame. 'Numerous are
the instances of this species of crime,' intoned an 1824 broadside;

> Let the frailties of human nature be what they may, and in an
> unguarded moment a female be led astray, and wander in the paths
> of illicit intercourse, it is much to be regretted that the laws operate
> so severely against them, and that the finger of scorn is for ever to
> be pointed at the deluded victim of man, and drive them to commit
> acts at which human nature shudders ...[1]

In the nineteenth century the criminal justice system, increasingly patriarchal, became increasingly lenient towards such offenders. The public was not terribly interested in this form of murder – and it clearly was murder, in terms of the law. It was familiar and very sad, but not terribly shocking. Often a woman tried for infanticide escaped with a conviction for concealment of birth, which did not carry the death penalty – but not always.

In the first third of the century, the state was much more zealous than in later years in exposing and punishing women who committed infanticide.[2] From time to time the justice system saw fit to remind unmarried women that they had better resist seduction, since unwanted babies could not be got rid of with impunity. Broadsides and newspapers record the trials and executions of hapless young women who had done away with babies they could not afford to acknowledge, let alone care for. There was, along with high-minded morality, a streak of smug Puritanism in English society that manifested itself in vindictive cruelty to the oppressed.

EARLY NINETEENTH CENTURY

The story of Hetty Sorrel in *Adam Bede* is based on an actual case described to George Eliot by her aunt, who in 1802 ministered to Hetty's prototype, Margaret Voce, in Nottingham. Unlike Hetty Sorrel, Margaret Voce was not saved from the hangman, but the newspapers disposed of her trial and execution in a few lines – an indication of the story's routineness.

In 1810 Mary Lockham, a nineteen-year-old servant, was tried at York for the murder of a baby found with a cloth stuffed into its mouth. Her employer testified that she 'was as kind and affectionate' to the children 'as a mother' and was 'always civil and obliging.'[3] A broadside distributed before the trial attempted to blacken her character,[4] but other accounts render her a pathetic figure. After the judge suggested that if the child had been born dead she would be guilty, not of murder, but of concealing the birth, the jury found her guilty of the lesser charge and she was sent to prison for five months.[5]

A sermon preached locally after the trial and then published refers to the 'many instances of unhappy young women, who have ended their days at the gallows, for the murder of their own infants ...' It warns:

> When we consider how common this crime is; when we consider the misery, not only of the unhappy creatures who commit it, but likewise the wretchedness in which it involves a wide circle of friends, relatives, and parents, one can scarcely select, from the catalogue of human woes, a more heart-rending affliction. Think of the feelings of a father and mother, who see their own child, whom they have brought up with all the tenderness of parental affection, led out to a public execution; think of the sorrow that would long prey upon the minds of brothers and sisters, and of the infamy which must, though doubtless unjustly, attach to the whole family. These are the dire consequences of this vice ...
>
>> O that female servants, and young women of the lower classes in general, would take warning from these admonitions, which address themselves so forcibly to the heart and conscience.[6]

Obviously there were enough 'young women of the lower classes' in danger of becoming pregnant to warrant such public advice. An unmarried woman who found herself pregnant was usually quickly abandoned by her lover, who would not have wanted the burden of supporting a child. She could not continue to work in a factory or as a servant if she had a baby to look after. 'The situation provided obvious incentives to hide one's pregnancy,' say Daly and Wilson, 'and such behavior evidently became epidemic.' They point out that the Industrial Revolution made things worse by isolating young people who went into service or apprenticeship away from their families.[7]

Hannah Halley, hanged in Derby for infanticide in 1822, worked in a cotton mill and had married a man who did not know of her pregnancy and was not the father. When the baby was born, she thrust it into a jug, poured scalding water over it, and hid it under her bed. She was implicated by her landlady and a friend of the landlady, who heard a child cry, demanded to see it, and found it after a search. The child died after four days.

'The whole history of this unfortunate woman's transgression ought to operate as a moral warning against the first deviations from the path of rectitude,' said the Derby *Mercury*. 'When led to the indulgence of an illicit passion, had she been told that it would issue in the dreadful crime of murder, she would have started from the prophetic warning with indescribable horror.' An 'immense multitude' watched her die.[8]

Caught in an equally impossible situation, Rachel Bradley, twenty-seven and unmarried, was hanged at Lancaster in 1827 after responding to a threat from the father to kill the baby or be killed herself. According to the *Star*, the child was murdered 'under circumstances of the most atrocious description.' A broadside entitled 'Rachel Bradley's Downfall' says she threw the baby into the canal while it was asleep because her lover had promised to marry her if she got rid of it. The trial and the execution, according to the papers, excited great interest.[9]

A year later Catherine Welch, twenty-four, was hanged in London for throwing her infant into a ditch because she had neither food nor shelter to give it. The *Star* reported that an immense crowd watched her die distraught, crying wildly for mercy, and shrieking when the drop beneath her feet was released.[10]

Such performances were repeated quite regularly until 1832, when Mary Kellaway was hanged at Exeter for killing a newborn.[11] Presumably methods for destroying a baby were discussed every time one of these cases was publicized.

METHODS

An 1839 textbook on forensic medicine lists the following as the chief varieties of violent death after delivery: smothering; haemorrhage from the umbilical cord; exposure; starvation; injuries to the head from falls, blows, or compression; wounds of the throat; puncture of the head, spine, ears, or heart; laceration of the intestine or throat by instruments thrust into the anus or mouth; drowning; poisoning; burning; strangling with the hand or a rope;

choking by foreign bodies thrust into the back of the throat or by doubling back the tongue.[12] A dead baby deposited in a hiding-place – a privy, a well, or a dunghill, for example – would not likely be traceable to the mother.

One broadside 'trope' concerns a young maidservant who secretly gives birth in the house in which she is employed. She then cuts the baby's throat and hides the body in her room. Later she throws it on the fire, where another servant discovers it. She is tried for murder, found guilty, and executed. This scenario seems to be derived from the true story of Ann Harwood, or Haywood, a servant executed at York on 18 March 1805 for the murder of her newborn daughter. She had attempted to conceal her pregnancy and insisted on the day she gave birth that she had merely caught cold. Some suspicious fellow servants searched the house and, in the ashes of a fire, found a baby that had been cut open and disembowelled. Several papers described a pathetic and horrific scene in the courtroom: on being sentenced, she fell to her knees and begged the judge for mercy.[13]

Broadsides gave a similar history to Margaret Harvey in 1819, Margaret Henderson in 1824, Mary Hardcastle and Mary Lavender in 1824, and Margaret Lewis in 1829. A ballad supposedly written by Ann Harwood includes this rather awkwardly phrased warning:

> When I am brought to the fatal tree,
> Young women all take advice by me,
> If by false man you deceived should be,
> From the crime of murder God keep you free.[14]

A whimsical variation on this is contained in an obviously fictitious, undated execution broadside on Ann Baker, a servant who had a baby, cut the child's throat, hid the body in a box, and buried it in the garden. After a dog uncovered the box, her mistress investigated and reported her to the authorities. The broadside tells us that after a ten-hour trial she was sentenced to death but left the court laughing. She dismissed the chaplain, telling him: 'You can do me no good; I had much rather you kept your preaching for another.' Just before the execution, she told him: 'I want no parson. I would rather have a fiddler and die merry.' When she got to the scaffold, she allegedly kicked off her shoes and danced until she dropped.[15] In a warning to frivolous young women, irreverence is here linked with immorality.

It is fair to conclude from these variations that the stereotype did manifest itself from time to time. Servants had babies out of wedlock and felt compelled to murder them. Their employers or fellow servants sometimes found them out and exposed them, forcing the justice system to react.

THE BLIND EYE OF JUSTICE

Most women suspected of infanticide were never prosecuted, and probably there were many who escaped suspicion. A letter from Thomas Wakley, the crusading coroner for Middlesex, to the home secretary, Sir George Lewis, notes an increase in infanticide in his jurisdiction in the late 1850s and adds that 'it is also true that infanticide is a crime which admits of being perpetrated in hundreds of instances without a chance of detecting the guilty parties.'[16]

Even when women were prosecuted for infanticide, there was a strong possibility of acquittal. There was always the loophole that murder or manslaughter could not be proved if the baby had not been born alive. (If the baby was not wanted, there was not likely to have been a midwife to witness the birth.) If the lungs would not float in water, doctors concluded that they had not inflated, and therefore the birth had not been a live one; because some doctors argued that inflated lungs were not conclusive proof of a live birth, sometimes judges gave an accused murderess the benefit of the doubt.[17] If the baby was born dead, the charge could be reduced to concealment of birth, a lesser offence punishable by up to two years' imprisonment.[18] This option became so popular that in 1895 the *Spectator* criticized the tradition 'in which, by a conspiracy of mercy among judges, doctors, and jurymen, a verdict is always returned of guilty of concealment of birth' in cases of murder right after birth.[19]

Puerpural mania, that is, derangement resulting from childbirth or suppressed lactation, was often a successful defence for women charged with infanticide. This diagnosis derived from the observations of medical men that a woman's difficulties with breast-feeding could cause her to become insane. In a study of insanity defences used at the Old Bailey, Joel Eigen found cases from as far back as 1822 and 1838 in which this debility was described, though only in the second case was the term 'puerpural mania' used. It was believed that even labour alone could cause such derangement that a woman might feel driven to destroy her newborn.[20]

SERIAL INFANTICIDE

The murder of one baby could be explained away, but the state could not condone a pattern of infanticide in one family, however pathetic the circumstances. In eighteen years of marriage, Rebecca Smith gave birth to ten children. Her neighbours in Devizes, Wiltshire, characterized her as inoffensive and industrious. She was simple, open, and honest. She went to church every Sunday, and prayed night and morning. Despite her prayers, her husband, Philip, a labourer and a drunkard, could not provide for a large family. Year after year she bore his children, but she found it necessary to murder them a day or two later. Year after year her babies died as she nursed them, gently inserting into their mouths a finger dipped in 'blue' rat poison or arsenic and then watching them writhe in agony: two Philips, two Sarahs, two Edwards, two Richards.

The last Richard, born 16 May 1849, died on 12 June. An inquest revealed that he had been poisoned. Arsenic was also found in the bodies of two of her other children, one who died in 1844 and one in 1841, marking the first time that it had been detected after as long as eight years. After she was convicted on 9 August of Richard's murder and sentenced to die, she confessed that she had murdered seven of his siblings. One other child died in infancy of a bowel problem; one survived. She was hanged on 23 August before a large crowd that was predominantly female.

The public, inured to serial poisoning and to infanticide, did not know what to think: could it be that in the underclass starvation was such a strong possibility that babies had to be killed soon after birth, just as kittens were drowned? Could harsh economic reality pervert the maternal instinct so that poisoning one's own children seemed a reasonable response?

As the *Globe* put it, 'While she was praying and thanking God for her own preservation for a period of years, she was the annual and deliberate destroyer of her own offspring – no sooner bringing them into the world than administering poison to get rid of them ...'[21] This woman, of nondescript manner and appearance, was clearly not a monster, yet she had not a trace of human feeling, poisoning babies as though they were vermin. People were so fascinated that at one point in the trial the judge upbraided spectators for their 'barbarous curiosity.'[22]

The local paper observed that Smith was so well behaved 'it might be thought she was totally incapable of the unnatural crime of which she was convicted.' She was also, however, 'extremely ignorant, and betrayed a want of any deep feeling.'[23] Another article in the same paper, aimed at members of her own community, urged compassion for her. She was not a monster, but rather an unfortunate human being ground down by 'calamity, sorrow and bitterness of heart' unknown to ordinary people, 'who pass easily through the world, unassailed by great temptations and unsullied by great crimes ...'[24]

LOOPHOLES

In 1855 Honor Gibbons was immortalized in Tennyson's *Maud* as the 'Mammonite mother' who 'killed her babe for a burial fee.'[25] She and her mother, Bridget Gerraty, enrolled her illegitimate baby daughter, Mary, in a Stockport burial club, and then killed her by feeding her sulphuric acid in April 1853. They were found guilty and sentenced to die, but were reprieved and transported for life.

The public was not often troubled by such glaring reminders of the grinding poverty on its edges. Far from attracting pity, the small number of women executed for infanticide after 1849, having killed other people's babies, were treated like monsters – anti-mothers, to use Margaret L. Arnot's term.[26]

In the few cases in the latter part of the century in England where women were convicted of having murdered their own babies, the death sentence was routinely commuted to life imprisonment or less. The home secretary's power to authorize releases was exercised more for those said to have acted out of puerperal mania than for any other group. 'Since infanticide was limited in its object and duration, fears about the spread of violence were overridden by other factors,' Roger Smith reasons. 'Infanticidal women were particularly well-suited to be objects of mercy.'[27]

Martin Wiener has observed that prosecutions for concealment of birth fell steadily, from 143 in 1865 to 82 in 1880, and sentences for infanticide grew shorter, from ten years to life in the 1850s and 1860s, to less than seven years by the 1880s. 'By the close of the Victorian era bureaucrats, judges and juries all considered the killing of a newborn by its mother ... as prima facie evidence of mental illness.'[28]

Carolyn Conley found that, in Kent, between 1859 and 1880, no woman was convicted of killing her newborn infant, but 62 per cent of those charged with murder or manslaughter in a baby death were convicted of concealment, most (86 per cent) receiving sentences of no more than six months. These figures led her to conclude that, since the state did not provide for illegitimate children, the courts felt it only fitting that penalties for infanticide be fairly light.[29] Not everyone saw this as a logical step. 'Infanticide must either be recognized as the custom of the country, or it must be stopped,' said the *Saturday Review*. 'If it is seriously intended never to hang a woman again, let this be announced.'[30]

There were legitimate reasons for discreetly condoning infanticide: many more babies were born than could be provided for, and it was better for a child to die immediately after birth than to die slowly, later, of starvation or neglect. In Arnot's view, infanticide and neglect sometimes operated as a means of family limitation in the nineteenth century because birth-control and abortion techniques were not yet in wide use but folk knowledge of alternative techniques had by then been lost.[31]

Too, in the words of the *Spectator*, 'one reason why infanticide has been so lightly regarded is that it is a crime of which no man can in his own person possibly be a victim.' Furthermore, as the English social system was based on the myth that single women did not have babies, it can be assumed that it suited society to arrange things so that they could not maintain them.

Unmarried mothers who killed their babies were not necessarily selfish or unfeeling, merely practical. Until the bastardy clause of the 1834 New Poor Law, if the father could not be persuaded to marry the mother, the parish had to give her an allowance. The bastardy clause relieved the parish of this responsibility, placing the burden entirely on the woman. Newspapers and broadsides contain many sad stories of poor and miserable unmarried mothers who could see no way to keep their offspring. Some who could not live with the guilt and pain of having killed their babies afterward took their own lives.

The *Annual Register* for 1847 records the case of Jane Taylor, a twenty-one-year-old servant, charged with the murder of her illegitimate baby in Warwickshire. Turned out of her mother's house, she had been staying with her brother and his wife, who testified to her being very fond of the child. But as they were evicted on her account, she was turned out once again. With nowhere to go, she simply waded into a canal with the baby tied in her apron, clasped in her arms. She was rescued by a man who could not swim, but the baby had by that time drowned.

The judge told the jury it would have to determine whether Taylor had gone into the water by accident or with the deliberate intention of drowning herself and the child. If it was for that purpose, it was murder, but they were to give her the benefit of the doubt. The jury not only voted to acquit her, but also took up a collection for her rescuer, to which the judge added five pounds from the county. The sheriff and barristers donated 'a considerable sum of money' to Taylor.[32]

Later in the century women who had obviously killed their babies were still liable to be convicted of murder and sentenced to die, and though they were certain to be respited, they were still given long prison sentences. In 1878, for example, a dispassionate story in the *Times* announces that Ellen Lanigan was given a death sentence for the murder of one of her infant twins on 17 May. She had actually murdered both. Her husband had been sent to a lunatic asylum four years previously, leaving her to support four young children. Eventually she entered into a living arrangement with a man who made her pregnant and then deserted her. When the twins were born in a Liverpool workhouse on 30 April, she realized she could not care for them. 'It was poverty and distress and cruelty that made me drown my children,' she told the court. I put them in a pool of water ... I remained in the field crying all night, and I have cried about my children every day since. I was destitute; I had no home or bed to lie on.'[33] Her sentence was commuted.

In 1895, Amy Gregory, a twenty-three-year-old Richmond laundress, was found guilty of murder and sentenced to die, setting off a wave of protest. She had strangled her six-week-old baby, Frances Maud Smart, whom she had left in the workhouse to nurse at six shillings a week, because she had neither means nor work. After giving birth she had sought help from her parents, but her father would have nothing to do with her.

After her conviction, the *Star* expressed sympathy for the 'heart-rending agonies' that she had gone through and 'the grim hardships which had transformed the instincts of a mother into the mad passion of a murderess.' The jury had recommended mercy, but even if she were reprieved, the paper said, the threat of execution would have been a terrible punishment.[34]

By killing the child, Gregory had made life possible for herself, as the *Spectator* put it in a lengthy article congratulating the home secretary, Lord Asquith, on having spared her life. But the article referred disapprovingly to the public clamour for her total exemption from punishment simply because she was a woman. The *Spectator* insisted that moral laws were as binding on women as on men:

What those who raise this point really mean, is that women, from natural deficiency of reasoning power and natural liability to obey impulse, are partially irresponsible, or at least less responsible than men are ... If they are right, women are not equal, but inferior, in their moral sense; and being inferior require more discipline from the law to brace their consciences up ...

... The plain truth of the matter is that some men are beginning to pity all criminals as victims of circumstance, and naturally pity those whom they think weakest, and who, if pardoned, will least terrify society.[35]

CHIVALRY OR EQUALITY?

This argument grew out of women's struggle for equality. Feminists did not want a double standard of justice any more than they wanted a double standard of sexuality. Chivalry was a two-edged sword. 'Many members of male juries probably shifted uncomfortably in their seats when confronted with the tragic results of another man's sexual transgressions,' Arnot has suggested. Furthermore, accepting that they were in need of protection would affirm that women were in some significant way inferior to men, less able to cope in the public world. At some level, she argues, men must have felt that if they were to retain their power in the political sphere women had to be defined as confined to some other, basically different sphere – like the home.

Feminists, in Arnot's analysis, objected not only to men's intrusion into what had traditionally been their responsibility, but to their assumption that there had to be poor mothers with sole responsibility for unwanted illegitimate children – that male sexual licence would prevail. To a suggestion in a letter to the *Times* that fathers of murdered babies be punished, the *Pall Mall Gazette* replied, 'It is always useless to punish legally what is not condemned socially.'[36]

Feminists felt that the measures proposed to deter infanticide would have attacked the symptoms, not the cause, of the problem. And they objected to the imposition of middle-class values on the working class, especially the prejudice against employment of unwed mothers and the assumption that working-class women would serve society better by staying home and taking care of their children.[37]

In 1871 the government proposed that anyone paid to take care of a child outside the child's home should have to register, prove herself of good character, and submit to frequent inspections. This plan was denounced by the woman's suffrage movement in a sharply worded pamphlet.[38] The resulting 1872 Infant Life Protection Act was watered down so that women who took in only one baby at a time did not have to register. Worse still, it soon became clear that municipalities were allowing establishments to evade registration.[39]

Until 1897, when the act was amended, infanticide continued in epidemic proportions, so that even at that late stage more than 30 per cent of murder victims were under a month old.[40] This is not to say that there was a dead baby beneath every park bench and in every ditch. But, for example, the *Times* reported that in London alone in 1871 there were 100 cases of murder or manslaughter, nearly all of them infanticide.[41] This was down from 150 baby murders in London in 1861, but the decrease may have been a delusion.[42] Daly and Wilson found that prosecutions for concealment of birth declined in England from more than 200 a year in the 1860s to fewer than 100 by the 1880s, 'but a good deal of suspicious infant mortality persisted.'[43]

While one group of women was engaged in upfront political action to affirm women's rights, another group was subverting the law. Reluctant mothers were becoming more proficient at disposing of babies they felt they could not raise. The same sort of underground network that had passed on folk wisdom as to how best to do away with a newborn was directing women with sufficient means to lying-in houses, where they could count on a secret confinement and an unencumbered future. Those with less money paid a small weekly fee to a caregiver who could be counted on to neglect the child so that it died after a month or two. For a few pounds women could be found to 'adopt' a child. So a large part of baby killing was being done professionally.

BABY-FARMING

By 1849 it could be seen by anyone who sought such information that getting rid of other people's unwanted babies was for some women an occupation. On the surface, these women were kindly, cheerful nurses, but few of them provided adequate food and care, many of them neglected their charges to the point of illness and death, and some of them murdered for profit.

In 1865 Charlotte Winsor's trial brought this line of work into the spotlight, and the *Pall Mall Gazette* and the *British Medical Journal* kept it there. In 1870 Margaret Waters, another practitioner, was executed for it. It continued, bubbling under the surface of respectable society, through the trial and execution of Amelia Dyer in 1896 and into the twentieth century. Once exposed, these women were regarded as sinister and witch-like, but there is evidence that in business they had been friendly and obliging and saw themselves as providing a needed service. As in other complex situations, much depended on the controlling point of view.

This sort of conflict is illustrated in George Moore's *Esther Waters*. When Esther, a kitchen maid, has a baby out of wedlock, she is given a chance to support herself by becoming a wet-nurse – but at the cost of sending her own child to a baby-farm to be looked after. To her employer, this sounds like a perfectly reasonable arrangement. From Esther's perspective, however, it is 'a life for a life.' As there was not an adequate substitute for breast milk, baby-farm babies often died, and sometimes baby-farmers helped nature take its course by neglecting them.

The baby-farmer cheerfully tells Esther that she sees neglect as deliverance for the mother and no particular hardship for the baby, since babies are not aware of what is happening to them. 'Yer know, all you girls are dreadful taken with your babies at first. But they is an awful drag on a girl who gets her living in service,' she says. 'I don't say I'm not often sorry for them, poor little dears, but they takes less notice than you'd think for, and they're better out of the way, and that's a fact; it saves a lot of trouble hereafter. I often think that to neglect them, to let them go off quiet, that I be their best friend ...'[44] This novel, published in 1894, is set a generation earlier, when wet-nursing was widely accepted by those who could afford to buy it and by those who could not afford not to sell it. Esther's story is worth telling because she is unusual. She rescues her baby at the cost of her wet-nursing job and manages to raise him to adulthood. But, being fictional, she has qualities and resources not found in ordinary people, as well as a substantial amount of good luck.

Baby-farmers took care of children whose mothers did not want them or could not have them. Their clientele comprised, among others, prostitutes, servants, factory hands, and unfaithful wives of absent husbands. For an upfront fee, they would 'adopt' a baby outright; for a weekly or monthly fee, they would feed it at a bare subsistence level that allowed them a profit. If, as was not uncommon, the mother did not want to see the child again, it was that much easier to kill it or neglect it.

By the 1860s, when journalists made baby-farming a public scandal, it was understood that handing a baby over with a fee for 'adoption' was tantamount to applying for its murder. These were difficult cases for the police to crack, since bereaved mothers who had wanted their babies murdered were unlikely to complain to the authorities, and bereaved mothers who had wanted their babies preserved could not risk the publicity of an inquest and trial. Baby-farmers were well protected by the secrecy that surrounded not only their own activities, but the origin of their charges.

Even after a spate of vicious publicity about Winsor, who in 1865 was twice sentenced to hang, and both times respited on legal technicalities, baby-farmers continued to advertise in major newspapers until campaigns by the *British Medical Journal* and the *Pall Mall Gazette* embarrassed the newspapers into policing their advertising. Waters was executed in 1870, probably to subdue public shock and indignation at the extent of baby-farming operations, but, as the *Pall Mall Gazette* predicted at the time, her example did not deter other baby-farmers: it merely made them more cautious.

Throughout the 1870s, despite the introduction of a law requiring the registration of baby-farmers, there was strong evidence of an industry out of control. J. Brandon Curgenven told a meeting of the National Association for the Promotion of Social Science in 1869 that about 35,000 of 50,000 illegitimate children a year were being put out to nurse, and quite possibly to be got rid of.[45] The rigid Victorian social code continued to push unmarried mothers to dispose of their babies, and though medical men like

Curgenven urged that the women they left them with be registered and inspected, advocates of women's rights resisted state
interference in women's concerns. So, despite a series of deaths in
obvious baby-farms (regularly reported in the *British Medical Journal* and elsewhere), women continued to patronize them and the
authorities were powerless to curtail their operations.[46]

In 1879 Annie Took was executed in Exeter for the murder of a
deformed baby apparently handed over to her for that purpose,
and Catherine and John Barnes, baby-farmers in Cheshire for at
least ten years, were sentenced to life imprisonment. In 1888 came
more baby-farming scandals,[47] and in 1897 a new law to regulate
them, but the parade of dead babies did not stop. In 1896, in one
of the grimmest revelations of the century, a quiet, bustling grandmother was exposed in Reading as a murderess of at least a score
of babies given into her care, and perhaps as many as fifty.

EARLY BABY-FARMING

The first baby-farming scandal was a rather low-key affair in comparison with the operations uncovered later in the century. 'A great
deal of excitement, not to say horror, has been created in the
minds of many in the neighbourhood ...,' said a local paper, when
Ann Barnes, who lived near Ely, in Cambridgeshire, was accused
in 1847 of having poisoned several infants whose parents worked
nearby as field labourers.[48] Barnes had had twelve children, only
two of whom survived to adulthood. Her second husband had
died five years earlier of suspected poisoning, but, by the time his
body was exhumed, nothing could be proved against her.[49]

When three babies in the tiny community of Purlsbridge died
after a few days' illness, the coroner became suspicious. They had
the same symptoms – vomiting, diarrhoea, and abdominal pain –
symptoms that no one else in the neighbourhood had. One of the
victims was Barnes's granddaughter, Mary Ann Youngs, four months
old. Three of Mary Ann's siblings had also died in infancy while in
the care of their grandmother.

None of the parents seemed particularly upset by this turn of
events, not even when Mary Ann's and four other baby deaths in

the community were traced to arsenic poisoning. It was obvious that Barnes had been hired to take care of the babies as long as they lived, but to see to it that they did not live long. She was arrested on 3 September 1847, but as the inquest concluded only that the children had died of arsenic poisoning by an unknown person, she was never tried.

The *Times* was sufficiently alarmed to reprint a leading article from the Cambridge *Independent* that suggested the parents had connived in the poisonings. At the inquest, said the article, the father of one of the dead babies had remarked to a reporter that he 'did not know but the old woman was right, after all. There was a deal too many of 'em, and nine out of every ten ought to be put out of the way.' The paper concluded in disgust:

> Here have three children been cruelly and deliberately murdered; a circumstance of so dreadful a nature that the contemplation of it fills the mind with horror; and yet, such is the ignorance and brutality of the wretched inhabitants, totally devoid of any moral feeling or restraint, that they laugh at the proceedings of the coroner, and devote the day of the inquest to revelry and drunkenness.[50]

The coroner's jury eventually decided that the children had died of arsenic poisoning by an unknown person.[51] At this point the idea of a nurse figure who made her living by murder was an outlandish one. However, such women did exist, as did mothers who hired them. Later, people to whom unwanted babies could be permanently farmed out were dubbed 'baby-farmers.' Not all baby-farmers murdered or neglected their charges, but it was evident by the 1860s that babies given into their care had a mortality rate far above the average.

CHARLOTTE WINSOR

Unlike Ann Barnes, whose baby-farming career was just one blurred episode in a decade marked by blatant serial poisoning, Winsor became a notorious criminal. The time was ripe for social reformers to expose the shocking lack of public responsibility for the children of the poor. In 1865, when Winsor was sentenced to death, the Victorian social conscience, as articulated by the press, was beginning to acknowledge that the law's liberal attitude to infanticide was encouraging enterprising third parties to go in for wholesale murder. The *Daily News* reprinted a savage editorial from the *Medical Times* that did not exonerate Winsor but suggested that the system was at fault for condoning child neglect. It criticized her not merely for murder, but for needless brutality, pointing out that to dispose of a baby she need only have given it stale or sour food – or gin – and she would never have been caught.[52]

Instead of tightening the law and ensuring that no further baby murders took place, society appeased its conscience by focusing its outrage solely on Winsor, a middle-aged woman of doubtful reputation cut off by her occupation and her chequered past from the rural community around her. Despite public awareness that it was an occupation that was by no means unique, she was depicted in newspaper reports, pamphlets, and broadsides as a perversion of nature, a monster for whom no punishment would be adequate.

Winsor was a child-minder who lived near Torquay, Devon, where police had been finding babies' bodies by the roadside. In February 1865 they found a baby boy wrapped in the 6 May 1864 edition of the local paper, the *Western Times.* They established the age of the child and traced all babies born about the beginning of October. Mary Jane Harris, an unmarried servant, had registered the birth of her son, Tommy, on 6 October but could not produce the child. She directed police to Winsor, who did not have Tommy either, but who did have a stack of newspapers with the 6 May edition missing.

Winsor had been paid three shillings a week. She had offered more than once to get rid of the child for five pounds, and it appears that all that stopped his mother was the lack of five pounds. At last the two women in charge of Tommy came to an arrangement, and Winsor proposed killing him in the bedroom while the mother waited in the kitchen. Harris agreed, and Winsor's six-year-old granddaughter was sent away on an invented errand. Harris, by her own account, sat and listened to her baby's frantic cries as he was placed between two feather beds and smothered.

Winsor and Harris stood trial in March 1865. The bereaved mother, twenty-three years old, described by the local paper as fair-complected and good-looking, wore a black cloak and fashionable white bonnet. Winsor, nearly twice her age and with a hard life behind her, was presented as a contrast. 'She boldly faced the court, with immoveable aspect. Her countenance is sallow, her features are long, and her cheeks sunken – perhaps from the anxious time she must have passed awaiting her trial.'[53] The jury was divided, eight for and four against acquittal. The judge accordingly dismissed them and dissolved the trial.

A second trial was held in July in which Harris appeared as a witness against Winsor. This time Winsor would not be protected by the mother's involvement. Consequently she was visibly anxious, covering her face with a handkerchief, and moaning and sobbing. However, this display of human weakness, inconsistent with the depiction of her as a hardened criminal, elicited no sympathy. She was found guilty of murder and sentenced to hang on 10 August. 'There is no bottom to the badness of human nature,' said a leader in the *Western Times* headed 'Moloch's Daughter.' 'The most soul-harrowing circumstances in these infanticide crimes, are, that they are perpetrated by women, and not women simply, but mothers.' Winsor, a 'miserable-looking hag,' was a 'Satanic nurse,' but the paper pointed out that Harris was as much the murderer as Winsor.[54] On the night of 9 August she was respited until a committee of judges could advise the attorney general about the legality of her retrial. (The judge probably should have tried harder to bring the first jury to agreement, and Harris, her co-defendant, should not have been used subsequently as a witness against her.) She was given another execution date of 12 February.

News of her respite came too late for the publisher of an execution broadside describing the scene of her demise. A crowd of thousands was supposed to have assembled 'at the usual hour' and 'expressed their abhorrence' by yelling when Winsor and the hangman appeared on the scaffold. A ballad composed especially for the occasion calls her a dreadful woman, a devil in human form, and extols God for having called her to account for corrupting mothers and murdering children:

> The tempter and the murderess,
> As you see by these lines,
> Has gone to face their Maker,
> And to answer for her crimes.[55]

It was not only street sellers who were disappointed that Winsor's life was to be spared for a while at least. The Exeter public, according to the *Western Times*, wanted her hanged as an example.

> There is no bloodthirstiness in this County, but public indignation and horror had been so excited at the fact that a miserable witch had been residing among us who for money had made a trade of child murder – that we never remember to have witnessed so general a feeling of resignation to the idea of the fullest legal vengeance being taken for this great crime ... We hear a good deal about child-murder not being considered in the category of murder; but there was no sign in the public conduct here of any abatement of the feeling of abhorrence in this case on account of the infancy of the victim.

The article describes her as 'a woman of low life, of no moral feeling, sordid in soul, and covetous of money.' But it conceded that she had some human qualities: she had learned to read in prison, and had been reading and discussing the Bible.[56] She appears to have been ignorant but canny rather than blatantly evil. None the less, a new execution date was set.

As 12 February approached, Winsor again prepared to die and made a written confession in which she admitted being an accessory to the murder in that she helped conceal it, but insisted that it was Harris who had murdered the child – by drowning him in a basin of water. Again at the eleventh hour, she was respited: the judges had not yet arrived at a recommendation. Shortly afterward her sentence was commuted to life imprisonment. Harris was tried separately in March and acquitted.

Winsor's punishment appears to have lasted longer than anyone intended at the time. As the *Pall Mall Gazette* observed, because the people who knew about baby-farming would not speak out, hers was the one case that the law had been able to find 'in a period of many years' in which 'what the law calls murders are perpetrated by the score all over the country.' A victim of 'that variability of opinion which makes people regard infanticide now as a murder, and now as a not unnatural means of getting rid of an intolerable inconvenience,' Winsor was saved by 'a tacit but over-ruling opinion' that infanticide was not, in fact, murder.

> Juries show this by refusing to convict, and Home Secretaries by perfect contentment that child-murderers should go unhanged. This is so well known that women kill their infants with a strong feeling of security that, even if discovered, their punishment will be inconsiderable ... That to murder a man is atrocious, that a garotter, is a brute, and a forger an intolerable member of society, is obvious to everybody; but it is not so easy to apportion the proper amount of blame and indignation to one who kills an infant with no position in the world, and scarcely any hold upon it. We do not admit it to ourselves, but our horror at a murderer is very much derived from the feeling that, were there cause and opportunity, he would serve us as he served his victim. This is not the case in child murder. Even Charlotte Winsor would probably have shrunk from killing a man; but to her, as to thousands of other people, it would seem that the life of a child, without mind, perception, and very little sense of body, is not at all to be valued like the life of one who has grown into some stature and importance.

The Winsor case, as the *Pall Mall* hoped it would be, turned out to be 'one of those lucky crimes or disasters which have caused many law reforms.'[57] As time went on, the justice system clamped down more and more on baby-farmers, and the Home Office evidently feared that to release her would be a step backwards. Unluckily for her, however, towards the end of her life she was judged by the standards of the day rather than the standards of the era in which she was convicted; and so, as she grew increasingly harmless, she was held to be more and more of a liability.

In 1865, at the time of her trial, the press was just beginning to challenge the assumption that infanticide was not really murder. Even in 1870, when Waters was hanged for baby-farming, there was a substantial body of public opinion that her punishment was excessive. As the *Pall Mall* noted after Waters's execution, in absolute terms the penalty was just, 'but relatively the penalty must be admitted to be in excess, not of the crime but of the estimate which has been lately taken of it.' Waters, the paper pointed out, 'was only one member of a class which has long been permitted to carry on its murderous trade with entire impunity.'[58] However, at the end of the century children's rights became more and more established, and infanticide more and more despicable.

Caught in the demands of changing public opinion, Winsor petitioned in vain for remission of her sentence. She wrote to the home secretary in 1870, then in 1874, then in 1877, and then annually from 1879, protesting that she was not the real murderer, and that in any case she had been punished enough. In 1886 she had served twenty years, the standard for life imprisonment. A note in the files of the Home Office says she 'professionally murdered babies for money.' Another, from Rowland Hill, indicates that her case has been reconsidered, but it is 'so atrocious a case that I hesitate to release her except for some strong reason.' In 1890 she turned seventy. She was the longest-serving female prisoner in England. Her behaviour was good, her health fragile. Her granddaughter was willing to care for her. Turned down, she petitioned again in 1891, 1892; four times, frantically, in 1893; and then, for the last time, in May the next year.[59] She died in obscurity on 19 June 1894, in Woking Prison, Surrey, of cardiac failure and senile decay.

THE WAR AGAINST BABY-FARMERS

As the sensation novel was enhancing the image of the murderess in the 1860s, the periodical press was making her look worse. There was nothing glamorous about murdering babies for money. The press had no use for either the women who gave babies into care or the women who took them. Arnot alleges – in my opinion, unfairly – that the newspapers' agenda must have been 'to confirm in readers' minds the essential rightness of their middle-class family life and the aberrant nature of all alternative arrangements.'[60] To do this she believes they created the 'anti-mother,' an irresponsible, uncaring, and mercenary woman who encouraged and accommodated unnatural attitudes in mothers. Certainly such women were condemned in the press. The public abuse heaped on baby-farmers accused of murder was much more strongly focused than it was on other murderesses.

The spate of publicity about baby-farming triggered by the Winsor case turned into a long-term campaign, led by the *Pall Mall Gazette*, to bring public opinion into line with the law so that infanticide would no longer be condoned.[61] The strategy for doing this was to make the crime concrete, so that the babies were seen as distinct human beings rather than abstract encumbrances and the baby-farmers as crude, heartless victims rather than convenient facilitators. It was at this time that the term 'baby-farmer' was coined.[62]

In the fall of 1867 an inquest was held into the death of a baby girl from starvation in the 'care' of Carolyn Jaggers, a London baby-farmer. The baby had been 'adopted' from an upper-class young woman whose solicitor advised the coroner that she would commit suicide if her name were made public. The *Pall Mall* pointed out that women in such a position would surely not be unhappy to be rid of the evidence of their shame.[63] Mrs Jaggers was let off with a reprimand, but her method of recruitment, through ads in the *Daily Telegraph*, was exposed and widely criticized. The *Pall Mall* ran two of them and, in a follow-up article, urged that the government impose standards on baby-farmers.[64]

The following January the *Pall Mall* quoted more *Daily Telegraph* ads and referred interested readers to the *British Medical Journal*, which was 'able to publish things that we cannot very well print here' – *viz.*, evidence of a thriving trade in abortions. Both the *Pall Mall Gazette* and the *British Medical Journal* sent replies to advertisements directed at pregnant women who wanted to deliver their babies in secret and dispose of them, or, better yet, terminate the pregnancy. They also advertised a child for adoption. (There were more than 300 replies to the *British Medical Journal* investigator.) The *Daily Telegraph* was soon shamed into dropping such ads, and by 1870 they were excluded from all the London dailies, but they were still accepted by the popular weeklies, notably *Lloyd's*, and they were also being distributed as handbills on the streets and in the post.

These early exercises in investigative journalism revealed an abundance of baby-farmers in the general vicinity of London providing various services, from taking in 'ladies in delicate health' to disposing of what the *Pall Mall* called 'the poor little consequence.'[65] The *British Medical Journal*, in a series that ran from January through September 1868, brought the operations to life by means of highly entertaining, offhand interviews whose sly narrative technique and attention to revealing detail owe something to Dickens.

Many of the advertisers catered to the mothers, not the babies, though they could place any child that survived its birth. One advertiser, who 'took in ladies, of course, and could get the child put away,' had a 'diplomy' in midwifery and struck the reporter as someone who would do anything if well paid. She felt that a better alternative to abortion was to dispose of a child by neglecting it at birth, 'and then it could appear as if it was still-born or had died in the birth.'[66] A grandmotherly abortionist told the *British Medical Journal* reporter: 'I'm a jokelar person, I am; and I says funny things and cheers 'em up ... I'm the old original, I am, and have had hundreds.' A 'buxom, energetic, smart woman of 42' insisted she did not do abortions because 'it's no use getting women out of it, for they go and get into it again.' She kept in a bottle a foetus that a rich widow had aborted two years before: she could not bury it in the garden because 'if one human bone were found there it would of course be thought that bad practices had been carried on there, which was not the case.'[67]

The *British Medical Journal* reporter, posing as a prospective customer, also visited establishments that took in children to nurse or adopt. At one such house he found this scene:

The children (each of whom had on a grimy-looking coarse napkin, but were not otherwise notably dirty) bore that peculiar expression of countenance which badly tended children generally acquire. The elder of the two, aged nine months, was fairly nourished; but still its appearance was not satisfactory. It looked, as so many of these children do, afraid to cry; while at the same time it was preternaturally sharp, its eyes anxiously following every movement of its foster-parents. The younger child, five months old, looked wretched. Its little face, being thin, showed painfully the bony structures, which, though hidden from actual sight by the skin, were yet only too palpable ... This child's bones were so scantily covered with flesh, that the baggy skin of the thighs could easily be folded on itself halfway round the bones ... I had noticed, on the side of the room furthest from the spot where a chair was placed for me, a couch whereon lay a bundle of dirty clothes, partially covered by a small quilt dirtier still. Towards this Mrs. ——— every now and then cast a furtive glance, and slyly lifted the coverlet more and more over the bundle as she passed it on her way to the fireplace ... I approached the couch, and there saw a most miserable infant, apparently a few weeks old. This child, Mrs. ——— said, on my asking her about it, was one she had to take care of for an hour while the mother went out – a statement which I took *cum granos salis,* and a large one too.'[68]

He later found that over the past two years the baby-farmer he had visited had registered seven infant deaths, two on the same day.

The investigation led to a demand from the *British Medical Journal*'s editor, Ernest Hart, that the government regulate baby-farmers' activities. He asked in exasperation:

If the partially helpless lunatic is thought worthy of a large and expensive commission of the Crown, of the inspection and guardianship of picked physicians and barristers, of Acts of Parliament, and of the special intervention of Lord Chancellors, is the utterly helpless infant to be looked after by nobody but the coroner? Why should not houses for the reception of pregnant women be as subject to inspection as lunatic asylums?[69]

The pressure moved the government to its first piece of legislation on the issue, the Infant Life Protection Act of 1872, which required the registration of baby-farmers, and it also moved the police to keep watch on baby-farmers suspected of murder. In 1870 police tracked down Margaret Waters, thirty-five, and her sister, Sarah Ellis, twenty-nine, who drugged and starved a child to death whose mother actually wanted it preserved. These women were operating a baby-farm in Brixton, south London, having advertised 'a good home and a mother's love and care.' They admitted to having 'adopted' about forty children. Many of these disappeared. Four more babies found in their care died after their arrest. To save on burial expenses, they had been leaving bodies around the neighbourhood: sixteen were found in the month before they were caught.

As a broadside ballad entitled 'Mothers Beware' described it,

> In a terrace, at Brixton, two sisters did dwell
> And of their sad doings the newspapers tell.
> How they tempted poor mothers their offspring to leave,
> To their tender care, but alas to deceive.
> They starved them to death, for of late has been found,
> The bodies of infants in the fields there around.
>
> Poor children half-naked, their state we deplore,
> Too weak for to stand, they laid on the floor
> Unwashed and neglected by night and by day,
> Till their dear little souls from life pass away
> And what cared the nurse for the dead ones, not she,
> The death of a child, why a saving would be.
>
> Will the hen drive the chicken from under her wing
> And leave it to perish, the poor little thing,
> Or will dumb brutes desert their offspring, ah! no,
> What proofs of affection animals show.
> Yet mothers alas their children will slay,
> Or else pay another to put it away.[70]

By this time baby-farming was an acknowledged evil. The *Times* index lists an astounding twenty-five stories on this case. The public had made the connection between baby-farming and murder, and was ready for blood. This it got in the form of Waters's execution on 11 October.[71] As the *Pall Mall Gazette* observed,

> The pleas she set up for herself are not of a kind to raise any doubt as to her guilt ... They attempt to show that the children died from a mere accidental concurrence of influences hostile to infant life ... But a woman who shuts her eyes to the fact that children in whose death she has a direct interest die rapidly and habitually under a combination of narcotics and insufficient food comes too near a murderess to claim the benefit of nice distinctions. If Mrs. Waters had been acquitted or reprieved there would have been a disastrous failure of justice.[72]

A leader in the *Daily News* after the execution noted that if capital punishment could be justified at all, it was in cases like this. The only grounds for appeal were that Waters was a woman and that she did not realize the full nature of her crime. 'But the law knows no distinction of sex in such matters ...' The paper suggested, as did the ballad, that women who gave her their babies were also guilty and should be exposed: 'There is a sort of feeling in such people that where it is "only a baby" the crime of murder is less ... These unnatural nurses and more unnatural mothers ... gradually fall into cruelty and murderous neglect.'[73]

The *Times*, too, thought it 'a most just sentence,' and offered the not uncommon view that 'a murder in hot blood, the deliberate gratification of revenge, or even a premeditated act of violence in the pursuit of some selfish object' – in other words, the kinds of murder that men committed – would be more acceptable. 'The deepest instincts of a woman's heart must have been deadened,' said the *Times*, 'and the most ordinary feelings of human nature extinguished before such slow murder could be perpetrated upon piteous little innocents.'[74] Beyond the normal revulsion ordinarily felt at murder, men were uncomfortable with the idea that women could subvert their traditional roles as nurturers and caregivers. Arnot argues that Waters functioned as a sort of scapegoat for all infant death. In the public mind she stood for all the women who made a trade out of motherhood and were blamed for infanticide.[75]

Even if she did commit murder, Waters was not a particularly despicable criminal. Though poor, she had respectable roots and, as the *Times* acknowledged, was 'a woman far above the average of her class in intelligence.'[76] Misguided but not evil, she was nothing like the sly, crass, brutally efficient baby-farmers depicted by the *Pall Mall Gazette* and the *British Medical Journal.* It was just that not only had she not considered neglect murder, she had not considered babies people.

Editorial opinion on her fate was not all in favour. The *Illustrated Police News* went so far as to suggest that had England not been distracted by the Franco-Prussian War she might not have been hanged.[77]

Even the *Pall Mall Gazette,* which had aroused public indignation against baby-farmers in the first place, recognized that Waters's hanging would not stamp out baby-farming. 'It would be a great mistake to suppose that the execution of a single baby-farmer has frightened the other members of the profession into seeking a livelihood in less murderous ways,' it said in urging readers not to be complacent. 'On the contrary, it would be no surprise to us to learn that the trade had decidedly profited by the publicity given to it by these proceedings.'[78]

ANNIE TOOK

The trade in baby-farming did not decline. Baby-farming scandals continued despite the Infant Life Protection Act, largely because small operations either ignored it or operated quite legally outside it. In 1879 three baby-farmers were tried for murder: John and Catherine Barnes, seasoned professionals under whose care twenty or thirty children died in Cheshire; and Annie Took, of Exeter, poor, ignorant, and clumsy, with four children of her own to look after.

Mothers in the Barnes case were reluctant to give evidence, and in the end the couple was found guilty of manslaughter and sent to prison for life. Took, who had dumped a dismembered body on a rubbish pile, had committed a particularly grisly murder on a malformed illegitimate baby boy. In October 1878 the mother gave her twelve pounds for a year's keep; the mother's sister said they never wanted to see or hear more of him. The following May, Took smothered the child and chopped off his head, arms, and legs on the edge of a coal bin. When the torso was found, the malformation led police to Took.

BABY-SWEATING

Baby-farming scandals continued through the 1880s and 1890s. In 1885 the *Observer*, complaining that not enough baby-farmers had been hanged, charged that infanticide stood 'at the head of a black list of our criminal statistics, far outstripping all competitors for infamy ... '[79] In 1895 the *British Medical Journal*, reacting to a scandal exposed by the *Daily Telegraph*, raised the point that, although by this time baby-farms had to be registered, there was a loophole: nurses of one baby at a time did not have to register, so that babies could be dispersed to them for disposal by midwives who ran lying-in houses. Thus, said the *British Medical Journal*, 'instead of a few baby-farms we find a number of unregistered nurses of single babies, together with a central emporium for the distribution of these unfortunate infants, unregistered and untouched by law because infants are never kept there.'[80]

Public indignation had now been aroused at the potential in England for baby killers to operate with impunity. Late in 1895 the *Sun* ran a series of articles that made Amy Gregory look like a madonna. By answering advertisements for lying-in houses, an intrepid *Sun* reporter, Herbert Cadet, exposed operations that disposed of babies by arranging ahead of time to kill them at birth, baby-farming, or 'baby-sweating' – charging the mother for an 'adoption.' The series, entitled 'Massacre of the Innocents,' made it plain that infants had no rights. 'The killing of children by slow torture is still a profitable and fairly safe means of livelihood.'[81] Inspection of baby-farms, it said, was only perfunctory, and not all potential baby killers had to register: it was perfectly legal to take one infant under a year old and as many as you liked over that age. Some took babies to kill one at a time by means of improper feeding, exposure, or neglect. Some charged a weekly fee and killed the child when payment stopped.

The *Sun* claimed that lying-in houses attracted wealthy and middle-class women who wanted to hide their pregnancies. When a child was born, an attendant could drop it into a pail of water, smother it with a damp cloth, or bash the head on the floor so as to break the skull. Baby-sweaters, it said, took most of the money for an 'adoption' and would hand a child over to 'some drunken and unscrupulous wretch ... in the certain knowledge that in a short time the child will be dead.'[82]

The *Sun* named names and was promptly sued (unsuccessfully) for libel. The state took no legal action as a result of these exposés, but it was all too plain that baby killing had become a viable business pursuit. In 1896 the English got some indication of just how viable when an experienced and ruthless multiple baby murderer surfaced in Reading, Berkshire. For three months the newspapers reverberated with shocking revelations of her career; and by the time she was hanged no one who could read could claim ignorance of the tactics of motherly souls who took babies away for money.

AMELIA DYER

Amelia Dyer did not need a coordinator: she advertised for babies on her own and did not have to split fees. As she did not have more than one live baby at a time, there was no need for her to register. She did not wait for the babies she 'adopted' to die of neglect. She would go to a railway station to meet the mother and pick up the child (and her fee), assure the mother that it would be well taken care of, take it home and strangle it with a tape, and then throw the body, weighted with a brick, into the Thames.

No one knew how many babies she had killed, but, for the three-month period before she was arrested early in April, police found evidence of her having had at least seventeen children committed to her care, none of whom could be found alive.

'After I got a baby something seemed to say in my ears, "Get rid of it,"' she confessed after her conviction.[83] She had apparently been doing this for so long, and to so many, that she grew careless: a body was found on 30 March wrapped in a piece of brown paper with her name and address on it. When she was arrested on 4 April she had recently deposited two bodies in a carpet-bag, which were taken from the Thames along with four other bodies. Newspapers dubbed it the 'travelling coffin.' Using correspondence found in her house, police tracked down the mothers of the babies found in the carpet-bag.

Dyer was charged with these two murders and tried for only one of them, but police speculated that she could have disposed of as many as fifty babies. Even she could not be sure of the total. On the basis of a confession she gave after her conviction, her daughter, Mary Ann (Polly) Palmer, was questioned and then charged with helping her mother murder a third child. 'I am afraid Mother I don't like to say it but I am afraid you have had so many that you have got mixed up in their names and don't know wich from wich,' Polly wrote to her in prison. Anxious not to be charged with 'purgery' as well, she asked for clarification. 'I get so confused and muddled up,' her mother replied, 'I don't know but sometimes I fancy if that child was the first one I did destroy if it was you had no hand in that I did it myself.'[84] Though it is plain from this statement that Polly was involved in some of the murders, there was no evidence to convict her, and she was eventually acquitted.

Dyer was what was known in the trade as a wholesaler. She ran newspaper ads offering to buy babies, whom she would then place in adoptive homes or, on occasion, adopt them herself. It is unlikely, considering the publicity that had been given to baby-farming in the previous twenty years, that her prospective customers did not understand that this was a code. At any rate, according to Polly, many of the mothers asked her not to communicate further with them.[85] There is no possibility that Dyer herself did not grasp the enormity of her activities, since at fifty-seven she had been in the business for many years and would have known the risks. There were suggestions in newspaper articles that she had been imprisoned for six months in 1880 for running a baby-farm in Bristol, and that before that she was an intermediary for Margaret Waters.

On 31 March Dyer travelled to the Cheltenham railway station to pick up ten-month-old Doris Marmon from her mother, Evelina Marmon, a Bristol barmaid, who had answered an ad in the Bristol *Times and Mirror*. She took her to Polly's house in London and strangled her with tape from Polly's sewing basket. The next day she acquired another child, Harry Simmons, in London, strangled him, and put both bodies in the carpet-bag along with a brick from Polly's garden. When she got to Reading, she threw the bag into the Thames and then wrote a note to Doris's mother to assure her that her baby was happy and well. She later told a newspaper reporter: 'When I packed the bag I kept pushing them down to make room for the brick, and, do you know, they kept warm for such a long time when I took them down to Reading ... I can hear the splash in the water now.'[86]

Since she had already confessed to having committed more than one murder, the defence pleaded insanity, but the judge would have none of it. It took the jury five minutes to agree that she was guilty. By that time, the public, inflamed by sensational press coverage, had already made up its mind. On the day the verdict was given, said the *Illustrated Police Budget* in a story headed 'The Doom of the Baby Slaughterer,' 'People flocked in, women standing on the seats, to see one of their own sex in the hour of her grievous trial. There was little to reward their enterprise, for if ever a woman looked a blameless, benevolent mother it was Mrs. Dyer.'

The *Police Budget*, lavishly illustrated and printed on pink paper, could hardly contain its excitement at the verdict: 'At last the curtain has fallen upon the terrible horrors at Reading, which for so long a time have kept the pulses of the British public at fever heat. Mrs. Dyer is to be hanged! The inhuman fiend who sacrificed the lives of so many children to suit her own base and sordid purposes has to enter now the gates of death herself ...'[87]

The public was incensed. 'A more diabolical, fiendish slaughter of poor innocent babes has perhaps never been recorded in the history of the nation,' said the Berkshire *Chronicle*, 'and if Mrs. Dyer were left to the tender mercies of the mothers of England, we feel sure they would be of the opinion that hanging was too good for her.'[88] This paper not only published photos of Mrs Dyer, her helpers (her daughter and son-in-law and an old woman and two children who had lived with her), and her house in Reading, but also conducted interviews with people who had visited her in prison. (The old woman, Granny Smith, thought she looked 'very peculiar – like a maniac.')[89]

By 1896, many English newspapers, influenced by the Americans and empowered with advances in typography and lithography, were running large, stacked headlines in lively, lavishly illustrated layouts. Factual stories were accompanied by speculation, rumours, trivia, and interviews. Scandal stretched the new journalism to the limits of its sensational inclinations. The story of Dyer, a hardened, ageing, patently evil woman surrounded by many bit players, had colour, variety, pathos, and staying power. For three months it dominated the news. There was no shortage of material, since she and her friends cooperated with the press in an apparent effort to persuade the public that she was insane.

The enterprising *Weekly Dispatch* interviewed the lock-keeper and ran sketches of Dyer, Granny, the house, the dragging operations, and the travelling coffin. Her confession was announced as 'Startling Admissions' and was accompanied by a story headed 'Is She Mad?' It interviewed her daughter and published 'Mrs. Palmer's Story,' which it billed as 'extraordinary and romantic.' (Mrs Palmer, who confided that she had received threatening letters illustrated with coffins and scaffolds and hangman's ropes, remembered that 'babies used to come and disappear in a very strange way.')[90] Its biggest coup was an interview in prison with Dyer herself.

The gossipy *Evening News* called the story the 'Reading Horror.' Among the bits that its crime reporter picked up at the prison was the information that, before her conviction, Dyer had sent a letter home asking for her sewing basket and some stockings that needed mending. On a list of books that she wanted were *Barnaby Rudge* and *East Lynn*.[91] She was reported to have shed tears every time she read the chapter describing the death of Willie Carlyle.[92] The *News* criticized her for having written more or less the same letter to prospective customers, expressing affection for children. 'This awful hypocrisy is the worst feature of this shocking case,' it commented righteously.[93] When she was hanged, it called her 'a murderess among murderesses ..., a perfect monster of crime.' She saw herself as making a little money by helping others to do what had to be done; the papers cast her as greedy and bloodthirsty. The *News* said bluntly: 'When a fellow-creature stands condemned to death, more especially when that fellow-creature is a woman, it is impossible not to feel some tinge of compunction, some feeling of remorse. But even the most gentle-hearted can have felt small sorrow for the fate of Mrs. Dyer. A woman with no love for little children is a blot on nature.'[94]

The sensational *Star* told the story of her conviction in graduated headlines:

Doomed!
Mrs. Dyer Sentenced to Death
The Judge's Last Stern and Awful Charge
Limp and Nerveless, She Can Make No Response.

Reporting on the execution, this paper interviewed the crowd outside Newgate. Someone said that she was mad; someone else replied: 'Mad your granny! Did she ever choke anyone till she got ten quid for doing it?' The reporter added, 'However crudely expressed, this remark does seem to fairly represent the philosophy of the situation.'[95]

The same sentiments were expressed in a ballad marking her execution, the chorus of which ran:

The old baby farmer 'as been executed.
It's quite time she was put out of the way,
She was a bad woman, it isn't disputed,
Not a word in her favour can anyone say.

The rest of the song, which is still sung today, tells the story:

The old baby farmer, the wretched Mrs. Dyer,
At the Old Bailey her wages is paid.
In times long ago we'd have made a big fire
And roasted so nicely that wicked old jade.

It seems rather hard to run down a woman,
But this one was hardly a woman at all;
To make a fine living in a way so inhuman,
Carousing in luxury on poor girls' downfall.

Poor girls who fall from the straight path of virtue,
What could they do with a child in their arms?
The fault they committed they could not undo,
So the baby was sent to the cruel baby farm.

To all these sad crimes there must be an ending;
Secrets like these for ever can't last.
Say as you like, there is no defending
The horrible tales we have heard in the past.

What did she think as she stood on the gallows,
Poor little victims in front of her eyes?
Her heart, if she had one, must have been callous;
The rope round her neck – how quickly time flies.

Down through the trap-door quickly disappearing,
The old baby farmer to eternity home,
The sound of her own death bell she was hearing.
Maybe she was sent to the cruel baby farm.[96]

The *Times* found in Dyer 'a depth of wickedness scarcely conceivable before.' It reminded readers that there were other baby-farmers, that 'year by year other children are done to death by methods less speedy and by so much the more brutal than those which Mrs. Dyer employed.'[97]

This proved to be so. The Dyer case inspired the *British Medical Journal* to launch a second investigation into baby-farming; the abuses uncovered ran in a six-part series from August 1896. The following year the Infant Life Protection Act was amended, but it still did not cover those who took in one child at a time. In December 1899, Ada Chard Williams was arrested for the murder of a twenty-one-month-old illegitimate baby, Selina Ellen Jones, handed over to her for a five-pound fee. Like Dyer, she had wrapped the body in brown paper and thrown it into the Thames – but she had first battered its head against a wall. The bodies of two other children tied up in the same way as Selina were also found in the river.

Chard Williams was executed in March 1900. She, Winsor, and Dyer were displayed in the Chamber of Horrors, Winsor until 1891, Chard Williams until 1909, and Dyer until 1979.

Certainly by the time Dyer was caught, public opinion was firmly against the murder of babies. Yet it was not illegal to pay a lump sum to be rid of a child. Civilization had progressed to the point where mothers scrupled to kill their own babies, but not quite to the point where unmarried motherhood was acceptable. Despite the scandals and the consequent protective legislation, there were still 'nurses' to accommodate those who had the money to get rid of their children. The cost of society's rigid expectations was the evidence of shame – the dead illegitimate child.

CONCLUSION

Infanticide was generally condoned as a fairly private crime of little threat to the general public, but aggressive reporting about baby-farming in the 1860s fanned it into a national scandal. It became a feminist issue once the government decided to clamp down on baby-farmers. In the same way that 'pro-choice' lobbyists in our own time insist that men, through legislation, should not be able to restrict women's control of their own bodies, and just as they later resisted Contagious Disease Legislation because it discriminated against their sex, women lobbied for less regulation than the government wanted to impose with the 1872 Infant Life Protection Act. Murder by baby-farmers continued because social conditions allowed for their function. Charlotte Winsor and Amelia Dyer were the most reviled of these. The poverty and desperation of Rebecca Smith, a serial poisoner of her own babies, and Amy Gregory, sentenced to hang but reprieved, made them sympathetic figures.

SEVEN

Murder of and by Servants

**Eliza Fenning / Ann Heytrey / Martha Brixey / Sarah Thomas /
Marguerite Diblanc / Kate Webster / Hannah Dobbs /
Esther Hibner / Sarah Bird / Theresa Sloane**

The line between privilege and dependence was nowhere more
sharply drawn than in a home where servants were kept. If their
power sometimes prompted employers to unreasonable demands,
accusations, and verbal and physical abuse, it also on occasion
provoked the abused to fight back against weak or elderly oppressors. For female employers especially, the risk of theft, abuse, or
even murder was considerable. The risks for female servants were
a function of their physical vulnerability along with the class and
gender bias so evident in nineteenth-century England.

In 1816 a London policeman complained of the easy mode servant
girls have of turning any thing they can bring away into money.
There is scarcely what is called a chandler's shop in any part of the
Metropolis ... but buys old bottles or linen, or any thing that a
servant girl, when she goes there to purchase things, can take with
her. The green-stalls will purchase things of them, and they find a
facility of raising money upon any thing they take to these kinds of
shops; and any girls lose their reputation by the encouragement
women keeping these shops give them. This is not a suspicion, it is a
thing proved and known ... This species of domestic robbery ... is
increasing still greatly ... Servants ... have become vile in the extreme; servant girls in particular; they are infamous.[1]

People were ready to believe the worst of servants. At mid-century Henry Mayhew estimated that they comprised one-third of London's prostitutes. It is true that they were kept poor, and that they had access to anything in the house that wasn't under lock and key, but it would be going too far to assert that therefore all maidservants were immoral. Nevertheless, those employers who oppressed their servants managed to justify their attitude as defensive. And servants accused of murder or attempted murder were assumed to have been acting under an impulse for revenge.

ELIZA FENNING

With such strong bias working against her, an accused murderess could be convicted by paranoid hysteria rather than solid evidence. The most pathetic example of this phenomenon is the case of Eliza Fenning, a twenty-one-year-old servant working for the Turner family in Chancery Lane, London, in 1815, accused by her master's son of attempted murder of his family. The Turners maintained that she had mixed arsenic into the dumplings that she served for dinner.

It is extremely unlikely that Fenning did this, since she herself ate the dumplings and apologized for their peculiar consistency. It is much more likely that someone who wanted to implicate her slipped arsenic or some other noxious substance into the mixture. The presence of arsenic in the food was never actually proved. However, something was put into the dumplings that inhibited their rising, and servant and family became ill. A scapegoat had to be found to quell the fear and indignation of the establishment. Who better than a maidservant? Fenning was promptly tried and convicted by the press.

The *Observer*, mounting a cruel and relentless campaign against her, announced in a headline: 'Poisoning a whole family!'[2] 'A circumstance of the most atrocious nature ... has recently occurred,' said the *Morning Chronicle*. 'A servant in a respectable family at the west end of the town, mixed a large quantity of arsenic in a pie ...' The story added that the unidentified servant, who had eaten some pie in order to avoid detection, was being watched by the police until she recovered sufficiently to be moved to prison.[3]

To her horror, Fenning was charged with attempted murder, swiftly convicted, and sentenced to death. The trial took place on 11 April. Her employer, Orlibar Turner, a stationer to lawyers, used a friend, a magistrate's clerk, as his solicitor in prosecuting her and had a large circle of legal acquaintances to turn to for advice and support. Though her parents were respectable and solvent – her father worked for a potato merchant, and her mother for an upholsterer – they were poor. They sold their furniture and moved into cheaper lodgings to raise money to help her, but she could afford only the skimpiest legal representation – no match for Turner's business associates. Her lawyers, who met her only briefly just before the trial, evidently did not grasp that someone else might have put arsenic into the dumplings, or that what made the family sick was not arsenic.

The most damning evidence against her was, as she herself admitted at the time, that the dumplings did not rise properly; also that a white powder was found in the mixing bowl the next day, and that knives used to cut the dumplings had turned black. A doctor who attended the family said it was his opinion that the powder was arsenic, and that arsenic would turn knives black. (In fact it will not.) There was no proof, however, that Fenning had access to arsenic, had put it into the bowl, or even had a motive for doing so. The only motive that could be pinned on her derived from a reprimand that she had had about a fortnight earlier from the younger Mrs Turner, who had reproved her for allegedly flirting with another servant. (It is more likely that she was fending him off.)

Not surprisingly, Fenning insisted throughout that she was innocent. However, there was no provision in English law until 1836 for the defence counsel in a murder case to cross-examine witnesses and challenge their testimony or to sum up the case for the jury. So although the prosecution's evidence didn't add up, the jury didn't notice. The recorder (judge), Sir John Silvester, impatient to get this case over with, made up his mind in a hurry.

Silvester was obviously unsympathetic to the defendant, and indeed may have regarded women in general, and lower-class women in particular, as objects – tools or impediments – rather than as people.[4] He refused to hear evidence at the end from Fenning and her father. He then reminded the jury that arsenic was found only in the dumplings, which she alone had mixed, and, failing to consider that she too had been made sick, he pointed out that common humanity should have prompted her to come to their aid. The jury consisted of two gentlemen and ten tradesmen, including a deaf bottle-dealer. It took them ten minutes to arrive at a verdict.

The judiciary could not be seen to heed the protests of a poor, ignorant servant in the face of her master's insistent accusations, no matter how unreasonable those accusations were. The newspaper press, conservative and tightly controlled, did its part to dehumanize her, dismissing the case as inconsequential. On being condemned to death, said the *Times*, as though she were barely human, 'the unhappy culprit instantly fell into a fit, screamed, and cried aloud most bitterly, and was carried from the dock in a state of insensibility.'[5] Only the *Examiner* gave her the benefit of the doubt. After a terse account of the trial, it ventured: 'We have seen nothing but a mere abstract of the evidence in this case, and from that, we confess we are not able to discover the necessary guilt of this woman. That she put the poison in the pan herself, knowing it to be poison, does not appear, as far as we have seen, though the jury evidently thought she did.'[6]

There was enough support for Fenning among influential citizens that the government delayed the hanging for two months as it attempted to justify the verdict. A reprieve would have had to be recommended by the judge to the king. The judge, of course, had a vested interest in upholding his original decision, and Orlibar Turner, the prosecutor, would not go back on his accusation against her. When it was made plain to him after the trial that arsenic could not blacken a knife, he almost agreed to ask for mercy for her, but the judge advised him not to, as suspicion would then fall on a member of his family – presumably his son.

The verdict was based on unreliable evidence, poor legal advice, and improper direction from the judge, but these objections were brought into the open only after the execution. Despite several high-level meetings in response to pressure from the public, on 26 July Fenning was hanged with two other prisoners. One, a rapist with whom she had been corresponding in prison, comforted her and helped her to pray.

Eliza Fenning went to the gallows in an embroidered white gown. The family arranged for her body to be on public view until the funeral on 31 July, when six young women in white dresses led eight mourners and about 1,000 supporters down Red Lion St and Lamb's Conduit St, through Brunswick Square, and into St George the Martyr burying-ground. The route was lined with grieving spectators. A man who spoke against her at the grave was set upon by other mourners.

Later the same day, a crowd attempted to set fire to the Turner house. The *Times*'s perspective on this event suggests a mounting fear of the mob on the part of the establishment.

> We regret to state, that yesterday evening the family of Mr. Turner, the prosecutor of Eliza Fenning, was again annoyed about eight o'clock by a crowd of persons of the lowest order, who had collected in Chancery-lane, round his door; it was found necessary to call in the aid of the police to disperse them. Several constables attended, and the crowd were forced back from the front of the house; they continued assembled in the vicinity till a late hour, but the vigilance of the police officers prevented any greater disturbance from taking place.[7]

After her death a debate was carried on in the press as to her guilt or innocence. The *Times*, the *Observer*, and the *Chronicle* assumed that the word of an employer was to be taken over that of a servant. 'The fate of this young woman,' said the *Times* after the execution, 'has excited in the public mind an interest which appears to us to be warranted neither by any circumstances proved at the trial, nor by any qualities which rumour has ascribed to her personal character.'[8] A spate of books and pamphlets appeared, including *The Case of Eliza Fenning, Innocence of the Crime of Poisoning, Five Cases of Recovery* (by the doctor who insisted that there had been arsenic in the mixing bowl), *Circumstantial Evidence, The Important Results of an Elaborate Investigation in the Mysterious Case of Elizabeth Fenning, Eliza Fenning's Narrative, Fullest Report, A Further Account, An Authentic Narrative of the Conduct* ... Many persuasively made the case for her innocence, while others argued that she deserved to be hanged. Newspapers summed up what had gone on, some even printing a transcript of the trial, which had taken place nearly four months previous.

It was rumoured that the younger Turner, Robert, was mentally unbalanced and had perhaps poisoned the dumplings himself; that Fenning's father had urged her to declare her innocence to the end (he insisted that he had not); that previous employers found her difficult (several signed testimonials to her good character); that she had been expelled from school at the age of twelve; that she had been writing love-letters in prison to a convicted rapist. The letters, entirely innocent, surfaced in the *Examiner*: the first was an effort to determine whether either of them had any chance of a reprieve; in response, he sent a religious message, to which she replied, touchingly: 'It's like a dream; for I know my innocence; I cannot prove it.'[9] To a righteous assertion by the *Chronicle* that newspapers ought to stop fanning doubt in the public mind, the *Examiner* indignantly replied that there was no direct evidence to obscure the doubts.[10] For more than three months after her death, this paper ran articles and letters defending her.

Eventually Fenning was seen as a martyr. The establishment's pangs of conscience reverberated throughout the last two-thirds of the century. In 1839, Matthew Davenport Hill, the recorder of Birmingham, in appealing for improvements in criminal-law proceedings, used her trial to illustrate the cruelty of the law before it was changed to allow counsel to plead for prisoners on trial for capital charges. In 1857, in a discussion of the right of defence counsel to address the jury, he pointed out that, if there had been enough arsenic to prevent the dumplings from rising, there would have been so much that anyone eating them would have died. He also noticed something that no one had mentioned before: there was hardly a motive.[11]

For many years the fate of Eliza Fenning was described in chronicles of crime as a stain on the English tradition of justice. Legend has it that Robert Turner confessed on his deathbed that he framed her to punish her for having resisted his advances.[12] This theory rings true, for there would then have been a motive, and contemporary descriptions of the man attest to his unstable mental state. This may have been the reason that the senior Turner would not respond to public pressure and withdraw the charges.

In 1850, in the controversy over whether Ann Merritt had poisoned her husband, the Fenning case was brought up.[13] The story was revived for *The Newgate Calendar* of 1863–4. It was retold in Dickens's *All the Year Round* in 1867–8, and he remarked to the author that he was never more convinced of anything than of the young woman's innocence.[14] *The Modern Newgate Calendar* (1868) observes that the jury 'had no sympathy with servant-girls attempting to poison those whom they ought to faithfully serve.' As to whether she was innocent, 'the people of London wept for her, and the great heart of London is seldom wrong in such a case.'[15] A penny dreadful issued in 1879 relates her 'sad undeserved end.'[16] *The New Newgate Calendar* (1889) suggests that she was innocent and that probably the sickness was not attributable to arsenic, since one person who ate much less than the others was just as sick as they were.[17]

In 1889, at the time of the controversy over Florence Maybrick's conviction for murder, an editorial in the *St. James's Gazette* reminded its readers that trial by 'the greater jury' of public opinion had taken place in the Fenning case as well.[18] Hill's son Berkeley, who years earlier, at the request of his father, had performed experiments to see whether arsenic would turn knife blades black, responded that the two trials were not comparable.

> One can easily reckon the weight of odds against the just verdict when on one side is an able prosecuting counsel and an indifferent medical witness, and on the other an ignorant servant-girl with no one to cross-examine the witnesses and disprove the accuracy of

their testimony. No comparison exists between the cruel mode of trying prisoners in those days and the merciful indulgent course taken in our time, which permits a prisoner to be defended by the ablest counsel of the English Bar, who may and should use his utmost skill to upset the case against his client.[19]

MURDER BY SERVANTS

There were some maidservants who did murder their employers, and their trials attracted a great deal of attention. Employers who mistreated their servants were justifiably afraid that they might one day be tempted to strike back. As a group the servant population did have high rates of drunkenness, immorality, and thieving. In defence of servants, it must be said, however, that they put in long hours for low wages, poor accommodation, and often inadequate food.[20]

If the employer was an elderly widow, physically vulnerable and alone in the world, there was an opportunity for the servant to get her own back by murdering, and then plundering. There were three such sensational cases in England through the nineteenth century – Sarah Thomas in 1849, Marguerite Diblanc in 1872, and Kate Webster in 1879 – and doubtless many more undetected ones.

The murder of her mistress, Sarah Dormer, by Ann Heytrey, or Aytry, near Warwickshire does not fall into this category. Though she appears to have been insane, the twenty-two-year-old servant was found guilty of petty treason[21] and murder, and hanged in April 1820. She had stabbed her mistress on a sudden impulse. The *Times* said she had been previously charged with stealing some money from the family.

This paper, whose readers would have been in a position to keep servants, reported aggressively that the crime had 'created a sensation.' Heytrey 'was a middle-size woman, and stoutly made,' with 'high cheekbones and on the whole a physiognomy well calculated to conceal a criminal heart. She preserved an undaunted firmness, and was dressed in a black gown; a gray shawl was thrown loosely over her shoulders, and she had on a fine muslin mob cap.[22]

According to the *Star*, the testimony of the victims' three teenage daughters 'could not but excite a feeling of sympathy in the bosoms of all who possess the better sensibilities of our nature. After they had answered all the questions thought necessary, they were permitted to leave a scene which at least must have been deemed a severe trial to their feelings.'[23]

An execution broadside designed to appeal to the lower class described her more sympathetically as 'unhappy girl' of sixteen who 'appeared truly penitent.' In a speech from the scaffold she was purported to have said:

> I dyed my hands in the blood of the best of mistresses; she was always kind to me, and I loved her as my own mother. I know not what possessed me to commit this heinous crime, but it must have been the d___ that prompted me to it; for as I was cutting cucumbers in the pantry for the family's supper, something whispered in my ear, 'You must murder your mistress.' I could not resist; without thought, and not knowing what I did at the moment, I ran and first knocked my mistress down while she was reading the Bible, and then cut her throat from ear to ear. I concealed the dreadful act as long as I was able; but it was to no avail as my conscience tormented me night and day, until I was obliged to confess my crime. Justice, you see, has overtaken me, and now I await my sentence.[24]

No matter what the excuse, no mercy could be shown to a servant who betrayed her position of trust. Such an aberration had to be very harshly and publicly punished so as to deter other servants from such action.

MARTHA BRIXEY

By 1845 the McNaughten Rules provided an obvious out for any killer deemed insane.[25] Thus it was that Martha Brixey, eighteen years old, was sent to Bedlam.[26] On 4 May she had nearly severed the head from the body of Robert Barry Ffinch, the ten-month-old baby to whom she was nursemaid, after the mother discharged her for repeated peculiar behaviour. She said she had turned the baby into an angel.

Like Ann Heytrey, Brixey immediately confessed and begged forgiveness. The murder, which took place at the family home in Greenwich, was widely publicized as the 'Greenwich Tragedy' and inspired a ballad of that name. References to her as the 'Greenwich Murderess' have led Smith to speculate that, though evidence of her insanity was decisive, her relationship to the child frightened the newspaper-reading public.[27]

Brixey's mental instability was supposed to have derived from menstrual irregularities. 'I have frequently had occasion to attend young women who have been subject to temporary suspensions of the action of nature,' the family's doctor told the court. 'I have known instances where the functions of the mind of a woman so situated have been seriously affected.'

But were the 'irregularities' a symptom of pregnancy? Not only had she been talking about leaving her job, but she seems to have been obsessed with the fit of her everyday dress. One day she ripped it off and burned it because it did not fit her though it had been altered several times. Her mistress had warned her not to have the replacement altered, but she was caught coming back from yet another visit to the dressmaker and was dismissed.[28]

Brixey was pardoned and released after thirteen years in the lunatic asylum. There is no record of whether she had a baby.

SARAH THOMAS

Sarah Thomas, an eighteen-year-old general servant in the home of Elizabeth Jefferies of Bristol, also appears to have been, if not mentally unbalanced, flighty, with relatives whose judgment also seems odd. Her mother was said to have announced in a bakeshop that the plum cakes she was buying were for her daughter, who was shortly to be hanged. On her final visit to the jail, the woman asked her doomed child whether she could have her clothes. The prisoner's two sisters had widely announced their intention of watching the execution, leading the Bristol *Mirror* to suspect that an upbringing in such a family 'may have produced that demoralization which has at length led to such deplorable and melancholy results.'[29]

For some in the underclass, which operated in a world reduced to the simplicity of struggle for survival, it perhaps made sense to kill for gain if one could get away with it. The world of their victims, however, was much more complex, with a justice system that worked to maintain the balance of power in society.

In April 1849, in one of the most sensational stories of the century, Thomas was tried and hanged for murder as the offended establishment and the more liberal general public argued about the merits of punishing someone so drastically on the strength of mere circumstantial evidence. On 7 March, Jefferies had been hit on the head with a stone and left to die; after a few days she was missed, and her servant was found, along with some of her mistress's silver, jewellery, and money, hidden in her mother's house.

'For a considerable time past,' said the *Weekly Chronicle*,

> the city of Bristol has not presented such a scene of anxiety as has been excited by the discovery at a late hour last night that an elderly maiden lady, possessed of very considerable independent property, ... had been murdered, as is supposed by her own servant girl, named Sarah Thomas, a young woman of remarkably prepossessing personal appearance, and under circumstances of the most revolting barbarity.[30]

The Bristol *Mirror* regarded the 'catastrophe' as 'a warning to all lone females similarly situated not to place unguarded wealth in the way of those who are not likely to be proof against the temptation.'

Two weeks after the murder, the Bristol *Times* responded to an 'absurd curiosity' about what the 'wretched young woman' looked like and what she was like. She was good-looking and 'neatly, almost genteelly, dressed.'

At her trial, held in Gloucester on 3 April, the Bristol *Mirror* said 'the court was crowded to suffocation. The curiosity of the public to hear the sickening details of this case seemed wound up to the highest pitch.' Thomas, though literate, did not seem to understand the gravity of her position.[31] The Crown conceded that the victim was an ill-tempered and demanding woman who had had many servants. Thomas, however, went farther than her predecessors, who had merely found other positions. The *Observer* noted that, 'while the jury was out, a horse stealing case was tried, which caused much laughter, and the prisoner ... laughed as heartily as anyone in court.'[32] The jury found her guilty, but recommended mercy. None the less, the judge sentenced her to death, observing that she did not deserve mercy, having shown none to her victim. The day after the trial she confessed.

Various groups, including one of 3,000 Bristol women, petitioned the home secretary for a reprieve, but he could find no grounds for one. Despite the controversy, she was hanged on 20 April, having been dragged kicking and screaming to the scaffold. Calcraft, who had been a hangman for twenty years, is supposed to have observed that he had never been so reluctant to do his job.

A huge crowd gathered to see the first woman hanged in Bristol since 1836. 'When the shrieking girl made her appearance upon the platform,' said the Bristol *Gazette,* 'half drunken men and women, with eyes bleared and voices thickened with their morning's debauch, stood watching the last struggles of a young girl dragged to her death for their benefit and warning.'[33]

The sorry spectacle was used by many to argue against capital punishment. One letter to the editor began with this vivid description:

> This day a girl in her teens, small in stature, and, it may be added, very comely in face, has been violently dragged by the officers of the law from the condemned cell to the front of the Bristol Gaol, and there by means of a rope and beam (the efficacy of which was consummated by two or three rough jerks and pulling of the victim's legs) has been publicly strangled within sight of her own grave, which was ready dug, and where this night her mortal remains will be ignominiously entombed. Thousands saw her dragged to the drop and watched her struggles there; and from amongst them many, with execrative shouts, hooted the executioner, who in the

fulfilment of his horrid duty, found it needful to pull and jerk her downwards while her body was suspended from the gallows beam. A clergyman was nigh, who had unceasingly striven to smooth that rough passage into eternity by converting the girl's evil-disposed mind, and whispering to her hopes of heavenly mercy and eternal bliss; but she could not forget that hempen collar; she could not shut her eyes to the dread reality of approaching strangulation; and when the functionary of the law and his assistants came, she shrieked, shrank back, struggled, fought, and would not submit. They soon overpowered her fragile strength, and, screaming for life, her spirit was most unwillingly hurled into eternity. Shrieks, from those who saw it, were her dying hymn.[34]

MARGUERITE DIBLANC

It was not until 1868 that public hangings were outlawed. Even then the public interest in hangings, particularly in hangings of women, was strong. But by the time Marguerite Diblanc was accused of murdering her mistress, Madame Marie Riel of Park Lane, London, in April 1872, the public was less sadistic and the justice system less rigid. Diblanc, a young Belgian cook, was at a particular disadvantage in court because its rules and proceedings were quite unfamiliar to her. Her vulnerability and foreignness, though seized on by some, made her an object of compassion to others. It was a foregone conclusion that she would be convicted; the question was whether she would be hanged.

Like Sarah Thomas, Diblanc aroused sympathy in some quarters – though presumably not quarters where servants were kept – because she had a sharp-tongued and unreasonable mistress. 'We are ... asked to take it for granted that a cook would not strangle her mistress if the mistress kept her own place and showed proper consideration for the feelings of her servant,' complained the *Saturday Review*.[35]

Diblanc and Riel became embroiled in a quarrel, the mistress insulted the servant, and the servant, younger and stronger, struck, and then strangled her. She then stole some money and fled to Paris. Once the body was found and she was missed, she was hunted down by the police, who were in turn responding to strong pressure from a public that identified with the victim. 'The ends of justice, the reputation of our police, and the security of London are all deeply concerned in the apprehension and punishment of the guilty person,' said a letter to the *Times*. The fear was, as the *Echo* put it, that 'at any moment a similar fate may befall any person similarly situated ... It is, we fear, too clear that not only property but lives are at the mercy of domestic servants.'[36]

Several papers described the missing woman as ugly, massive, and exceedingly strong, though she was actually short and dumpy. The *Penny Illustrated Paper* had a former employer confirm 'her great personal strength.' The *Pall Mall Gazette* speculated, from 'what we have heard of her harshness, her strength, [and] her robust and masculine look both in face and figure,' that she was actually a man.[37] The *Echo* said she was 'a stout, powerful woman, in the prime of life.'[38] The *Illustrated Police News* devoted most of its front page to sketches of various aspects of the crime, with a crazed and ferocious Diblanc pulling a rope around her victim, and congratulated the police on having caught 'this human tigress.'[39] The *Times* reported that the prisoner who shared her cell had 'become wild with terror' on learning who she was, 'and it is with the greatest difficulty that she can be kept in the same cell.'[40]

The hysteria abated once Diblanc was captured. The *Daily Telegraph* noted that 'when the wretched woman had been caught just as easily as a fox driven into a hole – when she had confessed her guilt, and the key to the mystery was known – popular interest in the case died away.'[41] None the less, public interest was such that a broadside was issued to mark her arrest, though by 1872 broadsides were rare and surfaced mainly at executions. The broadside ballad concluded:

> This deed has caused great excitement,
> And when in London she arrived
> To catch a sight of this vile monster,
> Both rich and poor alike did strive.
> And if the murderess is convicted,

When before the Judge she does appear,
She cannot expect for mercy,
For she had none for her mistress dear.[42]

In police court, far from looking large and fierce, she seemed frightened and dazed, said the *Telegraph*.[43] The *Times* reporter complained that she seemed sullen: 'Short in stature, stout, thick-necked, and of a coarse muscular type, she resembled the class of Irish costermonger women who are almost daily charged with assaults and drunkenness ...'[44] The *Daily News* prefaced its transcript of the conclusion of the trial with the pathetic picture of the prisoner about to receive the verdict.

> She must stand while the sentence of the jury is delivered. Then the white bonne's cap and lappet and the broad shoulders draped in black are seen, and in another second the awfully anxious face and the frightened eyes of the prisoner are turned to the jury and the judge ... The prisoner stands with downcast eyes while the Judge's remarks are translated to her sentence by sentence, and though her lips move as if she were trying to speak, no word comes forth. Again does the exceeding ghastliness of a trial for life or death, in a tongue unknown to the person principally affected, come forcibly home ... and then without further word or gesture she turns obediently ... and disappears from sight ... and then laughter and conversation are resumed, ladies and gentlemen and the motley crowd are to be seen and heard pressing eagerly out into the bright sunshine to resume the business or pleasure of their lives, the drama they have taken part in is over, and the murdered woman avenged.[45]

The *Daily Telegraph* also called attention to her vulnerability, observing, 'If she had received the summons to be led out to instant execution, she could hardly have looked more cowed and terror-stricken than she appeared when the Judge proceeded to pronounce sentence of death.'[46]

The jury had strongly recommended mercy because the murder was not premeditated, but rather an angry response to a slur on

Diblanc's morals. 'It's true I killed her,' she told the police who arrested her, 'but I did not intend to murder her. She told me that if I left her I should come to be a street-walker, and that put me in a passion, and I said, "You say that again and I'll throttle you." She said it again, and I laid hold of her by the throat and shook her, and then threw her down, and when I looked at her I found that she was dead.'[47] This was the sort of murder that the French excused as a crime of passion, but, as the *Times* remarked, the English had not followed their lead:

> We have hitherto deemed the French practice on this point lax and perilous, but we seem to be drifting towards it when such a case as the present is thought by an intelligent Jury to justify a strong recommendation to mercy. It is the object of the law to restrain furious and less than malignant passions, and it is a grave question whether the capital penalty is not as necessary to control the one as to control the other.[48]

Predicting that Diblanc would be reprieved, the *Echo* demanded in a front-page headline: 'Death, or fifteen months retirement?' There was, in fact, a reprieve, but Diblanc was kept in prison for more than the standard maximum of twenty years.[49] Arguing that 'the law-making and law-executing public' kept female servants, the *Echo* said the murder had 'struck terror into a thousand households, and consequently demands the most summary and exemplary repression.'[50]

When the sentence was commuted to life imprisonment, most people were relieved. But the *Saturday Review* remarked on the 'growing disinclination to inflict capital punishment, especially on women ... It seems to us difficult to imagine a more savage or atrocious murder; and nothing can be more dangerous than to countenance the argument that because a mistress uses hard words her servant has a right to spring upon her like a wild beast and choke her.'[51]

Despite the commutation of her sentence and her release on licence in 1893, Diblanc was installed in the Chamber of Horrors and remained there until 1901.

KATE WEBSTER AND HANNAH DOBBS

More savage and atrocious murders by servants were, of course, possible. After Kate Webster killed her mistress, Martha Thomas, at Richmond in March 1879, by pushing her down the stairs, and then strangling her, she cut off the head and boiled it, presumably so that it could not be identified, thriftily selling what liquefied as 'best dripping.' She then burned what she could of the body in the fireplace and threw what remained into the Thames.

Hannah Dobbs, a twenty-five-year-old servant in the Euston Square house in which a lodger, Matilda Hacker, was robbed and murdered in October 1877, was thought to have strangled her and lugged the body to the coal cellar, where it languished for nearly two years. As the trials were held at the same time, one in Richmond and the other at the Old Bailey, England seemed to some to be in the grip of a rebellion by servants. 'It was presumed,' as the *Spectator* said after the trials, 'that there was a mania among female domestics for murder and robbery, and that no feeble person living alone with a servant ought to be considered safe.'[52] She was enshrined in the Chamber of Horrors until 1891.

Yet Dobbs, despite a mass of circumstantial evidence, was acquitted. She had been alone in the house with Hacker on the day the murder was thought to have been committed, and she was found to have pawned pieces of Hacker's jewellery. There was some suspicion, though, that the landlord of the house had been involved in the murder, and there was no proof that Dobbs had not, as she claimed, simply been given these trinkets by him some time after the murder.

It was assumed from the outset that Webster, a tough Irishwoman of about thirty depicted in the press as having long been a drunkard and a thief, was guilty. She had, after all, posed as the dead woman as she attempted to sell her furniture, and she had been seen disposing of a heavy box. The trunk in which some of the body was found was known to have been Mrs Thomas's, though the body was never identified. By this time Webster had fled to Ireland, where she was arrested. She then tried to implicate two friends, one whose son carried the box for her and the other who was going to buy the furniture, but they were cleared. She was found guilty and hanged on 29 July.

'Seldom,' said the *Daily Telegraph*, 'has a deed more absolutely wicked in all its aspects been brought to punishment.' It would have been safer for her victim 'to have taken into her household a tigress than to have lived alone with that strong and cruel Irish charwoman ...'[53]

A few days before the execution, the *Illustrated Police News* published a full page of sketches of scenes and incidents connected with the murder; the entire front page of the next edition depicted the execution.[54] Webster's image remained on show at the Chamber of Horrors well into the twentieth century.[55]

MURDER OF SERVANTS

If there was an undercurrent of fear running through England's privileged class that servants might turn on their masters, this was in part attributable to an uneasy awareness that many domestic servants were mistreated. The lowest of the low were maids of all work, who had to put up with small, dark, sparsely furnished, and poorly ventilated rooms that were cold in winter and hot in summer, and spent life more or less in captivity.[56]

It would be natural for the constraints of such a life to simmer in some unhappy servants into a perpetual state of resentment. Occasionally, as a result of a particularly abusive remark by an employer, the resentment would flare up. Those servants who murdered their employers were motivated by strong passions. In contrast, employers who murdered their servants did so out of callous indifference.

A servant in a household with several other servants was to some extent protected by the mere presence of potential witnesses, but the mistress of a house with only one servant could exploit or abuse her with impunity as long as the master, if there was one, did not interfere or object. A servant who had no one outside the household to look out for her was particularly vulnerable.

Dickens created Charley and Guster to call attention to the tendency of employers to exploit and abuse the poor and friendless young women who waited on them. *Bleak House* (1852–3) shows Judy Smallweed in the act of 'girl-driving' and Mrs Snagsby happily finding fault at the top of her lungs with 'a lean young woman from a workhouse' to which, despite this, she decidedly did not want to return. These were relatively gentle jabs at the system of workhouse apprenticeship, which had been severely criticized as a result of two recent widely publicized cases of servant abuse. Parish officials routinely handed over orphaned or deserted children of pauper parents without checking or following up.

The tradition of the sadistic female servant-abuser was established by Elizabeth Brownrigg, who was hanged in 1767 for starving and beating a servant-girl to death. It was continued by Esther Hibner, hanged in London in 1829 for similar ill treatment, and two couples, the Birds and the Sloanes, tried in 1850 and 1851, though in the Sloanes' case the abused girl was rescued in time to save them from a murder charge. In the latter two cases it can be assumed that the mistress of the house was the primary abuser, but because Victorian households were nominally ruled by males, the justice system assigned the blame equally.

ESTHER HIBNER

Eight apprentices had been given into Hibner's care by the local parish so that they could learn to do fancy weaving and embroidery. Their training included, according to the newspapers, 'a series of cruelties of the most revolting description.'[57] The girls were fed on small amounts of potatoes or bread and milk (and dog food when they got the chance); put on the floor to sleep with only one blanket, even in the coldest weather; forced to rise at 3:00 or 4:00 A.M. and work until well after dark; and frequently beaten with a rod, cane, or slipper. The weaker they became, the less work they did and the more they were punished.

Hibner, sixty-one, was assisted by her daughter, also named Esther, twenty-four, and her forewoman, Ann Robinson, twenty.

Each midday these three enjoyed a rich and alcoholic repast. When one of their apprentices, Margaret Howse, died, they celebrated with a pint of gin.

The three were charged with murder after the death of another apprentice, Frances Colpitts. It was alleged by other apprentices that the younger Hibner dipped Colpitts's head in cold water several times, flogged her when she was too ill to clean the stairs, and rubbed her nose in urine that she left on the stairs when she was too weak to go to the toilet. She died from starvation and lack of exercise.

Hibner exhibited not a scrap of remorse as the surviving apprentices detailed acts of cruelty they and their deceased companions had suffered at her hands. 'Although you have been the mother of a child yourself, you saw her sufferings without any of that feeling which one would imagine could never have been absent from a female breast,' said the judge as he pronounced a sentence of death. According to the newspapers, their tormentor said several times that she regretted not having jumped out of the dock and attacking the little girls who testified against her.[58]

Hibner was said to have protested that her daughter and Robinson were acquitted even though their treatment of the children was worse than hers.[59] The younger Hibner was found guilty of cruelty to children and sent to prison for a year.

On the same day, 13 April, her mother was executed 'before an immense assemblage of persons, who in the most unequivocal manner expressed their detestation of the crime of which she had been convicted ... Thus perished one of the most hardened and unrepenting culprits that ever disgraced society or the female character,' said the *Star*.[60]

The *Times* described her 'dreadful appearance: her dress, a black gown, over which was a white bedgown, and the white cap on her head contributed, together with the sallowness of her complexion, to give her a most unearthly aspect.'[61] William Calcraft, the hangman, on his first assignment, was cheered as the drop fell. She had cut her throat in a suicide attempt, and 'just as the platform fell the cheering increased and the blood gushed from the wound.'[62]

Hibner was judged by all who came in contact with her as a miserable wretch. She was more like a fiend than a woman, said the governor of Newgate. The chaplain, whose comfort she refused, found her conduct shocking.[63] 'From the moment of her conviction till she ceased to exist,' said the *Herald*, 'she displayed the most hardened disposition ... and her sullenness to all about her was beyond precedent.'[64]

A *Times* leader called on workhouse authorities to be more careful in placing apprentices: 'The conduct of the woman – (if we may give her a name of which in life she was unworthy) – of the woman Hibner, should make parish-officer extremely cautious in selecting the people with whom they place their children as apprentices.' This was a warning that had to be repeated.[65]

ROBERT AND SARAH BIRD

The Birds, a farm couple, were tried at Exeter in March 1850 for the murder of their servant, Mary Ann Parsons, fourteen years old, whom they had taken from a workhouse. On 4 January, weak from beatings and starvation, she had died, apparently after stumbling and hitting her head on the fireplace. Her mother, who had happened to visit on the day she died, complained that the Birds had mistreated her daughter, and the death was investigated. They were arrested and charged with murder.

This was a sensational case from the start. The girl's body was a mass of bruises, though the actual cause of death was a blow to her head. The inquest inspired an angry article by Harriet Taylor and J.S. Mill in the *Daily News* and an accusation in a *Times* headline of 'Horrible Brutality.'[66]

Sarah Bird volunteered that her husband, Robert, had hit the girl last, thereby admitting that both had been beating her. It is impossible from this vantage point to assess the guilt of husband and wife separately, although it seems reasonable to assume that in a farmhouse the wife would have had more involvement, but the husband more responsibility. At any rate, their intertwinedness saved them. They were acquitted in March 1850 because it was impossible to tell who, if either of them, had struck the fatal blow. There then followed a debate in England's editorial columns as to the solidity of the judge's position. A vicious condemnation of the decision appeared in the *Weekly Times*, which headed its commentary 'Atrocious Wrong and Scandalous Impunity': 'We are forbidden to be silent not more by the atrocity of their crime than by the infernal sophistry which, emanating from the semblance of a representative of the majesty of justice, has let loose upon society two such fiends.'[67]

Pressure from the newspapers was probably responsible for the retrial of the Birds in the next assizes. They were rearrested, and charged this time with assault. On this charge they were convicted, but there was some question as to whether they were being tried twice for the same offence, and the case was not resolved for several months. While a decision on their appeal was pending, another case came to light that had an even greater impact on public opinion because the victim lived to tell about it.

GEORGE AND THERESA SLOANE

George Sloane was an up-and-coming London lawyer and businessman, not a simple farmer. His office and residence were in the same place, the Temple. His wife, Theresa, had charge of the household and was assisted by a maid of all work, who had not only the Sloanes, but their lodger, to see to. They were not well-to-do, but they lived comfortably. Mrs Sloane was assisted by Jane Wilbred, seventeen years old, who had come to her from the workhouse. This one servant did all the work but the cooking. She cleaned the offices and other rooms, made the beds, washed the clothes, served the meals, and ran errands. For all this she received only her board and room, and no wages.

Her board was effectively starvation. For breakfast she was given bread with mustard, and coffee with caraway seeds. At midday she had bread, and soup with mustard in it. Her final meal of the day was bread with pepper or mustard on it, and nothing to drink, not even water. She was allowed to use the chamber-pot – there was no toilet – once a day. If she was caught using it at night, she was punished the next morning by being forced to eat the contents. Mrs Sloane devised these rules and punishments; Mr Sloane enforced them.

The servant's troubles had begun when she inadvertently frightened the family's pet linnet by walking through a dark room with a candle. The bird subsequently died, and her mistress held her responsible. 'Never was such fiendish vengeance excited in a female mind for so trifling a cause as the supposed loss of a favourite bird,' said the *Sun*.[68]

Besides beating and overworking her, the Sloanes kept her on the edge of hunger. They once forced her to eat her own excrement as a punishment for having taken a spoonful of broth made for the cat, an offence she denied. Another perversion of her employers was to have her work topless in winter, so that she would feel the cold. As one ballad put it,

> Now Mrs. Sloane did poor Jane beat,
> For drinking broth made from cat's meat,
> Which to poor Jane Wilbred was a treat,
> Oh! what a cruel monster.
> They made poor Jane as I've been told,
> Work almost naked in the cold,
> Both Sloane and his wife in crime are old,
> But justice has pursued them bold.[69]

Having come from the workhouse, she had no friends or relatives to complain to, so she bore this state of affairs. As she neared death, a neighbour and colleague of Sloane's noticed her condition, questioned her, removed her from the household, and sought medical help. Much to the surprise of even her doctors, the girl recovered. Once the extent of the abuse became evident, the Sloanes were reported.

By December 1850, when the story came out, the English public had had enough of the law's toleration of servant abuse. Two trials had still not settled the fate of the Birds, and now here was an even more blatant case. The Sloanes' sadistic behaviour was a disgrace to the professional class, and their near-escape from justice shook the public's confidence in authority.

The workhouse administration apparently had no provision for assuring the welfare of former inmates. 'Shall we admit,' asked the *Morning Advertiser,*

> that it is a proper thing in parish authorities to lease out the services of young girls, without ever inquiring whether the servant is worthy of the mistress, or the mistress of the servant? ... We trust that, whatever may be the result of Mr. and Mrs. Sloane's trial, it may be productive of a more vigilant anxiety for the welfare of parish children, on the part of parish authorities.[70]

A preliminary inquiry at which the servant was a witness revealed the indignities to which she had been subjected by her apparently respectable employers. George Sloane appeared at this hearing, but his wife, the more active abuser, claimed she was too ill to appear when summoned, and then fled to France. Eventually, with an indignant and relentless press at their back, the police found and arrested her.

> Old Mother Sloane they've caught,
> And to London they have brought her,
> And to Newgate they have walked
> This chip of old Nick's daughter.[71]

But it was her husband who bore the brunt of public indignation. The Victorian assumption that a man was likely to have been the leader in such behaviour protected her to some extent.

The case was covered extensively for the two months between the preliminary investigation and the trial. A month before the trial, the *Weekly Times* devoted nearly a full page to various aspects of the case, starting with a history of legal cases of abuse of servants. This was headed 'The law, as it affects the Sloanian school of domestic tyrants.'[72]

The trial drew a large crowd eager to see the young woman. They were not disappointed. As she was brought in to testify, said the *Morning Advertiser*,

a deep groan seemed to break from every person present involuntarily. She was, as far as it was possible to judge in her then wasted and famished condition, a rather mild and good-looking girl. She was placed in an easy chair, and supported on pillows, and during the whole course of her examination, it was almost impossible to perceive that she was living, but for the motion of her eyes and lips.[73]

The couple pleaded guilty to a series of assaults, presumably to avoid more publicity, and were given two years. The *Weekly Chronicle* pronounced the sentence a 'very cheap price' for child torture. 'A mere pickpocket would fare worse at the bar of an English Criminal Court than those heartless monsters ...'[74]

Though the case involved neither a murder nor an execution, broadside sellers had a field day. 'I declare to you, sir, the knowingest among us couldn't have invented a cock to equal the conduct of them Sloanes,' one of them told Henry Mayhew. 'It was women that bought him most. They was more savage against him than against her. Why, they had fifty deaths for him ...'[75]

Soon after the verdict against the Sloanes came the announcement of the judgment in the Birds' case. They were sent to prison for sixteen months.

At mid-century, when these trials took place, the public was used to the idea of women as cruel and strong. Harriet Parker had recently been hanged for suffocating two children as a lesson to their father. Mary May, Sarah Chesham, and others had been implicated as multiple poisoners. Maria Manning had been exposed as the mastermind of the murder of her former lover. Sarah Thomas had been dragged to the gallows to pay for the murder of her mistress. Rebecca Smith had confessed to repeated infanticide. Thousands of people witnessed their executions, and thousands more read about them. These murderesses, legends in their own time, were memorialized in broadsides and ballads. They had demonstrated that women were not always passive, submissive, and easily led. None the less, the public was not willing to believe that Theresa Sloane was primarily responsible for the suffering of Jane Wilbred or Sarah Bird for the death of Mary Ann Parsons. The image of women as benevolent nurturers was virtually unassailable.

In 1865 Jane Smith was sentenced to five years in prison after her twenty-four-year-old servant, Martha Turner, died at Great Yarmouth, Norfolk, from starvation and exposure. She had been sleeping on straw on a damp cellar floor, subsisting on stolen table scraps, and enduring savage beatings from her mistress. *Lloyd's Weekly* took the opportunity to issue 'A Warning to Mistresses' in a leader that suggested that a great deal of suffering was being borne by poverty-stricken domestic servants who did not know enough to complain to the police and 'never dream that the law is made for them as much as for their mistresses.' But clearly the law did not expect to have to discipline mistresses. 'We have missionaries spread over the globe, and we have savage life like this at home?' asked *Lloyd's*.[76]

CONCLUSION

Subversive behaviour by servants was widely feared by their employers. Eliza Fenning, hanged in 1815, was an innocent victim of this syndrome. Ann Heytrey, also hanged, admitted her guilt, but seems to have been insane. The murder of her shrewish employer by Sarah Thomas aroused more curiosity than hostility in the public, but no allowances were made for Kate Webster, who cut up the body of her mistress and was rumoured to have boiled the head.

The tendency to abuse maids of all work and apprentices was no figment of Dickens's imagination. The infamous Esther Hibner, who starved and beat probably more than one of her assistants to death, acted the part of the witch figure to the end. More civilized, and perhaps more frightening on that account, were Sarah Bird, a farmer, and Theresa Sloane, a lawyer's wife.

EIGHT

Murder of the Elderly

Mary Bateman / Jane Jamieson / Mary Ann Higgins / Eliza Ross / Mary Ann Burdock / Martha Browning / Mercy Catherine Newton / Alice Holt / Louisa Taylor

A sizeable proportion of the nineteenth century's most avaricious murderesses picked on their elders, who tended to be not only weaker, but more credulous, than most people. It was relatively easy to get the elderly to swallow poison as medicine. If necessary, they could be throttled or smothered. And sickness and death at their age could be passed off as natural.

If murder was detected, however, there was a good chance that it would be well publicized and the murderess execrated. For one thing, the public had a vested interest in discouraging such activity. Anyone in a position to leave money to a relative could identify with victims like this. Another disquieting factor in these murders was their impersonality. The quality of the relationship between murderess and victim was irrelevant. The perpetrators saw the victims as barriers to their own prosperity and happiness. What they were like as individuals had no bearing on their fate.

Some were relatives whose death meant an inheritance for the murderess. Kitty Newton told her mother flatly that if she didn't hurry up and die she would have to kill her. Alice Holt registered her mother in a burial club. Mary Ann Higgins thought she needed her uncle's money to get married. These women operated in a simplistic, narcissistic frame of reference. Their own needs were paramount: therefore the relative had to die. They had no moral training to restrain the power they had over these weaker, older people.

Like child murder, murder of the elderly required only access and a motive. Those with more distant connections to their targets had to demonstrate a certain amount of cunning by cultivating positions of trust. Mary Ann Burdock, probably the most notorious nineteenth-century poisoner, doctored her wealthy lodger's food. Louisa Taylor slowly poisoned an old woman she was nursing, hoping, apparently, to marry the widower. As a fortune-teller, Mary Bateman was able to administer poison to someone she had swindled. Martha Browning strangled her bed mate for a banknote in her pocket. Eliza Ross created a sensation as a 'burker' – someone who killed merely for the money a body would bring. She chose a street hawker whom she thought would not be missed. These women, with the exception of Browning, who appears to have been dull-witted, were, next to baby-farmers, perhaps the most reviled murderesses of the century. They may have represented the unknown figures that newspaper readers might have to turn to and trust when *they* were old and vulnerable.

Impulsive, violent murder of an old person by a woman was rare. Jane Jamieson of Newcastle achieved notoriety for this in 1829. She is the only one of these murderesses who attracted any sympathy – and the only one who murdered in the 'masculine' way.

MARY BATEMAN

A legendary figure known as the 'Yorkshire witch,' Mary Bateman, a fortune-teller, appears to have been a sort of guru. So bizarre was her story that it was retold many times through the century, beginning with a pamphlet published at the time of her execution and reprinted in *The Newgate Calendar* of 1864.[1] The pamphlet points out that the 'guilty deceiver and the deluded victim each furnish an appropriate and an impressive lesson.'[2] The fatal flaw in each was greed.

A woman in her late thirties, Bateman had made her living for many years swindling gullible clients. In 1806–7 she managed to defraud an elderly couple, Rebecca and William Perigo of Bramley, near Leeds, of all their property by promising them bags of gold. She then attempted to do away with them to make sure they did not expose her when the gold was not forthcoming. As a charm, they were instructed to consume certain powders that she gave them. If the powders made them ill, they were to take some honey that she provided as an antidote. The honey contained arsenic, and Rebecca Perigo died in May 1807.

When the widower explored some of the other charms Bateman had sold them, he discovered the fraud. She was arrested in January 1809, and tried and hanged at York in March. She refused to confess.

The *Morning Herald* provided a colourful account of the execution, which drew 5,000 spectators, many from Leeds:

> The child which had been sucking for a year past, at her breast, was taken from her, some little time before her execution; dreadful to tell! – she gave it up – without a pang!! – she parted from it – without one emotion!!! When the anatomist comes to dissect her heart, will he find it, as Mrs. Hardy, the recorder of Leeds, well expressed it ... 'A heart of flesh?'[3]

One paper reported that her followers were expecting 'that some miracle would be worked in her favour, and that she would fly off the scaffold in a cloud, or on a broom, and be saved by the interposition of Heaven ... Jack Ketch however was of a different opinion, and his opinion prevailed.'[4]

There had been speculation as to whether Mary Bateman's husband had been her accomplice. The 1809 pamphlet put that theory to rest, arguing that a man would have behaved more reasonably. 'We do believe that no man could have been guilty of so much cruelty with so little motive. Women, as they are naturally much more amiable, tender and compassionate than the other sex become, when they pervert the dictates of nature, more remorseless and cruel, and can conceive and execute the most diabolical of crimes.'[5] As we have seen, this was a commonly held belief reinforced every now and then by extreme deviance.

JANE JAMIESON

Jane Jamieson killed her mother by accident, in a rage. Such an offence is not as threatening to the general public as premeditated murder, which, if successful, is likely to be repeated, and Jamieson was not treated harshly in the press.

The story was that she flew into a drunken passion on 2 January 1829, when her mother, Margaret, accused her of having murdered two illegitimate babies. Or, as a broadside ballad tells it,

> Oh when my eyes beheld the blood,
> In horror and amaze I stood,
> My soul was sick – my eyes ran o'er
> And her who bore me lay in gore.
> No sooner had she fallen down,
> Then I did see my fatal doom,
> The blood in streams ran down her breast,
> And so her soul it sunk to rest.[6]

The woman died of a stab wound from a red-hot poker, but not before attempting to persuade doctors that her daughter had nothing to do with it. Despite her efforts Jamieson was executed on 7 March.

Jamieson, in her thirties, was described as slovenly and ignorant. 'She was formerly a smart, clean, good-looking woman; but lately she has been little less than an object of disgust,' says one broadside. 'She is very coarse-featured,' says another, 'but her countenance does not present any peculiar indication of ferocity.'

The *Times* reported that the trial lasted eight hours, an unusually long time, and was crowded with spectators.[7] The testimony suggests that the murder was accidental and that violence was normal in her family. The mother and daughter had quarrelled frequently and noisily, sometimes throwing pots, knives, or pokers at each other.

Jamieson was a model penitent. In the two days between the trial and the execution, she cooperated with the chaplain, joining the final prayers 'with great fervency of spirit.' Her ordeal was described as 'a dreadful example to the licentious and those who give way to unbridled passion.'[8]

In fact, murderesses did not often give way to unbridled passion. In particular, those who murdered the elderly were clever and methodical. They picked their victims carefully and took the time to cover their tracks.

MARY ANN HIGGINS

Mary Ann Higgins was immortalized in Calcraft's memoirs.[9] An orphan, she had been raised by an uncle. She came under the influence of a suitor who wanted the old man's money. Soon he fell ill and died. However, the woman who came to help nurse him noticed a powder in his rennet and another in a bowl of soup in the kitchen. Higgins and her suitor, Edward Clarke, were immediately suspected. She confessed before the double execution at Coventry in August 1831, but found little sympathy from the crowd.

ELIZA ROSS

'Ordinary homicides slay from passion or revenge,' said a pamphlet on the London burkers;

> the murders they commit are the product of an ungovernable and overmastering impulse which hurls reason from her seat, and in the wild conflict of guilty passion, precipitates them into the commission of acts, which are no sooner done, than they would perhaps give the universe if they were undone. But Cook [i.e., Ross] and her criminal predecessors possess the horrid and anomalous distinction of having, without the palliation of passion, or of any other motive which a

just view of human infirmity can admit in extenuation, and from a base and sordid love of gain ... established a traffic in blood, upon principles of cool calculation, and an utter recklessness of either God or man, which would have done no discredit to Mammon himself.[10]

Eliza Ross's cool callousness was barbarity in the extreme, but it was not wild and uncontrolled. Ross went after what she wanted with boldness and tenacity. In London's east end, she had a reputation as a woman best left alone. She was an Irishwoman, large, raw-boned, and coarse-featured, said the *Courier*, a drunkard and a thief of 'masculine proportions and strength.'[11] She had served three months in jail for skinning a neighbour's cat and throwing it back at her. It was rumoured that she supported her gin habit by relieving children of their clothing or any valuables they might have on them. Some said she was a body-snatcher. It was suspected that she had a business relationship with an anatomy lecturer whose office was nearby.

Ross was convicted of homicidal suffocation even though the body of her victim, Caroline Walsh, eighty-four years old, but hale and hearty until she moved in with Ross, was never found. Ross's story was that there was no body because there was no murder. Others, however, suspected that there was no body because it had been sold for dissection. Walsh's clothing, at any rate, had been sold by Ross.

The friendly old woman disappeared on 19 August 1831. Her granddaughter, who disapproved of her connection with Ross, came to call on her the next day and was told she had gone out. This she did not believe. She hunted for her none the less, but could not find her. She went to the police, who did nothing at the time but, by October, realized what had probably happened. By then rumours of burking activities of John Bishop and Thomas Williams in London would have reached their ears, and they were hearing from others whom Ross had tried to entice to her lodgings to sleep.

Ross's twelve-year-old son confirmed their suspicions. His description of the murder was consistent with the needs of an anatomist for a body that bore no marks of violence. The boy had seen his mother give Walsh something to drink, and then, when she lay down, put her hand over the old woman's mouth and nose and press down on her chest until her eyes rolled. His mother carried the body away, and the next morning he came upon it in a sack in the cellar. That evening he saw his mother leave the house with the sack over her shoulder.

It appeared that his father was well aware of what was going on but declined to involve himself. As a broadside ballad put it,

> Before his eyes that cruel deed,
> The aged woman's life she took,
> While he did at the fire stand,
> And his father out of the window look'd.[12]

The *Times* reported that, on hearing that the boy had talked, his mother exclaimed: 'Good God! How could I have borne a son to hang me?'[13] She was tried on 6 January 1832, and sentenced to hang the following Monday, 9 January. Her husband, Edward Cook, was acquitted.

Protesting her innocence to the end, she told the authorities that, if she was to be hanged, Cook should be hanged as well.[14] The night before the execution, she called out in her sleep: 'Oh, my child, my deluded child, thus to hang her who suffered for you!'[15] But there was little doubt that she deserved her fate. When the drop fell, the crowd cheered. She was an unsavoury, tough creature brought to justice for an abhorrent crime.

MRS BURDOCK

Ross's crime, as the prosecutor pointed out at the outset of her trial, was shocking because she killed, not for her victim's property, but for her body. Mary Ann Burdock, hanged for murder in Bristol three years later, was more socially acceptable but far greedier. Walsh's body would have fetched very little, particularly in August, when there were no anatomy classes. Clara Ann Smith had money and jewellery.

When Mrs Smith died in Bristol on 23 October 1833, she had been a widow for five years and a lodger of Mary Ann Wade's, as she called herself then, for a month. After fourteen months Smith's relatives heard of her death and demanded to know what had happened to her property. When it was not forthcoming, the body was exhumed, and yellow spots, evidence of arsenic, were found in the stomach. It was established that the landlady had sent a former lodger to buy arsenic a few days before the death. After that the maid saw the landlady put a yellow powder in the old woman's gruel. She recalled being told to carry it back to the kitchen later but not to eat anything left over, as Smith tended to spit into her food. Mr Wade, also a shady character, had been seen with a gold watch after the lodger's death and had apparently been transformed from a working man to a gentleman. Not long after the transformation, he unfortunately died suddenly at home, as he was drinking a glass of grog. The widow, newly wealthy, bribed another lodger to marry her.

A youth named Clarke had also died suddenly while in her orbit. There was some suspicion that she might have had something to do with either or both of these deaths, but it was not pursued. The trial in April 1835 attracted attention far beyond Bristol. It was faithfully covered in the three local papers, the *Gazette*, *Mercury*, and *Mirror*, and picked up by the London papers. The accused woman, who gave her age as thirty-four but looked closer to forty, said the *Gazette*, had a good though portly figure, and a handsome face with clear skin and large, dark eyes.[16] She was, however, 'deplorably ignorant, could neither read nor write, and appears to have received no religious or moral instruction.'[17]

When she arrived at the court-house, said the *Times*, 'the populace set up the most discordant yells and groans.' If the jury had not found her guilty, 'serious consequences would have ensued from the fury of the lower orders.'[18]

Burdock stubbornly denied the murder and insisted that her execution would be murder. A crowd estimated by the papers at 50,000 gathered to hiss at her as she died. A local country paper explained that her 'whole conduct serves to show the fearful extent of wickedness of which human nature is capable, when devoid of those restraints which are induced by moral and religious culture.'[19]

A transcript of the trial was published in pamphlet form. There were broadsides in several competing versions to mark the inquest, trial, and execution.[20] There were at least four ballads, one of them in the first person, and three versions of a confession. It is safe to say that at the time of her death Mrs Burdock's name was a household word. She remained a legend for some time, appearing in the memoirs of Calcraft the hangman and in the 1889 *Newgate Calendar.*[21]

The publicity given to this murder appears to have started a wave of arsenic poisonings in England. It also started a panic about the possibility of poisoning by the preparers of food and drink in a household.

> In Trinity Street, this murderess liv'd,
> A lodging house did keep,
> To which one Clara Ann Smith did go
> A home in hopes to seek

began one ballad about Mrs Burdock, which went on to describe the mixing of arsenic in the gruel by her trusted landlady. In 1836, the year after Burdock was tried and hanged, Sophia Edney admitted to having been inspired to poison her husband in Cross, near Bath, by the Bristol case. (See chapter 4.)

In the 1840s more and more women were suspected of using this method, some were caught, and doubtless many more got away with it. (See chapters 3 and 4.) As cases of poisoning were publicized, more and more people became aware that arsenic, a substance whose presence in a house could be easily explained, was being used on human beings as well as rodents.

But the subtlety of poison was not necessary to accomplish the murder of someone older and weaker: a woman could depend on her own strength. In 1846 a young servant stranded in London strangled her benefactress for a paltry five pounds, which she did not collect.

MARTHA BROWNING

Martha Browning killed Elizabeth Mundell, a widow in her sixties, for what she thought was a five-pound note. However, the note she coveted and finally obtained was issued, not by the Bank of

England, but by the 'Bank of Elegance,' and her possession of it implicated Browning. Initially it had been thought that Mundell had committed suicide.

Browning, twenty-three, had persuaded the kindly old woman to let her stay with her in her lodgings in Westminster and sleep in her bed until she found another position. After three weeks she decided to strike. To get the note, which Mundell kept on her person at all times, she strangled her with a cord in her sleep. The woman's philanthropy, observed the *Times*, 'deserved a better requital.'[22]

The London newspapers ran story after story on her arrest, confession, trial, and execution in December 1845 and January 1846. The *Illustrated London News* devoted a full column to a story headed 'A Girl Convicted of Murder.' *Lloyd's* said it would 'be of some satisfaction to those who may have considered it almost impossible for such a person to have committed so fearful a crime' that Browning had confessed. She could read and write well, said the paper, but didn't fully see the note until after the murder, when she tried to change it. Mundell's son-in-law was with her and, realizing where it had come from, had her charged.

Dickens used this case as an example in a letter to the *Daily News* shortly after the execution. Arguing that the prospect of capital punishment was unlikely to prevent murder, he noted that in murder for gain

> there is little calculation beyond the absorbing greed of the moment to be got ... it would have been more safe and prudent in the woman who was hanged a few weeks since, for the murder in Westminster, to have simply robbed her old companion in an unguarded moment, and in her sleep. But, her calculation going to the gain of what she took to be a Bank note; and the poor old woman living between her and the gain; she murdered her.[23]

A desperately poor and ignorant young woman could not be expected to act out of reason. Such a creature would operate according to the instinct for survival, and in the present rather than the future. Nor would she consult the past. As long as society continued to deny large numbers of its members access to the necessities of life, the strong would wrest them from the weak.

MERCY CATHERINE NEWTON

One of the most merciless daughters in the annals of crime was Mercy Catherine Newton, known as Kitty, who on 4 December 1848 brutally and fatally attacked her seventy-two-year-old mother, Anne Newton, for no other reason than that she was impatient to receive her inheritance. She was tried for murder three times and, after two hung juries, acquitted in March 1850 on account of some legal doubts as to exactly how her mother died. A *Times* leader said bluntly that, despite the verdict, 'there can be no doubt on the mind of any reasonable man that the wretched woman was guilty.'[24]

A fire on the fatal night made it look as though the woman had been burned to death, but it was established that her nose had been severely flattened, probably as she was being smothered. The suspicion was that the daughter had started the fire to cover up the murder and had poured oil on it to advance it.

Kitty Newton, thirty, was a housekeeper in Bridgenorth, not far from Wolverhampton. On her mother's death she was to inherit £200 outright and the interest on £300 for life. The woman lived in lodgings and came occasionally to visit at the house where her daughter worked. Usually they drank and quarrelled.

A fellow servant testified that, a year before Anne Newton's death, her daughter had whipped her so that pieces of flesh were torn out of her arms. To a doctor who came to dress the wounds and admonished her, Kitty said she was sorry she had not finished her off. A few months later the fellow servant rescued the mother as Kitty was trying to force a handkerchief down her throat. Her mouth was torn and bleeding, and blood was also coming from her ears. Not long after that the woman was beaten so severely that the flesh above her knees was blackened and one ankle sprained. Kitty had recently implored her mother to commit suicide and offered to furnish her with the means. She was heard to say she would never be happy as long as her mother was above ground, or that she would like to see her mother cut into quarters and roasted on a gridiron.

The *Daily News* commented that, even when she was sober, the daughter did not treat her mother civilly: 'the evidence given on the trial goes entirely to prove a barbarity and fierceness of disposition not merely irreconcilable with filial feelings, but absolutely with those of the sex which she disgraces.'[25]

Because of its complications, this case had extended coverage. By the time it was over, the public was well aware of the arbitrariness of the law. Headlines had called the accused woman a female fiend; news stories had taken it for granted that she was a murderess. Referring to the case of Robert and Sarah Bird as well (see chapter 7), the *Times* worried that murderers were being 'allowed to walk unpunished through the land.'[26]

ALICE HOLT

By 1863 murder for burial insurance money was an old story, but it was unusual for a daughter to target her elderly mother. At the urging of her husband, Alice Holt (also known as Hewitt) registered her sick mother, Mary Bailey, in a burial society in Stockport by having a friend impersonate her. On the night of 26 February 1863, Mary Bailey drank some brandy and water with what she thought were grounds in the bottom. The next morning she was dead from arsenic poisoning. The trial was delayed because Alice was pregnant. She was tried on 9 December at Chester, found guilty, and hanged on 29 December in what the *Daily News* described as 'one of the most dreadful, sickening spectacles which has ever been associated with a public execution.'[27] The weather was cold, the hangman could not get the bolt to release the drop, and, when it finally did drop, the rope was too short for her height and weight, so he had to pull on her legs.

An execution broadside that was obviously not written ahead of time records her piteous moaning and notes that the crowd contained a preponderance of women. It reports that she insisted to the end that her husband was the murderer, which was probably true. A ballad re-creates the couple's bickering over the prospect of killing off her mother, the daughter resisting pressure from her abusive husband:

> Now that the old gal's life's insured,
> Holt to the daughter did say,
> Better in the grave she were immured,
> And the money will make us so gay.
> Now that you have got me in the family way,
> And from me my virtue you've wrung,
> You'll never be happy a day,
> Till on the gallows I'm hung.[28]

LOUISA TAYLOR

The motives behind Louisa Taylor's murder of Mary Ann Tregillis were much more complex. Her late husband's friend, William Tregillis, was a naval pensioner with an income that apparently attracted Taylor. Though he was eighty-five and she only thirty-seven, she proposed that he leave his wife and run away with her. He had previously been in a lunatic asylum and it is possible that her plan was to get her hands on his money once his wife was dead, and then institutionalize him again. At any rate, that was his theory once his wife realized that she was being slowly poisoned.

Mrs Tregillis, who was eighty-one, took sick soon after Taylor moved into their rooms in Woolwich, south London, as a lodger in August 1882. Taylor obligingly nursed her, administering medicine prescribed by the doctor. Despite this attention, she got sicker. The nursing care ceased early in October, when Taylor was arrested for having stolen ten pounds that she had asked Mr Tregillis to put under his wife's pillow.

Taylor's absence arrested the sick woman's symptoms, but it was too late. She was found to be dying of lead poisoning. Taylor had been adding sugar of lead, which she obtained from the doctor

for an alleged skin condition, to Mrs Tregillis's medicine. In a
dying statement, the victim testified that she had seen her 'nurse'
blend in a white powder.

Mrs Tregillis died on 23 October. The death could not be attributed directly to lead poisoning, but it was at least accelerated
by lead poisoning. Taylor was found guilty of murder, without a
recommendation for mercy – a recommendation that would have
been automatic for a woman, the *Times* pointed out, 'had the
crime been less deliberate and revolting.' A 'wicked attempt to
prey upon two aged and weak people even at the expense of the
life of one of them' would receive the punishment it deserved.[29]
As the *Telegraph* said in a leader approving of the death sentence,
it was an inhuman crime, a story of 'barbarous cruelty and shocking immorality.'[30] There could be no question of premeditation in
a case of slow poisoning. She was executed on 2 January 1883.

Eliza Ross got perhaps a pound for the body of Caroline Walsh;
Martha Browning's prize was a fake five-pound note; Mrs Tregillis
was killed for an annuity of forty pounds, or less than a pound a
week. Mr Justice James Fitzjames Stephen, who presided over the
jury that tried Louisa Taylor, remarked that if a person were equal
to the commission of murder at all, a paltry amount might very
well be as much temptation to the crime as a larger sum.

CONCLUSION

The women hanged for the murder of old people were a singu-
larly unimaginative and insensitive lot. They seem to have been
oblivious of the humanity of their victims. Kindness and generos-
ity were lost on them. Mary Ann Higgins's uncle took her in when
there was no one else to raise her. Elizabeth Mundell allowed
Martha Browning, a stranger, to share her bed because she had
nowhere else to go. Mrs Tregillis, too, took Louisa Taylor into her
bed when she begged to be allowed to move in. Mrs Walsh was a
chatty old woman who liked company. But the women who murdered them appear to have been emotionally flat. They seem to
have neither liked nor disliked their victims, but merely to have
used them as a means to an end.

Abuse of the elderly is by no means a twentieth-century phe-nomenon. Greed most often motivated the murderesses in this chapter, and their victims' vulnerability encouraged them. The most notorious were Eliza Ross, a burker, and Mary Ann Burdock, probably a serial poisoner. Mary Bateman, the Yorkshire witch, became a legend. Alice Holt was remembered for her difficulty in dying at the end of the rope, and Louisa Taylor for her apparent lack of a motive.

Part Three: Meaning

NINE

The Image of the Murderess

Until the 1880s, when the plight of Adelaide Bartlett, and then of Florence Maybrick, attracted the attention of middle-class women, the image of the murderess was controlled by men. In the courts and in the press, they evaluated her behaviour in terms of their own needs and expectations. Needless to say, she fell short. The murder of her own child by an insane mother could be forgiven, but the murder of women's social betters – and in that category I include their husbands – could not even be understood. It was monstrous, unnatural female behaviour.

It is clear from the foregoing stories that not all accused murderesses were evil. Almost certainly Eliza Fenning, and probably Maybrick, were framed. Many of them were, by our standards, temporarily insane – for example, Martha Brown, Constance Kent, Frances Stewart, Eliza Gibbons, and Eleanor Pearcey. Some, like Ann Heytrey, Martha Browning, Sarah Thomas, and Mary Ann Cotton, were either feeble-minded or mentally unstable.

Others were misguided. Murder afforded socially and economically oppressed women a measure of control over their unfortunate circumstances. If we look on it as a means of asserting control used by those who feel otherwise powerless,[1] we can gain some understanding of why women like Catherine Foster, or even Sarah Chesham, solved their problems through murder.

'Lower-class individuals are "pushed around" by those in authority more than middle and upper class people,' Terence Morris and Louis Blom-Cooper say in explaining the aggression theory.

'They are subject to external authority but never exercise it for themselves ... Where external pressures are strong by virtue of sub-ordinate social status – or intense involvement in relationships with others – aggression turns outwards.'[2] When life becomes unendur-able, in other words, the oppressed, because they are not used to being responsible, blame and punish others for their misery.

Such dreariness is not the stuff of which novels are made, but it is none the less fascinating. It tells us how a subordinate social group behaves in the face of what would seem to be a hopeless combination of powerlessness and poverty. Until they took mat-ters into their own hands, these women had no control over their lives. Murder liberated them, at least until they were caught – and it is fair to assume that probably many others who behaved in this way remained undetected.

The indifference of many condemned murderesses and the be-lated conversion of others suggest that the moral education of lower-class girls was neglected. Probably there were not many de-sirable female role models in what Mary Carpenter called at the time 'the pariah caste ..., those families where there is no fear or love of God, no regard to human law, no self-respect, no pleasures but those of animal gratification, no perception of anything pure or beautiful.'[3]

The realities of poverty left little room for ideals for either sex. Men abused their wives with impunity, and young children were often battered. Some women murdered as a response to abuse; others were themselves abusive.

What education girls of the lower class had consisted largely of rote learning without comprehension.[4] Their world was limited and concrete and isolated, largely because the rest of society wanted it that way. Within this 'pariah caste' women were further isolated in domestic employment.[5]

As Mary Wollstonecraft observed long before this, cunning is the natural opponent of strength.[6] Women depended on men to provide for them and had little recourse if the provision was inad-equate or the provider abused them, or even if they had tired of the provider. Some women simply wanted to replace their mate, others to reduce the number of mouths that had to be fed. Mur-

der was a way of showing resistance to their lot in life. Behind
many of the murders by women in the nineteenth century, particularly infanticide and poisoning, was a persistent desperation.
They were motivated less by greed than by need. 'With the elimi-
nation of social inequity and desperation,' Martin Daly and Margo
Wilson have written, 'we may yet see homicide become an almost
negligible source of human mortality.'[7]

In his chronicle of female criminality, Patrick Wilson notes with
reference to serial poisoners that 'there is also present in ... multiple family murders a curious quality, the need for the women,
even to their own danger, and by killing those they might nor-
mally be expected to love, to create space about themselves, to
seek liberty.[8] If for some of these women murder was a way of
getting through life, for others it was a way of making a living.
Occasionally they used it to remove someone who was a nuisance
or an obstacle, but in general for these women murder was a
practical solution to the problem of surviving, and a solution that,
though it sometimes shocked the middle and upper classes, must
have been accepted by their peers, since several of them had ac-
complices or helpers and the collusion of the community. It is
entirely possible that simple desperation provoked tenant farmers'
wives with not enough food for the family, or ill-used servants, or
urban women who were too old for prostitution, to murder. It was
a way out.

Women of all classes, as the subordinate group, are socialized to
help one another. This way of life does not rule out murder: in
fact, it can facilitate it. In the first half of the century at least, girls
of the lower classes did not have much formal schooling, but as
women they learned from one another. Their world was limited
and concrete. The society above them operated in many ways on
abstractions, and by doing so excluded them. Life in the underclass
was very much a matter of survival of the fittest. Though their
crimes were sensational, the serial poisoners were not themselves
colourful. Their crimes almost all turn on the betrayal of trusting
husbands, children, invalids, or employers. Perhaps because society, too, had trusted them – to collude in their own oppression by
accepting it – it reacted strongly to news of these betrayals. Those

murderesses who could not be dismissed as insane were condemned as inhuman – not simply because they had killed, but because they had killed 'unnaturally.'

The justice system, which in many ways bent over backwards to keep crime a male preserve, does not seem to have known what to do with them. It was hard to come to terms with the fact that a group of people traditionally regarded as trustworthy, some of whom one trusted oneself, as an employer or an invalid, could be dangerous. Yet, in the 1840s, report after report confirmed that this was the case. It was almost as though reports of their trials, convictions, and executions inspired rather than deterred similar efforts. The Earl of Carlisle recognized this possibility when he declined to elaborate on poisoning methods while trying to get a bill through the Lords restricting the sale of arsenic. (See chapter 3.)

The justice system expected women to be the victims, not the perpetrators, of serious crime. It was 'natural' for them to be scrutinized in court and corrected in prison, but in many ways women were actually treated more harshly than men in these settings. Prison policy was designed by men, who evidently had no understanding of how difficult it would be for women to work in congregate silence or how dehumanizing it was for them to be regimented and watched. Lucia Zedner, in *Women, Crime and Custody in Victorian England*, shows that female prisoners were harder to control than their male counterparts. Florence Maybrick's account of prison life for a woman at the end of the century, when it was presumably much improved, suggests why this was the case. Maybrick, who believed that the men responsible for prison policy were well-meaning but ill-equipped to extend it to women, remarks on the indignity of a woman's having no mirror, no privacy, and virtually no personality once she took up residence in a prison.[9] Russell P. Dobash, R. Emerson Dobash, and Sue Gutteridge attribute the humiliation and degradation to 'patriarchal and paternalist' attitudes towards female prisoners.[10] Those who worked in the justice system thought that prison was easier for women than for men because women did not have to do heavy work outdoors, but that is not an opinion shared by historians.

For crimes other than murder, the justice system did treat women more leniently than men, but feminists are now questioning their motives. Was this simply because women were already in the power of people who could discipline them? Was this a way of maintaining the fiction that women were docile and domestic? At any rate it was a utilitarian rather than a chivalric approach, as Ian Bell has observed, in that, 'by having so little power, women were thought to pose less threat to the community and so could confidently be treated with less severity.'[11]

Murder was the great leveller. Men who killed were treated more harshly than women who killed only when the insanity defence could be applied. Until the Kent case, the law and the press threw the book at any woman who violated the taboo against murder. The public showed much less tolerance or pity for aggressive, sociopathic women than for the same sort of men. The upper classes applied their own rigid definition of femininity to women living on the fringes of society, where survival from day to day was the primary consideration, and the lower classes had even less tolerance or pity for aberrant women than did the upper classes. Lower-class women maintained their respectability by establishing a distance from their erring sisters.

A pattern was established in the 1830s of public vilification of murderesses. It began in 1829 with Esther Hibner and was augmented in the next few years by Eliza Ross and Mary Ann Burdock. These callous, greedy women became witch figures, hated viciously and spontaneously not merely for what they had done, but for what they stood for, as though ordinary people were projecting their own dark tendencies onto them.

By the 1840s, when murder by women seemed very prevalent, the press was regularly registering profound shock, contempt, disgust, and dismay at the increasing evidence that women were killing members of their own families for money. There was no attempt to find out why. What seemed like a relentless wave of arsenic poisonings resulted in the Sale of Arsenic Act of 1851, which at one point in its evolution had a clause, later removed, barring women from the purchase of this poison.

Maria Manning showed the public that a murderess could be a glamorous figure, and even that the pursuit of murderesses could be a sexual turn-on. By mid-century the press had become adept at exploiting public interest in the criminal *because* she was a woman.

The most sensational murder trials were of women who had had some sexual motivation, or at the very least were young and attractive. Along with a marked increase in detected murder in nineteenth-century England, there was a corresponding awakening of interest among the public in such details as what provoked the murder, what means were used to kill, whether and how the prisoner was apprehended, incriminating accounts of his or her past, exact testimony at the inquest and trial, and the behaviour of the condemned criminal in the face of death.

Possibly the increase was one manifestation of pressures on the lower class of the transformation from an agrarian to a manufacturing society; another explanation is simply that, as the quality of law enforcement rose, so, too, did the exposure of lawlessness. Whatever its cause, the accumulation of murders brought to light was disquieting, and the perceived preponderance of murders by women[12] at a time when the female sex was conventionally esteemed for its virtue was regarded with particular fear and perplexity, and a distaste so strong that these attitudes translated at some levels into a general distrust of females, or at least of collective female potential.

Murder by a woman was so unthinkable in the patriarchal ideology of Victorian England that it had to be explained away as the action of a whore, witch, monster, or madwoman. In a period when the family was thought of as the glue that held society together, any crime that threatened it was bound to be regarded by the establishment as particularly vicious. So the murderess was subjected to what the feminist criminologist Frances Heidensohn in *Women and Crime* has termed 'double jeopardy' – punishment for being unfeminine, and therefore unnatural as well as for breaking social rules. This response was instinctive, but later in the century Cesare Lombroso, the celebrated Italian criminologist, lent authority to it when he wrote in a scholarly analysis: 'The born female criminal is, so to speak, a double exception, as a criminal and as a woman ..., and she is therefore more monstrous.'[13]

Women were thought of as emotional, not rational, beings. Rational, calculating women who killed were despised for making a mockery of this stereotype as well as for the killing. In the nineteenth-century culture, those who killed were derided as not merely wicked, but also perverse.

The punishment was supposed to be determined by the crime, regardless of who had committed it or why. For many years the public was comfortable with this policy. But by the time Kent confessed to the murder of her stepbrother, there was some hedging in the newspapers. She was saved from the gallows and ultimately released because the justice system did not operate in a philosophical vacuum. Judges and home secretaries were human and could, in their general approach, be swayed by public opinion. The influence of new theories of criminal responsibility was shifting the emphasis away from the rigid scale that had prevailed in the justice system to a consideration of individual circumstances and the potential danger of an offender to the community.[14] 'Criminal offenders ... came increasingly to be described in terms of the external forces acting upon their will,' Martin Wiener has written. 'They were less likely to be portrayed by reformers ... as simply people who deliberately chose to break the law, but more likely to be described as problem personalities that manifested pathologies.'[15]

From about 1880, Home Office documents show a concern that the punishment be appropriate. There is evidence in its files on Alice Rhodes and Elizabeth Staunton, Louisa Taylor, Charlotte Winsor, Eliza Gibbons, Amy Gregory, and Ada Chard Williams[16] that, in the last part of the century, perhaps conscious of a previous bias, the government took a special interest in the disposition of cases in which women had been convicted of murder. By the end of the century, it was acknowledged that women, weaker physically and having fewer means of employment, were more likely to be driven by stress of circumstances to certain types of crime. A report to Parliament in 1895 acknowledged a tendency not to prosecute a woman for an offence for which a man would be prosecuted, and not to convict a woman on evidence on which a man would be sent to prison.[17]

By 1889 society was more sensitive to individual circumstances, and the justice system, though still highly moralistic, had abandoned its rigid attitude towards crime and punishment and was taking into account such variants as mitigating circumstances and the likelihood of recidivism. Criminality was increasingly seen as a disturbance of biological or psychological balance. Female promiscuity continued to be regarded as an indicator of criminality well into the twentieth century, but, in general, as the repression of male sexuality diminished at the end of the nineteenth century, so, too, did the image of the murderess.

Despite sporadic assaults, the ideology has prevailed until now that killing is more 'unnatural' for women than for men because women have traditionally committed substantially less crime than men, and their offences are usually less dangerous to society. This state of affairs probably has less to do with women's inherent virtue than with the fact that their socialization has limited the opportunity for them to commit crime. None the less, where there are other people, there are opportunities for murder. As we have seen, for women to take advantage of such opportunities was unusual but by no means unheard of.

In the 1890s a more charitable male attitude to female deviance and steady public pressure from women toned down the bias of the English justice system against murderesses. At the same time, the Italian criminologist William Ferrero was reinforcing it with his claim that it was women's destiny to suffer rather than to cause suffering.[18] But by this time public abhorrence of the murderess had given way to a more general interest in the 'science' of women.

The historian V.A.C. Gatrell has observed that crime always symbolizes the threat of anarchy, and that those who break the law provide the establishment with opportunities to demonstrate its authority. Gatrell makes this remark in a discussion of theft and violent crime as a power struggle between the ruling order and the underclass, but it serves equally well in an analysis of the male/female dynamic in society.[19] At mid-century, in a leading article about the alarming increase of murder by women, the *Weekly Chronicle* expressed concern that 'the decencies of life and social purity once violated, the most disastrous and calamitous results may follow.[20] The police and the courts provided the press with evidence of these results.

The simple truth is that at a time when the sociological reper-
cussions of the Industrial Revolution included independence for
women, men were obsessed with the need to keep society a patri-
archy. Which of them would not have wanted to live with Virginia
Woolf's Angel in the House?

> She was intensely sympathetic. She was immensely charming. She
> was utterly unselfish. She excelled in the difficult arts of family life.
> She sacrificed herself daily. If there was chicken, she took the leg; if
> there was a draught she sat in it – in short she was so constituted
> that she never had a mind or a wish of her own, but preferred to
> sympathize always with the minds and wishes of others.[21]

Behind the righteous indignation of educated, articulate men
there must have lurked a fear that the angel was a figment of their
imagination who might disappear at any moment – that women of
their own class, as their social equals, might subvert their power.
Piety, selflessness, domesticity, virtue, and submission were only
male fantasies imposed by the establishment, preached by the
Church, documented by artists and writers, and even achieved by
some in everyday life.

TEN

The Feminine Perspective

It stands to reason that, if murder by women is to be properly reassessed, it must be done from a feminine perspective. Until the 1880s murder by women was detected, reported, and judged by men, who, reacting to cultural and emotional conditioning, had trouble seeing them as human. Once women threw off the patriarchal standards that had been imposed on them and took up their own causes, with their own point of view, they looked for and found different things in the justice system from what men had.

Female spectators were always a part of the spectacle in murder trials, though, on the whole, the establishment took a dim view of their move from the domestic to the public sphere. Both judges and newspaper reporters remarked on their presence in any numbers, always disapproved of at executions but condoned at trials. The *Times* noted the presence on the first day of the Edmunds trial of 'many persons of consideration, including ladies.' The *Observer* seemed almost disappointed that, on the first day of the Manning trial, there were relatively few women in attendance.

> Though the court was densely crowded there were not more than about 20 women present – a number infinitely below the average of the fair worshippers of the 'horrible,' who in past times have been wont to fill the courts of justice when any noted criminals have been put upon their trial. The Lady Mayoress, Mrs. (Alderman) Lawrence, Mrs. Sergeant Wilkins and Mrs. Dennistoun were the only celebrities among the softer sex on this occasion. At the trial of Courvoisier

fully one-half of those present were fashionably attired individuals of the same gender.[1]

The Bartlett, Maybrick, and Pearcey trials attracted large numbers of women, who followed the proceedings closely. No longer were they content to have events that concerned them filtered through male biases. They inferred from his hasty retreat that Adelaide Bartlett, as well as her husband, had been exploited by their minister, who wanted nothing to do with her once their affair was made public. They inferred from the evidence against her given by neighbours, servants, and her brothers-in-law, that Florence Maybrick had been too trusting in a sinister household. They inferred from the love-letters published in the newspapers that Eleanor Pearcey had pulled the real world down around her ears once she could not control it with her imagination. And they must have sensed that the justice system did not take account of such circumstances.

In the 1880s women made significant inroads into the outside world, substantially broadening their educational and professional opportunities, and in the process gaining support in their struggle for a fair deal. They followed trials and commented on verdicts. They applied pressure when they felt that justice had not been done. Some were bold enough to mock rather than attack the establishment. In a letter to the editor of the Liverpool *Daily Post* after the verdict against Maybrick, one exasperated woman explained the behaviour of the jury thus: 'Husbands must be protected from adulterous and murderous wives, and they [the jury] gave their judgment accordingly.'[2]

In discussing this case, Mary Hartman comments on the 'most remarkable ... emergence of women ... inside and outside the courtroom, from their previously subdued roles to new articulate and active ones.'[3] They crowded the courtroom, flooded the papers with letters, circulated petitions, and in general made known their dissatisfaction with the double standard. Maybrick noted in her prison memoir that, after the verdict, as she was being driven back to jail, she was cheered; on the first day of her trial, as she entered the court, she had been hissed.[4] Presumably the change was a result of women's hearing at first hand just how likely it was that she was a killer.

Bartlett and Maybrick were, to some extent, tried for sexual impropriety, even though the charge was murder. Bartlett had a brilliant lawyer who played on the judge's chivalry, but Maybrick's lawyer could not manipulate the judge. Both these women were able to persuade most people that, though they were unconventional, they drew the line at murder. They were subjected to intense scrutiny by the newspapers, and in this they doubtless fed a public craving for sex by sublimation, but they appeared in the press to be more sinned against than sinning.

The women at their trials brazenly challenged the conventional male culture of the courtroom. They were much in evidence at women's murder trials, despite being told repeatedly that they did not belong. Clearly women like this did not have to be protected from references to birth-control devices, adultery, and so on. Their obvious presence eventually affected press coverage of trials: in the 1880s the popular press catered to readers who wanted to know about the humanity of the prisoner under scrutiny. In the 'naughty nineties' some papers gleefully covered divorce and promiscuity. Female sexuality was, by the end of the century, unremarkable in a courtroom, and far less incriminating than it ever had been.

ADELAIDE BARTLETT

Adelaide Bartlett's trial at the Old Bailey attracted more female than male spectators. So great was the anticipated demand for seats that a stand was added and tickets were issued. 'It is an unfortunate circumstance that in narrating its progress one has primarily to regard it as a show – a carnival time for City matrons and damsels, and in a much smaller proportion, for City men,' complained the *Daily News*.[5] The *Times* observed that, on every one of the six days of the trial, the building was filled with 'a preponderating number of women.'[6] When the *Pall Mall Gazette* remarked on how odd it was that women would crowd a criminal court just to see another of their sex in a painful position, despite the 'delicate details' of the case,[7] the *Evening News*, in a thinly veiled reference to the 'Maiden Tribute of Modern Babylon' exposé of the previous year, chided W.T. Stead's paper for its false modesty and squeamishness. (Stead went to prison for having 'bought' a young girl for immoral purposes in an effort to mobilize public opinion against the practice of selling children into prostitution.) 'Perhaps, when our contemporary has purged itself,' said the *News*, 'it will have a better right to fling stones at women who only go to a sensational trial.'[8]

The judge, Sir Alfred Wills, also disapproved of women's attendance at a trial so open about sex. They were, he said in his summing up, exposing themselves to details that were 'distasteful and disgusting.' In the *Times*'s view, the judge

> spoke strongly, but not at all more strongly than the occasion warranted. There is some excuse when the audience of both sexes consists of the witnesses in other cases, who must either sit in Court, or hang about dismal corridors and anterooms; and such is occasionally the explanation of the presence of women in Courts when they seem out of place. But this explanation does not account for all the facts at which Mr. Justice Wills glances. It is, perhaps, useless making rules as to a matter which should be governed by good feeling. But plain words on this subject will do no harm, and if other Judges took occasion to speak to the same effect as Mr. Justice Wills proceedings in Courts would not so often be made the means of gratifying an idle or prurient curiosity.[9]

The women's response was to laugh at the judge's prudery. They were not in need of protection. At least some of them already knew about the ease with which Stead had 'bought' a thirteen-year-old virgin to do with as he wished, and had read his description, later claimed to be mere fantasy, of her defloration. Some were members of Josephine Butler's Ladies' Associations, which had pressed for the repeal of legislation providing for the compulsory medical examination of any woman suspected of being a prostitute.[10] From the 1870s female activists had been advocating a more sympathetic attitude towards female criminals.[11] Now they were beginning to campaign for higher education, broadened career opportunities, and suffrage. They were loosely organized but highly visible. As John Glendening suggests, their presence assisted Bartlett in two ways: by contrast with them, she appeared sensitive and genteel; and, whatever their motives, they not only supported but celebrated her as someone who had escaped male exploitation.[12]

Meanwhile, her lawyer, Edward Clarke, manipulated the system by presenting Bartlett as defenceless and dependent. He told the judge and the jury, which of course was all male, that she had had but one friend, her deceased husband, and that it was now open to them to take his place.[13]

When the jury obliged with a verdict of not guilty, the crowd outside cheered and the spectators in the courtroom, to the judge's consternation, applauded.

FLORENCE MAYBRICK

The system was much more sympathetic to Bartlett than was the general public. Quite the reverse lot fell to Maybrick, who had the bad luck to draw a judge who seems in hindsight to have been mentally ill.[14]

At first the papers were not on her side, though many were won over later by her frankness and gentleness. Spectators at the preliminary hearing groaned and hissed when a waiter at a London hotel testified that she had slept in the same room as a man who was not her husband.[15] The *Evening News* accused her – falsely, as it turned out, of being pregnant by this man.

In his charge to the jury *before* the trial started, Sir James Fitzjames Stephen indicated that, if Maybrick proved to be an adulteress, she was probably also a murderess. 'I hardly know how to put it otherwise than this,' he said,

> that, if a woman does carry on an adulterous intrigue with another
> man, it may supply every sort of motive – that of saving her own
> reputation; that of breaking through the connection which, under

the circumstances, one would think would be dreadfully painful to the party to it. It certainly may quite supply – I won't go further – a very strong motive why she should wish to get rid of her husband.[16]

In his final charge, he reminded the jury that she had indeed proved to be an adulteress. 'Nothing can exceed the strictures of Judge Stephen's language in condemning the lady's infidelity to her husband,' wrote Butler, registering 'surprise that such strong expressions should be reiterated *ad nauseam* when dealing with a woman, while they are not made use of at all in the case of men of high rank, who have been notoriously unfaithful to their wives.'[17]

The jury found her guilty, but the press, by and large, did not agree. A flood of letters to the editor and several petitions (one from a group of doctors assessing the medical evidence, and another from a group of lawyers assessing procedure) insisted that there was a reasonable doubt as to the condemned woman's guilt. One man was so incensed that he offered to take her place on the scaffold.[18]

In a front-page editorial on the verdict, the *Star* asked 'the great jury'

whether the case has been proved against the unhappy woman so completely as to leave no room for even the smallest doubt in the mind of any rational man. How can any man seriously contend that there is no room for such doubt in face of the enormous number of people who are still in doubt? The editors of newspapers – and they are a body of intelligent men, accustomed to scrutinise severely evidence in such cases as this – are in doubt; the people who were in the court and heard all the evidence are in doubt, for the verdict came upon them with the shock of a terrible surprise. And there is another body of still more expert opinion to whom the case presents terrible and grave difficulties ... Above and beyond all that, there is that huge mass – the opinion outside, the opinion of the people at large who have sufficiently indicated their feelings – some with the solemnity and decorum which the terrible issues suggest, others in that rough and ready but not wholly uneloquent fashion in which the strong common sense, the generous emotions, and the keen human sympathy of the common people, manifest themselves.[19]

Maybrick needed all the help she could get, and the papers gave it to her. From the outset, though she was a young, good-looking, apparently loose woman, reporters were kind and fair to her – perhaps because she was also rich, but more likely because she was brave and seemed, in the American way described at the time by Henry James, open and well-meaning.[20] Unlike her predecessors on Death Row, she was seen as a normal human being, not a freak.

Coverage of the trial bore very few descriptions of her body. *Lloyd's Weekly Newspaper*, which fed its readers a steady diet of crime scandals, was restrained and admiring:

Mrs Maybrick walked alone, with a light and easy gait and perfect steadiness of manner. She was attired in deep widow's mourning – a crape bonnet with streamers behind, crape jacket with open short sleeves, and white cuffs. She also wore black gloves. She had on a black veil; but this was quite thin in texture, and in no way obscured her features. Observers pronounced her to be a woman of exceedingly attractive appearance – slight, graceful, and neat in figure, and in profile at least more than passably pretty. She hardly looked her age, which was given as 28. Her complexion was light, her hair 'frizzed,' and her features small and regular.[21]

At the end of the trial the *Star* reported: 'When the foreman of the jury made his terrible deliverance Mrs. Maybrick seemed thunderstruck. She gasped for breath, and bent her head in her hands. Her face had the pall of death; her eyes were wild and unearthly, and never a tear came to relieve them.'[22]

After she heard the verdict, said the *Daily News*, she

rose to her feet. The wonderful nerve that she has shown all through the trial came once more to her aid. She stood at the front of the dock, and with her hands clasping the rail she held herself erect, and drew her head well up. Looking steadily at the judge, she essayed to speak, but at first the words would not come ... her voice gathered power and her demeanour acquired afresh the air of dignity which has so often been remarked in her.

As the judge beseeched the Lord to have mercy on her soul,

the prisoner, her head by this time bowed upon her hands, stood clinging to the dock rail. At a motion from the principal gaoler standing behind, the female attendant, who had been with her throughout the trial, touched her softly upon the arm. The prisoner raised her head and turned. The female warders, one on each side, gently assisted her to walk, but their aid was soon not required. After a couple of steps Mrs. Maybrick's fortitude returned.[23]

The tone here is gentle, the attitude sympathetic. The writer is clearly distressed to see the woman destroyed. This degree of consideration by the press of a convicted murderess was unprecedented.

The sympathy for Maybrick's position did not extend to the top echelon of many newspapers. Middle-class women agitated against the double standard, but many men of class and position, among them newspaper proprietors, were attached to it.

The response to this case reflects the influence that women were having on social reform, particularly in their questioning of the institution of marriage. The question 'Is Marriage a Failure?' had first been raised in August 1888 in a magazine article by Mona Caird, who believed that marriage should be a partnership of equals. For weeks the *Daily Telegraph* carried a spirited dialogue from 27,000 letters it had received on the subject.[24] The subject was revived in the summer of 1889 by a run of *A Doll's House* in London.

There were rumours – valid ones – that the dead man, who had beaten his wife for her infidelity, had been keeping a mistress, and had even had a child by her. The *Star* said of the Maybrick marriage:

In accord with a public opinion which to us appears a relic of the savage degradation of the rights of woman to a lower level than those of man, he married, when elderly, and ill, and gloomy, a young woman in all the freshness, the lightheartedness, the eager joyousness of girlhood, and especially of American girlhood. It requires the greatest virtues of unselfishness, loftiness and purity to make such a match anything but a failure ...[25]

The case was used by more than one writer to attack women's emancipation. In the Maybrick controversy the *Spectator* discerned

something of a claim for women of the right to observe or disregard the obligations of marriage at their own pleasure ... There seems to be at the present time a sort of partisanship for unfaithful wives, which has long disappeared, if it ever existed in precisely the same form, for unfaithful husbands. Doubtless there was a time when libertinism was regarded almost as a sort of distinction in a man. But we cannot remember that there ever was a tide of the sentimental sympathy and admiration for it which seems to have been felt towards Mrs. Maybrick.[26]

The *Standard* derided 'sentimental ladies who were prepared with bouquets of flowers for the self-confessed adulteress and possible murderess.'[27] A street ballad warned wives not to flirt with other men:

When once you start like Mrs. Maybrick perhaps you couldn't stop,
So stick close to your husband and keep clear of Berry's drop.[28]

In the view of the Liverpool *Courier*, the sentence was 'a warning to women who have severed themselves from women's attributes that they cannot henceforth hope to enjoy immunity from the just consequences.'[29] But most people could not in all conscience endorse such a warning. It was the first time that public opinion gave an accused murderess the benefit of the doubt. Her lover, Alfred Brierly, was seen as the villain, his paramour as the victim. 'Popular feeling is incensed against the man who seduced Mrs. Maybrick from the path of duty and rectitude and honour, and dragged her down to a position of degradation and shame,' said the Liverpool *Post.*

> For men who, for the mere gratification of their own brutal in-
> stincts and passions, thus wreck homes and ruin reputations no
> sympathy is possible. They are legitimate objects of popular con-
> tempt and reprobation, and the public conscience revolts against
> their going scot-free while their victims have to bear the full burden
> of their guilt and sin.[30]

Maybrick's predicament was also used to point up the need for
legal reform. *Truth,* which endorsed the verdict, noted disapprovingly that people were asking how many of the jury were married
men and why women couldn't serve on juries.[31] It was also felt that
an appeals court rather than the monarch or her representative
should be reviewing controversial decisions. A London correspondent for the Toronto *Globe* explained 'the conquest of England by
the American young woman' thus:

> Pretty women have languished under the shadow of the noose here
> before and have gone to their doom in dozens, but the oldest in-
> habitant does not remember any case which has created a tithe of
> the commotion in the public mind that now exists over this young,
> bright, attractive American widow ... What it all means is that the
> interesting personality of the condemned woman has acted as a
> spark to ignite a long accumulating store of combustible material.
> The state of the English law practice in murder cases is simply
> shocking ... Here there is no appeal from a capital conviction.[32]

Even those who believed Florence Maybrick to be guilty did not
want her to hang. A letter to the editor of the *St. James's Gazette*
insisted that the public outcry was due not to the impropriety of
the verdict but to the public sentiment that almost unanimously
'revolts from the idea' of executing a woman for any crime, especially 'a young lady like the one just condemned ... '[33] A leader in
the *Times* referred to 'the large number of people who shrink

from contemplating the death of an attractive and outwardly re-
fined woman upon the scaffold.'[34]

The *St. Stephen's Review*, a fashionable weekly, found it incon-
ceivable

> that men outside a lunatic asylum should declare that the case did
> not admit of reasonable doubt ... We can only account for the
> conduct of the Maybrick jury by supposing them to resemble a man
> we encountered the other day in an omnibus. He was holding forth
> on the vexed question, and he gave vent to the following opinion: –
> 'What I say is this, whether she poisoned 'im or not, 'ang 'er!' ...
> Men of this kind look upon Mrs. Maybrick's admitted offence as
> something it is their duty to society to stamp out ... Mrs. Maybrick
> has been sacrificed to the prejudices of hypocritical morality, and to
> the apprehension that husband-poisoning would be extensively prac-
> tised if not at once nipped in the bud.[35]

But the public would no longer subscribe to the notion that
husbands ought to be preserved at all costs, even if now and then
an innocent woman was hanged.

ELEANOR PEARCEY

It was one thing for a woman who might or might not have killed
a domineering, unfaithful, abusive husband to galvanize public
opinion against the justice system, but quite another for someone
obviously guilty of the murder of her lover's wife and child to
inspire compassion. 'The public mind has been excited in no
small degree by the whole story,' said the *Times*, 'a tragedy of low
life of singular completeness and horror.'[36] Not everyone who
followed the case felt pity for Eleanor Pearcey, but the *News of the
World* expressed surprise at the 'sympathetic interest taken by such a
large number of the fairer sex ... It is to be feared,' said this paper,
'that many women whose training and social surroundings should
teach them better regard such cases much in the same way as they
would a sensational drama at the theatre ...'[37] Gibbons, Bartlett,

and Maybrick were of their class; Pearcey, though highly literate, was poor and dissolute. Yet, according to the *Pall Mall Gazette*,

> no sense of decency restrained them; no amount of personal discomfort kept them outside the doors of the grim forum. Wives came with their husbands, brothers brought the female members of their families, mothers sat side by side with their young daughters. Hour after hour did these ghoulish women, armed with opera-glasses, sherry-flasks, and sandwich-boxes, hang with eager curiosity upon every movement and look of their miserable sister, whose fate was so firmly fixed from the outset. To the end they stayed; for the solemn closing scene had special attractions for them. These women were not the wives and daughters of labourers and costermongers, but ladies of gentle birth and no inconsiderable position.[38]

'We would gladly publish the name of every woman who disgraced her sex by rushing to that wretched sight as if it were the finest kind of raree show,' fumed the *Evening News*.[39]

It is impossible to know what proportion of them came for sensual gratification and what proportion for political reasons. But it is undeniable that women's presence at sensational trials served to call attention to biases against them in the justice system, and that men, through the press, continued to resist their incursion into the courtroom. No longer could criminal women be displayed as curiosities and punished as a purgative exercise for the rest of society, their bodies stretched and squeezed metaphorically by the press, and then literally by the hangman.

By 1890 newspaper accounts acknowledged women as part of their readership. They did not spare the gruesome details that sold papers, but physical analysis gave way to psychological analysis. 'Evidently she is a woman of small brain and imperfect education,' said the *Echo* disapprovingly of Pearcey, 'but with strong animal passions, who was in the habit of drugging herself with cheap and pernicious sensational literature.'[40]

Hardy was in London at the end of the trial and remarked in a letter to his wife on the extent of the newspaper coverage. His biographer Michael Millgate speculates that he may have been 'so deeply affected by what he heard of the case that it became an integral part of the imaginative and emotional context of his most socially conscious novel,' *Jude the Obscure*.[41]

'What young girl who has seen Mrs. Pearcey in the dock, and listened to the horrible story ... from the lips of those directly connected with it,' asked the *Evening News*, 'can be expected to feel an interest in the pasteboard and tinsel of stage tragedy? Here was a real breathing, quivering woman sitting before them ..., listening to the bald story of her own shame ...'[42] Inferring the thought processes behind the actions that led to the murder, the same paper later theorized that the murder was committed out of sudden rage rather than simmering jealousy.[43]

What was Mrs Pearcey's real name? Had she wanted to marry Frank Hogg? Was she protecting an accomplice? What had provoked the attack? Was Hogg worth all the attention that she had given him? What was she feeling? The *Illustrated Police News* observed:

> Not once throughout the hearing of nearly four hours did she betray her feelings by succumbing to emotion, but frequently a slight twitching of the mouth was observed as the more repulsive portions of the evidence were given. For the most part she listened with unabated attention to the testimony of the numerous witnesses, and her blue eyes were directed with almost reproachful tenderness towards those whose acquaintance she had enjoyed for many years.[44]

At the beginning of the affair, the *Evening News* observed somewhat salaciously that spectators in police court

> must have been struck by her appearance, for she is a young, good-looking, and well-made woman. And this was patent in view of an exceedingly ungraceful attire, for all her own [blood-stained] clothes have been taken from her, and she was forced to appear to-day in workhouse garb. This consisted of a faded alpaca dress and bodice, and a shawl and hat of a dark green colour. Still more striking was

her appearance while the evidence was being given. She did not seem to be listening to, indeed, to be hearing, anything that was taking place.[45]

By the time she came to trial, her appearance was of less concern to this paper:

She was dressed precisely as on former occasions, in the hat which is incontestably green and the black mantle which is unmistakably of the dolman order of sartorial architecture. A slight nervousness, shyness almost, was evident in her bearing as she walked to the dock, glancing furtively at the crowd ..., but once settled in the dock ... she speedily subsided into her normal state of gentle placidity ...[46]

And again: 'She was dressed as on former occasions, and looked considerably more alert and cheerful than during her previous appearances in this court.'[47] Perhaps for the benefit of a female audience, her paramour was described in much greater detail, and far more critically:

Mr. Hogg recovered from the condition of near imbecility which was his distinctive characteristic in the earlier stages of the case, and with a face unblotched by tears, is seen to be a rather unpleasant-looking man. His features are good enough, but the eyes are set close together and furtive in expression, and the grey, sandy, arid look produced by a uniformity of dingy yellowish-brown in beard and complexion and hair is decidedly against his claims to good looks. There is a want of manly dignity in his carriage and aspect which impresses one unfavourably, and he does not look over-clever. Once during the afternoon he smiled a sickly, thin smile, which exaggerated the weakness of his face.[48]

In the coverage of this case can be found evidence of a subtle change in the construction of female criminality. There was very little of the double standard in the trial of Eleanor Pearcey. After delivering the verdict, the judge did lecture her for 'giving way to prurient and indecent lust,' but the same would have applied had Frank Hogg stood in her place. At some level, despite her savage conduct, middle-class women identified with her. In allying themselves with a fallen woman, they were not only doing their duty to the less fortunate members of society, but also acknowledging the potential for darkness in their own souls.

ELEVEN

The Body of the Murderess

THE DOUBLE STANDARD

It was widely believed that, though women were by nature morally superior to men, those who were 'unnatural' – violent – were much more of a menace than the same sort of men. The murder of Constance Kent's little brother was characterized by one paper as 'the revengeful act of a woman – morbid, cruel, cunning – one in whom the worst of passions has received a preternatural development, overpowering and absorbing the little good that she ever had in her nature.'[1]

'History teaches us that the female is capable of reaching higher in point of virtue than the male,' George Manning's lawyer argued, 'but that when she gives way to vice she sinks far lower than our sex.' In the words of Elizabeth Windschuttle, 'the double standard prescribed different attitudes toward male and female criminals. Men could commit crime, but be reformed. If women committed crime, they were destroyed utterly. They were irreclaimable.'[2] This theory provided another convenient justification for the enthusiastic punishment of women.

Female criminals were for years thought of as subhuman, less controllable and predictable than male criminals because they were predisposed by their reproductive function to animal-like behaviour. Henry Mayhew and John Binney, who collaborated on a study of London prisons in 1862, believed that the behaviour they saw in prisons was 'the *true* female nature,' rather than 'the *disguised* and *polite* form of it' that the rest of society saw.[3] Women in prison were seen as thoroughly and irredeemably depraved. Murderers were bad, but murderesses were worse.

BODY PARTS

Part of a transgressive woman's punishment was public scrutiny. When she was accused of a crime outside the norm for her sex (infanticide, theft, or prostitution), the justice system put her body on show. What Helena Michie has called the 'culturally selected parts of the female body ... to stand for unnameable body parts' implied the rest.[4] The way an accused murderess wore her hair, the movements she made with her hands, the tint of her complexion, the focus of her eyes, the thickness of her lips, the firmness of her step, the construction of her frame (robust or delicate, depending on her class) – all these were described and commented on in the newspapers. The breasts, the legs, the ankles were never mentioned, but crime reporting used synecdoche to summon up the whole figure. Wherever it was in evidence, femininity was dissected and displayed by the press.

What men accused of murder wore to court was not dwelt on. Rachel Short found that description of men's appearance in early-nineteenth-century English broadsides and newspaper accounts was rare: it was far more likely that reference would be made to a man's past experience and lifestyle. Female criminals received different scrutiny from the press. Once they had described her crime, reports concentrated on a woman's appearance, social status, and behaviour in court. Short also noticed that there was more interest in a woman's response once she had been caught.[5] These tendencies to gender bias in the press only intensified as the century progressed.

For example, the *Standard* noted approvingly the fur-trimmed black velvet jacket and 'fashionably plaited chignon' that Christiana Edmunds wore to her trial.[6] The *Telegraph*, which specialized in colour stories about major trials, described her as slight and olive-complected, with a high narrow forehead, hazel eyes, soft, fair brown hair, the upper part of her face 'certainly not wanting in feminine charm,' but the effect marred by full, thick lips and 'a somewhat heavy and protruding jaw.' Her thickly braided 'coronet' of hair seemed to this paper 'a fashion now long out of date.' Her hands were small, tightly gloved, and folded across her knees[7] – an appropriate posture, twentieth-century psychology would say, for a middle-aged spinster said to be suffering from repressed sexual urges. But this was 1872.

When it was time to pronounce the death sentence, the judge shrank momentarily from using his power over a frail, vulnerable creature who was clearly out of her mind and in need of protection. According to the *Times*, he 'was much overcome with emotion, and at the dreadful words "hanged by the neck till your body be dead" he broke down and hid his face, during a pause when a pin might have been heard to drop.'[8] Something about her plight was projected onto the judge: it was as though her impending death would destabilize *him*.

Here is firm evidence of the irrational fear that men felt in the face of female volatility. Perhaps if women like Edmunds did not see their secure, established world, it did not exist.

In psychoanalytic terms, in the words of Elisabeth Bronfen, 'femininity and death inspire the fear of an ultimate loss of control, of a disruption of boundaries between self and Other, of a dissolution of an ordered and hierarchical world.'[9] Bronfen contrasts 'masculine order, where self-identity depends on accepting a set of codes, whose laws must be clearly defined and preserved, and a feminine disruption and transgression of such an order.'[10]

Edmunds appears to have picked up the cue that her sexuality could save her from death. Asked at this point whether she had anything to say for herself, she announced (falsely) that she was pregnant. The *Daily Telegraph* observed that at this point 'her eyes flashed with a sort of defiant look, and ... her hands were tightly grasped.'[11]

This form of reporting savours the feminine body, which is about to be ravished by the hangman, by analysing its outward composition. As Mary Poovey has pointed out, around the middle of the nineteenth century it was accepted that women's dependence on men was attributable not so much to their 'fallen nature' as to their biological difference.[12] Poovey mentions this belief in discussing a debate among medical men about anaesthesia; the emphasis on physiology in crime reporting is even more odd, as if the one measure were being used to confirm the other. If we consider that, in the courtroom, murderesses were defined both ways, as sex objects and as fallen, we can see why they were overpunished.

FEMININITY

Accused murderesses were represented in the press as what Lyn Pykett calls 'proper' or 'improper' feminine, the improper variety being unrestrained, immoral, and energetic.[13] This phenomenon is evident as early as 1815, when some newspapers uncharitably construed as carnal Eliza Fenning's bond of compassion with a man whose execution was scheduled for the same time as hers.

Defiance in a 'proper' female like the ladylike Edmunds would have been out of place, but, by the same token, an 'improper' female could be criticized for 'proper' characteristics, as in this description from the Somerset County *Herald* of Sarah Freeman, who, it complained, was

> possessed with excessive vanity in reference to her personal appearance. She was a stout built woman, nearly five feet in height, and of particularly repulsive countenance – her eyes were very prominent, and, when she was excited, most remarkable for malignity of expression. Previous to her trial she was very particular in getting up her dress, but it will hardly be believed that on Friday last she made herself a cap to appear in on the morning of her execution, saying to one of the matrons, 'I am not going up there (alluding to the gallows) a perfect fright.'[14]

In a similar way, the fiery Maria Manning's meticulous grooming set tongues wagging, though she appears to have been admired for it. And Mary Ann Burdock's thrift made people uncomfortable: it was reported that, on his farewell visit, she firmly instructed her brother to tax her solicitor's bill and get her 'a good, strong coffin, but mind, you are not to give more than two pounds for it ... It must be full-sized, and let it be lined with flannel.'[15]

This was said as she reviewed what money had been left for her children. A 'proper' witch figure would not jeopardize her comfort in the next world to assure her children's comfort in this one. All the publicity about Burdock had dehumanized her. She had been depicted as cold, callous, and grasping. Could such a person be maternal?

The Manning case provided a prime opportunity for the establishment to set down a definition of proper and improper behaviour of male and female criminals.[16] At the time of her arrest, the *Observer* judged her 'utter absence of any ... depression' to be a mark of 'very masculine character.'[17] The *Morning Chronicle* later referred to 'the more than masculine violence of her character.'[18] Frederick's lawyer urged the jury to discount 'those urbanities of life which clothe the female with obedience and the male with the domination of power and strength.' He argued that Maria was the brains behind the murder, and that her husband had been imprudently chivalrous in assisting her to avoid discovery. Maria's lawyer asked the jury to believe 'that this woman did not forget her sex, and do that which few women were recorded to have done – commit a cold-blooded and atrocious murder ...'

The *Times*, explaining why the press was far more interested in the wife than the husband, noted that she died 'exhibiting an amount of courage and nerve which contrasted strangely with the terror-stricken aspect of her husband. There has been a diabolical energy of character displayed by her throughout, which has attracted to her conduct a still larger share of public attention than to that of Manning.'[19]

On the same subject, the *Chronicle* said:

If we turn away from the male criminal with sensations of loathing and disgust, we cannot gaze upon the woman without the deeper emotions of execration and horror. The murderess of her paramour, she has also – if her partner in guilt has not left the world with a lie on his lips – been, as far as in her lay, the murderess of her husband too. If, as his tale – corroborated in no small degree by the more than masculine violence of her character – would lead us to believe, she, and not he, was the actual assassin, she must have deemed it at least within the range of possibility that a full confession from her might save his life.[20]

Viewed thus, her energy, courage, and nerve were masculine, her refusal to subordinate her own survival to that of her husband unfeminine, and his cowardice unmasculine.

The *Chronicle* maintained that in committing murder Maria had 'sold her body to the hangman and her soul to the Powers of Darkness.'[21] If so, the hangman handed it over to the newspapers for a post-mortem. Newspaper reports of the most sensational trials constituted a nagging reminder that femaleness and criminality were not mutually exclusive, and signalled an effort to define the mix by detailed description.

Early in the century the bodies of hanged criminals were donated for dissection. Later the dissection took place metaphorically, *before* the execution. The discourse on what constituted femininity appears to have been a reflection of society's unsatisfied appetites and a sublimation for sexual activity. When the mysterious Maria first appeared at police court, said the *News of the World*, 'All eyes were directed to the door through which she was to enter, and as she appeared in the distance, cries of "Silence," "Hush," "Here she is," escaped from the lips of many in an under tone. She walked forward firmly, and took her place in the dock without showing the slightest tremor or want of self-possession.'[22] Would any normal woman have had the decency to show her fright? Boldness was thought of as a 'masculine' quality.

Summing her up, the *Herald* told readers:

She is a woman about five feet seven in height, rather stout made, and rather good-looking, but not by any means what might be termed a handsome woman. She wore a tight straw bonnet and white lace veil, the latter of which partly concealed her features on her first entrance; but on taking her position in front of the bar, she threw back her veil, and exhibited her whole countenance, which at first was extremely pale, but soon assumed a flush which improved her appearance ...'[23]

The description of the white veil and tight bonnet shading a ruddy countenance suggests latent sexuality, passion that could not be confined.

Maria's wardrobe was much discussed. 'There is no foundation for the report that ... Maria Manning was occupied in the jail in preparing a dress in which to appear in Court,' said the *Globe*. What had happened was that she had asked for more clothing from a trunk confiscated by police when she was arrested.[24] It was reported that, on the first day of the trial, Frederick Manning wore a black suit and black neckerchief. His wife wore a black dress, plaid shawl of subdued colours, and stylish cap 'with an extraordinary profusion of lappets [ribbons], fastened tightly under the chin, the extremities of which were richly laced and frilled, hanging down to the waist.'[25] On the second (and final) day, she wore a black satin dress, a plaid silk shawl, a cap with black and yellow embroidered ribbons, and kid gloves. There is no mention in the papers of what her husband wore that day, merely the intelligence that they 'took their position in the dock as far apart from each other as possible.'[26]

The persistent association between female guilt and female sexuality, which is at least as old as the story of Eve, was fed in the late Victorian period by science, which, for example, asserted that the most important bone structure in a woman was the pelvis, while in a man it was the skull. There seems to have been a direct connection between these two in the case of Elizabeth Berry, whose head, according to a Scottish phrenologist working from a photograph, revealed, among a mass of other undesirable qualities, excessive 'amativeness' but little 'conjugality.'[27]

THEORIES OF FEMALE CRIMINALITY

Carol Smart shows in *Women, Crime, and Criminology* that as recently as 1950 women's criminality was explained as a function of their bodies. Otto Pollak, in *The Criminality of Women*, thought that

women learned to be devious first in their monthly efforts to conceal their menstrual periods from the world, and later in feigning
orgasms. Another way of putting this would be to say that men
have always been insecure in the realization that they have no way
of assessing their power in sexual relationships.

Pollak describes female crime as being biologically determined.
It is true that deaths from poisoning and infanticide, traditionally
female crimes, were easily concealed, but it does not follow that
women are at the mercy of their reproductive organs. Yet, for a
hundred years, experts had been arguing that the animal nature
of women was at the root of female crime. Around the middle of
the nineteenth century, criminology had moved from moral to
biological explanations of deviant behaviour, reasoning that, as
women matured, the onset of menses, childbirth, and menopause
could prompt criminal activity.[28]

In 1865, Alfred Swaine Taylor, in *The Principles and Practice of
Medical Jurisprudence*, noted that disordered or suppressed menstruation, childbirth, or lactation, 'owing to sympathy of the brain
with the uterus,' could be causes of homicidal monomania. This
condition, first described by J.E.D. Esquirol,[29] was thought to be a
state of partial insanity in which an uncontrollable destructive impulse could motivate someone to kill a loved one. According to
Taylor, the disorder could strike not only people exhibiting depression or irritability, but 'those who have been remarkable for
their kind and gentle demeanour and quiet habits' – in other
words, women.

These explanations of the mysteries of female reproductive power
are all valid to a point, but they hardly lead to the expectation that
women will be driven to extreme remedies by their bodies. They
do tell us why newspaper reports harped on female sexuality, and
why the death sentences of some murderesses were commuted.

Though there was a suspicion that the lack of a sexual outlet
had driven Christiana Edmunds mad, a more logical reason was
the heredity of madness acknowledged by the home secretary and
mocked by the *Spectator*: three members of her immediate family
had had mental problems. The *Lancet* asserted that the combination of these factors practically guaranteed madness:

If there be one thing certainly proved in mental medicine, it is this
– that for any woman, belonging to a family which (like that of the
Edmunds's) was a prey to insanity and other nervous diseases, and
living an involuntarily single life while struggling with hysteria and
suppressed sexual feeling, it would be almost *impossible* to go on to
the critical age of forty-three without actual derangement of mind.[30]

Constance Kent's deceased mother had been insane. But in
excusing her, the *Times* argued merely that it was normal for ado-
lescent girls to go through 'a period of almost utter heartlessness'
in which the line between fantasy and reality was blurred: 'Constance
Kent, it is said, only did what myriads of her age and sex only wish
should come to pass by other agency than their own, and cared as
little for what she had done as they for the spontaneous event.'[31]

The implication that women's sanity depended on their bodies
made it easier to regard all women as on the edge of criminality. For those to whom this rationale did not appeal, two late-
nineteenth-century criminologists, Cesare Lombroso and William
Ferrero (*The Female Offender*, 1895), provided the reverse biological
explanation: the female criminal was acting against nature, which
intended her to be gentle and nurturing.

This was hardly a new theory, and indeed was behind the vicious attitude to female poisoners in the middle of the century.
The public simply attempted to dissociate from their treachery by
deeming it inhuman. If murderesses were not human, not only
was the rest of humanity not indicted by their behaviour, but they
were prime candidates for inhuman punishment.

TWELVE

The Murder of the Murderess

Until the end of public executions in England in 1868, men and women of all classes avidly devoured stories about women who killed, delighted in their trials, and came from far and near to see them hanged. If the hanging body was a message to society that disorder could result in death to the body politic,[1] the hanging female body carried even stronger overtones. Destructive forces would be eliminated. Passion, sexuality, and volatility were short-lived.

There were fewer executions after 1838, when the death penalty no longer applied to theft and fraud, and there is no reason to doubt Thomas Laqueur's finding that they were a bigger draw than before: 'Railways, better publicity and public hunger born of rarity made nineteenth-century hangings far larger and more boisterous occasions than their earlier counterparts ... The crowd, and particularly the carnivalesque crowd, was the central actor in English executions.[2]

The ritual of the carnival, in which the world is turned upside down, gave both sexes a holiday from the conventions that ordinarily restricted them. It would not have been possible for people to enjoy the suffering of someone they could relate to, but once they imagined a condemned murderess removed from the realm of humanity, they were free to celebrate.

The most interest was aroused by young women brimming over with passion, like Sarah Thomas or Maria Manning. This is not surprising, given the traditional linkage of sexuality and death.[3] There was always a strong female contingent at the hanging of a young woman, perhaps because it was titillating to see someone called to account for giving in to temptations one might have had oneself.

In 1849 the *Globe* had devoted an entire editorial to deploring the attendance of 'a respectable and honest woman' at the execution of Rebecca Smith in Wiltshire. The woman had had her pocket picked at a pub to which other members of the crowd had also repaired afterwards. 'The evident carelessness and lightness with which she beheld the extreme penalty of the law carried out in the person of one of her own sex, are both surprising and repulsive,' said the *Globe*. 'The imagination can scarcely realize, in the form of a woman, such indifference to another's suffering.'[4]

Hanging was a cruel end to any life, as V.A.C. Gatrell argues in *The Hanging Tree*, but it is my impression that murderesses, actual or accused, had a worse time of it because they were seen as hopelessly abnormal. They had ventured into a man's world in which they were not understood. The barbaric arena that Gatrell describes was not meant to accommodate women except as victims or spectators. Consequently most of them were treated as though they were not important (like Eliza Fenning and Martha Brown) or they were inhuman (like the serial poisoners), though those who had committed infanticide were viewed sympathetically by the mob.

In the first third of the nineteenth century, the hanging of a woman was less remarkable than later on. Obvious villains like Esther Hibner and Eliza Ross were reviled for their outrageous behaviour; for run-of-the-mill infanticides, a one- or two-line announcement was standard in the *Times*'s reports on spring and fall assizes in England's various judicial districts: 'Jane Doe was found guilty of ... She was left for hanging.'

Removing a criminal was supposed to erase the stain of murder and make society pure once more. This cleansing was cause for celebration: the crowd at a hanging generally hooted and sang. The stain-removal was a pagan ritual, the practical object of the swift and dramatic punishment being deterrence.

This process of law was more effective as theatre than as justice. For a short time it focused the attention of the community on the crime and the criminal, endowing murder with a peculiar grandeur. As Gatrell has suggested, spectators would have experienced terror at the thought that they, too, would die, but also relief that this was happening to someone far removed from them.

> The tableaux on scaffolds were not pictorial, but witnesses could still see them as *representations*. Enacted upon stages, hangings also signified something other than themselves as their reality was filtered through ascribed meanings: they could just as efficiently be dissociated from the witness's own death as pictures were. They might be emblematic of one's own death. But thankfully and cheeringly they were not *it*.[5]

Elisabeth Bronfen, discussing the aesthetic of female death in literature, provides an explanation in Freudian terms that can be applied to the tableau of an execution: 'Identifying with the dead, the survivors feel their own vulnerability (melancholy), while identifying with the process of destruction, which is possibly due to a denial of any identity with the other, they feel their own triumph and power (sadism).'[6]

There were, of course, in all this ritual and ceremony, fatal errors, Fenning being the prime example.[7] Hangings were the grand climax of a sometimes fairly arbitrary chain of events. Murder trials were hasty affairs presided over by a travelling judge, a jury that would not be let out until it came up with a verdict, and a prosecutor. A lawyer would be appointed, often at the last minute,[8] to conduct the defence, but there was no provision for the accused to speak.[9] There was no avenue of appeal until 1907, though the king, and later, after Victoria came to the throne, the home secretary, could recommend the commutation of the death sentence or the early release of a prisoner.[10] In Patrick Wilson's view, such decisions were made on the basis of public opinion.[11] A petition to the home secretary had to be quickly organized if it was to be of any use: usually the execution took place within days, or, at most, weeks, of a capital conviction.

Some female criminals were able to get their capital sentences commuted to transportation (up until 1853), life imprisonment (which could later be shortened), or less. A woman could have her execution postponed if she could successfully 'plead her belly,' – prove that she was far enough advanced in pregnancy that the child was 'quick' or moving.[12] We know from the cases of Christiana Edmunds and Kate Webster that, even into the 1870s, a woman in such a position was still required to submit to examination by a panel of matrons that reported to the judge on the validity of the claim.

Though sometimes the reprieve of a pregnant woman was permanent, it was not meant to be,[13] and there are descriptions in broadsides and newspapers of women mounting the scaffold with babies clutched to their breasts until the last possible moment.[14] It was only around the middle of the century that reluctance to hang non-pregnant women developed, and these scruples did not extend to the lower classes.

Why were people so interested in the way women died at the hands of the justice system? 'At all times – even when there was a constant succession of company beneath Tyburn Tree – most curiosity has been shown with regard to the weaker sex,' said a newspaper report of the execution of Catherine Wilson in 1862.

> 'The crowd was greater,' says Hugh the gipsy in Mr. Dickens's tale of 'Barnaby Rudge,' 'because it was a woman.'
>
> This ... description refers to a period ... at which women as well as men were strung up for offences less grave than are now punished by a week or two of healthy exercise on the treadmill; and if a vast crowd would then go forth to see a wretched girl's light form shaken in the wind, how much more is it to be expected that people will flock in multitudes to witness the death struggles of a Manning or a Wilson, in days when such hideous sights resemble angels' visits in the one characteristic of being few and far between![15]

It is highly likely that men got a sexual thrill out of seeing a once aggressive woman subdued, quaking in terror and then submitting to the relentless, devastating force of the law as she turned before their eyes from a wild, thrashing creature to a limp, discarded form swinging helplessly above the ground. There is an aggressive component of male eroticism – derived from denial of

men's initial dependency on their mothers – that delights in seeing a woman helpless and degraded. For women at a hanging,
there was the thrill of seeing what happened to those of their sex
who transgressed.

Martin Wiener has described execution as 'a pornographic inva-
sion of the integrity of the body, carried out in public by the
agents of the state. Such spectacles pandered to the worst instincts
of human nature and identified government in the popular mind
with wilful violence.'[16] Thomas Laqueur has found 'ribald sexuality, male potency and death – intimately bound together in the
carnivalesque' in the imagery of eighteenth-century executions.[17]
Gatrell remarks on the potential for obscene fantasies triggered by
the sight of 'the bucking female body as it hanged ... By the end of
the eighteenth century and into the nineteenth the secret gratifi-
cations some men might extract from female execution were cau-
tiously admitted.'[18]

The general fascination with the public punishment of murderesses derived from the perception of female criminality as rooted
in sexual excess. Though normal women were thought to be un-
troubled by sexual desires, criminal women were assumed to be
driven by them. 'Even when the sexual origin or content of a
crime was not immediately apparent,' says Lucia Zedner, 'it still
tended to be characterized as sexually motivated and made the
subject of much pious moralizing.'[19] Both sexes were able to project
repressed guilt over their forbidden desires onto 'fallen' women,
women who had carried out forbidden fantasies.

The newspapers all but wolf-whistled over Maria Manning's final
appearance in a black satin gown with a large white collar and a
black silk blindfold (a handkerchief) covered by a black lace veil.
The *Chronicle* admiringly observed that 'even the distortion consequent upon the mode of death she suffered could not destroy the
remarkably fine contour of her figure as it swayed to and fro by
the action of the wind,'[20] an image that was retained by Dickens.
Still brooding about it three years later, the novelist recalled her
limp black-satin form as 'a fine shape, so elaborately corseted and
artfully dressed, that it was quite unchanged in its trim appearance as it slowly swung from side to side ...'[21]

Maria died 'game' (fighting); her husband did not. The *Advertiser*'s description suggests the image of the crowd as voyeur: 'Manning gave a few convulsive jerks, and all was over, but his wife had a long struggle with death, and it was some moments before the immortal spirit had quitted her body for ever, and passed the threshold of eternity. A slight shudder – a murmured expression of horror – escaped the multitude, and the terrible drama closed.'[22]

Another sexual allusion occurs in the last stanza of a ditty that appeared in *Punch*. A ruffian expresses his excitement and delight at the scene and his admiration of the way in which Maria Manning died:

> But, arter all, what is it? A tumble and a kick!
> And, anyhow, 'tis seemingly all over precious quick,
> And shows that some, no matter for what they've done, dies game!
> Ho, Ho! if ever my time comes, I hope to do the same![23]

A letter to the editor of the *Times* from Sidney Godolphin Osborne (signed 'S.G.O.') expressed disgust that men of respectable society had gathered to watch the execution with opera glasses, 'studying the dying convulsions of a murderess, just as they have criticized, through the same instrument, the postures of the ballet dancer!'[24] Given all the pre-execution publicity, though, the wide and intense appeal of this final appearance was hardly surprising. It was reviewed like the theatrical performance that it was.

The *Times*, admiring her 'handsome figure,' remarked that even on this occasion Maria 'had omitted nothing of that care for her personal appearance which marked her when pleading for her life at the bar of the Old Bailey.'[25] Her husband's attire, a black suit and a shirt with the collar loosened and turned in so as to accommodate the rope, was only briefly mentioned in the papers.

Maria Manning was by no means the only criminal reviewed like an actress. The body language of a condemned murderess as she met her fate was of great interest to the English throughout the nineteenth century. For example, in 1822 a broadside about Hannah Halley, convicted of infanticide, announced that 'when the time of execution arrived, *she was weak, and pale, and powerless. Still she*

ascended the steps which led to the fatal platform with more firmness than was anticipated, and when brought out upon the drop
she behaved with becoming fortitude.'[26]

From the 1830s, when Victoria came to the throne and the
ideals of sexual restraint, domesticity, and female delicacy became
more and more persistent, fantasies and fears about the opposites
of these qualities bubbled under the surface of English life. Mary
Hartman has described the accused murderess as 'the multipur-
pose scapegoat for all the fears, obsessions, and anxieties of men
who, whatever their motivation, professed to understand her and
held power over her life.'[27] Once convicted, she was finally in the
power of the establishment. The familiar nineteenth-century woodcut image of a female body swinging from the gallows can in some
sense be seen as symbolic of spent sexual energy or the weight of
general sexual repression.

Catherine Foster, the disappointed bride, was imagined to have
been terrified at the thought of 'a death that would leave me *dangling
in the air*, while I could not even gratify the natural impulse of
holding up my hands to save myself, because those hands would be
bound before, and a *cord would connect, my arms behind me.*'[28]

The public was horrified to think of her being executed. A
creative pamphlet, apparently designed to deter other wives from
poisoning their husbands, describes, in the first person, what hap-
pens as one is hanged:

> I thought I was the most wretched, miserable being in the world
> doomed to a fearful death – the death of strangulation – the death
> of apoplexy – death by a gush of blood to the brain, the tenderest
> part of the human body ... Oh! heavens, such a death as this for a
> human being, gifted with the most acute feeling. Death by strangu-
> lation, hanging, falling by one's own weight and then the gush of
> blood through bursting arteries and veins to the head. Oh! the idea
> is horrible, most horrible![29]

People went to hangings, particularly those of women, to see a
proven sinner suffer. The more formidable a sinner, the greater
the glee at her downfall. But Catherine Foster, young, poor, igno-

rant, penitent, and tortured, did not have far to fall. While there was undeniably a festive air in the crowd of 10,000 or so that gathered in Bury St Edmunds to watch her execution, the poignancy of her plight was not lost on these people. This was the final act of a tragedy, a twisted version of *Romeo and Juliet*, though it had as well something of the grave scene from *Hamlet*: the local paper describes how two London correspondents 'placed themselves at the foot of the gallows, [and] commenced a cry of "Shame! Murder! etc." at the hangman.'[30] There was a softness about Catherine Foster that lingered in people's minds.

In 1849, a few months before the Manning execution, when the terrified Sarah Thomas was finally dragged to the drop, said the Bristol *Mirror*,

> all eyes were upturned to the half-fainting form of the wretched criminal. She cast her eyes once around her and took her last look of animated nature. Almost immediately she threw down her eyes, as if overcome at her situation ... She did not appear to undergo much pain; the only thing that could be remarked was *a slight convulsive clutching of the hands, which remained afterwards fast clutched in each other*, one gyration of the rope, and apparently all was over. There the body hung for one hour before it was cut down, a warning and an example, to deter others from crimes of a similar atrocious nature, which can only lead to the same ignominious results.[31]

The same attention was simply not paid to men on the gallows. One reason may be that the rope scene bore a remarkable resemblance to a rape scene.

If for the spectators the execution of a woman was a once-in-a-lifetime carnival, for the victim it was a crushing, terrifying, and humiliating ordeal from which the end of life must have been a release. Nowhere is this more evident than in the local newspaper report of 'the ignominious end of Martha Brown,' as the Dorset County *Express* termed it. The woman, about to die for the murder of a habitually drunken, abusive husband, had made a formal confession and appeared to have come to terms with her fate. Her body was surveyed and the parts inventoried:

She was dressed just as she appeared at the trial – a black silk gown, with white collar, and black bonnet. Her attire appeared to be even more particularly attended to than on the last occasion she came before the public. The firmness of her step was truly astonishing, and she freely engaged in devotional conversation with the Rev. H. Moule, holding her hands together all the time, as if in prayer, as the procession moved along. On coming in full sight of the scaffold she looked up and gave an involuntary *shudder* ... The culprit was then assisted up the first flight of steps, which were rather steep, and about half-way up she made a sort of *stumble*, as if her dress had got *under her feet.* Her courage appeared about to desert her, and she faintly exclaimed, 'Oh, dear! I wish I had spoken the truth at the beginning.' If, however, she felt at all overcome, she quickly regained her self possession, and arrived on the first stage, which was a boarded passage leading to the second flight of steps, approaching the platform on which the scaffold was erected. In this passage it was arranged that the pinioning should take place. Calcraft, who had been in the gaol all the night, having come down from London on the previous evening, here commenced the first portion of his sad duties. He was dressed in a neat suit of black, with a hat, and had a very respectable appearance. The wretched woman's *arms were fastened together* behind her by a strap *above the elbows,* so that she could not put her *hands* together in front. She made a faint exclamation, but did not flinch during this operation, which having been performed, Calcraft proceeded to *take off her bonnet* and to *untie her cap.* She expressed an objection to be divested of her cap, and it appeared to have been tied rather tightly, as there was *some little difficulty in undoing it.* It was not, however, yet taken off; and the Rev. Mr. Moule urged her to think nothing of such matters, but to look to the Saviour. After receiving a restorative draught she was with little difficulty assisted up the second flight of steps to the platform, and thence up to those leading to the drop, making altogether an ascent of about thirty-six steps ... She gave a slight glance at the crowd before the lodge, and then immediately cast down her *eyes.* The Rev. Mr. Moule shook *hands* with her and bade her farewell while on the drop, and she faintly exclaimed 'Thank you, sir –

thank you, sir; goodbye.' Calcraft then *removed her cap*, and placed *over her head and face* the one used for such purposes, and the rope was put *round her neck* and adjusted to the beam above. She was placed in a proper position, and the executioner descended to draw the fatal bolt. He had just got his hand on the instrument when he seemed to be aware of an omission. He again ascended and placed a cord round her dress *just below the knees*. During this time the wretched woman did not move a muscle, and her firmness astonished every beholder. Calcraft returned to the bolt – in an instant the drop gave way – and the wretched woman was launched into eternity almost without a struggle. For about a quarter of a minute there was *a muscular contraction of the legs, a slight quivering of the muscles* of the body, and all was still.[32]

The piling on of details makes Brown pathetically human, and the deliberately impassive tone conveys the inevitability of her situation. At the same time there is an appreciation of the woman as a sexual being. Hardy attended this hanging at the age of sixteen and remembered as an old man 'what a fine figure she showed against the sky as she hung in the misty rain, & how the tight black silk gown set off her shape as she wheeled half-round & back.'[33]

In the opinion of many who wrote to the newspapers and complained to legislators in vain, this execution was nothing less than judicial murder. (See chapter 4.) More than that, it can be argued that this was judicial rape. The pinioning of the arms so that the shoulders were forced back and the bosom out, the resistance to the untying of the cap, the placing of her body 'in a proper position,' the almost-forgotten cord below the knees, the hangman's hand on 'the instrument,' and the involuntary muscular contractions are evocative of a fantasy rape scene.[34] The sexual impact on Hardy, like that of Maria Manning on Dickens a few years earlier, is unmistakable.

Even more disturbing (because it is more explicit) is the titillating vision summoned up by a broadside ballad of 1865 as Constance Kent (who was actually reprieved) was imagined preparing for her execution. Addressing herself to 'maidens dear,' she laments:

Oh what a sight it will be to see,
A maiden die on the fatal tree.

She then reminds her audience, 'I am a maiden in youth and bloom.' Later she emphasizes her sexuality by remarking on

How many maidens will flock to see,
A female die upon Salisbury's tree.
Constance Emily Kent is my dreadful name,
Who in youth and beauty dies a death of shame.

At the end, she is about to submit to metaphorical rape by the justice system:

I see the hangman before me stand,
Ready to seize me by the law's command,
When my life is ended on the fatal tree,
Then will be clear'd up all mystery.[35]

THE BODY

After 1868 the suffering had to be witnessed by representatives of the press and duly publicized. In 1884 followers of the case of Catherine Flannagan and Margaret Higgins, the serial poisoners, were told that on the way to the scaffold they 'clung to the warders for support, and slowly and with effort ascended the cruel flight of steps.'[36] Three years later, the execution of Elizabeth Berry attracted a crowd of about 800, who, according to the Oldham *Chronicle*, 'while waiting to see the flag hoisted, discussed the woman's crime, and wondered what her feelings were.' Since they couldn't see how she looked as she died, they were reduced to imagining what she thought.

The body of a hanged prisoner had to be viewed at an inquest so that the public was satisfied that death had occurred. Usually there was a curt published statement to this effect. However, the lengthy description of Berry provided by the *Chronicle* had tender, seductive overtones. The body was *decently covered by a white sheet*, which came *up to the chin*, and was tucked up almost *to the left ear*, so that the part of the *neck* which had been caught most violently by the rope was not visible ... The body had evidently been recently washed, as the woman's *hair* was damp. It had been brushed back, but not combed, and lay in a tangled disorderly mass ... For all that, the expression was placid, nor was there anything indicative in its appearance that she had died in pain. An observer, who did not know the woman's history, nor how she died, would not have suspected that her end was violent, unless he had lifted the coverlet, and looked at the mark on the neck. The *face*, however, seemed to have grown smaller about the lower part, and the *cheeks* were not so full, and the same remark will apply to the *lips*, which were closed.[37]

This is a violated body. Society has had its will of her. The white sheet covers marks of violence; tangled curls frame the pale face, the lower part of which (once full and sensual) has contracted; the lips are closed. Death, femininity, and the aesthetic, which Bronfen sees intertwined in literature, are here presented as spot news.

Mary Ann Burdock's (1835) was the first widely documented female execution in twenty years, after Fenning's, in which the subject's sexuality can be inferred from both the commentary and the attendance. The Bristol *Mirror* estimated that an unprecedented crowd of 50,000 assembled in a dense mass. When she appeared on the scaffold, 'there was a shuddering and anxious silence, and when, on the signal of dropping the handkerchief, the unhappy convict fell beneath the heaviest vengeance of the law, a thrill of terror pervaded every countenance.'[38]

This sort of report persisted until public hangings were abolished. In 1849, describing a crowd of about 20,000 that gathered to watch Mary Ball die, the Bath *Chronicle* observed, 'A subdued thrill of horror appeared to pass over this immense multitude as the fatal bolt was drawn.'[39] Even after 1868 people sometimes gathered outside a prison to watch for the black flag, as they did when Berry was hanged, but they had to rely on the newspapers for the thrilling details.

Fortunately for true-crime addicts, the *Illustrated Police News*, established in 1864, filled the vacuum left by the abolition of public hangings. This paper covered its front page with the work of artists skilled in imagining how criminals must have felt on such various red-letter occasions as their exposure, sentencing, confession, and last hours. It shows Mary Ann Cotton in despair, leaning on one elbow, as she contemplates execution, and then standing, pinioned, waiting for the noose to be slipped over her head.[40] Mrs Pearcey's dreams the night before her execution are depicted, along with the condemned prisoner herself, trying frantically to sleep.[41] Florence Maybrick is shown, haggard and in shock, as she gets news of her reprieve.[42]

In the last third of the century, the public appetite for the suffering of murderesses abated somewhat. The justice system flirted with the idea of hanging middle-class women like Constance Kent, Christiana Edmunds, Adelaide Bartlett, and Florence Maybrick, but the closest it came to the middle class was Eleanor Pearcey, who, though poor, as a kept woman lived in a largely imaginary world apparently inspired by cheap novels. Marguerite Diblanc and Eliza Gibbons were reprieved and eventually released. Although there had been six executions of women in the 1860s and ten in the 1870s, there were only four in the 1880s and four in the 1890s. The newspapers noted that hardly anyone stood outside as Annie Took was executed in 1879.

The voyeuristic exercise of pursuing a murderess until she was forced to submit to the law all but ceased with the women's movement of the 1880s. There was a growing reluctance to hang women, but at the same time a strong sense of the moral obligation to deter others from similar crimes. In a peculiar way, this shift of attitude came about as a result of the increasing implication of middle-class women in murder. Whether women's emancipation produced this activity is a question I will leave to others to argue, Freda Adler having thrown down the gauntlet in *Sisters in Crime* (1975).

In 1890 the *Daily Telegraph*, which had always excelled in the description of criminals, merely noted on the day of her execution that Eleanor Pearcey 'looked pinched and wan' and her face had 'lost all its roundness and attractiveness.'[43] We know nothing of the way in which she met her death save for the information in the *Evening News* that she 'submitted quietly,' her 'drawn features and pale skin' showing the suffering she had undergone.[44] Only *Lloyd's* provided a full physical description of her, derived from the inquest viewing. Linking sexuality and death, this report noted

> an unusual suffusion of blood visible under her delicate skin, and the purple hue of her lips, curled back and showing her prominent teeth, gave evidence of pain ... Her long luxuriantly curling hair was spread down her back and over her shoulders, her hands, outstretched and without any appearance of contortion, were at her side, and her feet, though denuded of boots, appeared small and well shaped. She was dressed in the striped stuff gown she wore at the trial ...[45]

There is no smugness here, but rather a tone of regret that conveys a sense of tragedy at the final struggle between sexuality and death. The blood, purple lips curled back in pain, outstretched hands, and feet stripped naked evoke suffering and punishment.

We know from reports of the Boxing Day crowds at Madame Tussaud's model of Pearcey in her kitchen that interest in her was intense even after the execution. It is likely, though, that the interest was piqued by curiosity, and even compassion, rather than hatred. A hanging was no longer a celebration marking the reinstatement of social purity; it was simply a disagreeable but inevitable piece of business dictated by the social contract.

Conclusion

Though the women whose transgressions and punishments are documented in this book are not admirable, some of them are likeable, and many of them endured far more humiliation, deprivation, terror, and pain than they deserved. Throughout the nineteenth century, until the 1880s, and especially in the first half of Victoria's reign, their trials and executions served not only to deter prospective murderers, but to assert the power of the ruling class in general, and men of that class in particular. The limp feminine form twisting in the wind after an execution, once a boisterous crowd had had its will of her, signified more than justice done. The punishment had an erotic component that was in part attributable to perceived subversion of the 'angel in the house' ideal. Patriarchal Victorian society, fearful that other spirited women, not just murderesses, were straining at their limits, focused derisively on the body, bearing, and appearance of murderesses. Before the nineteenth century was out, though, vocal upper-class women working for social reform, though they did not sanction criminality, insisted on more humane treatment for female offenders.

Murderesses tended to be poor, ignorant, and oppressed. They sought escape or control. Their victims, almost always in the domestic sphere, were mostly nonentities. Yet these murders tended to be a threat to people higher up the social ladder in the way that the revolutions in Europe in 1848 were a threat to class stability in England. If their murders showed that not everyone who was oppressed would passively accept her lot, their punishment showed their oppressors' determination to prevail.

Killing people is wrong. Still, it is hard to be unsympathetic to murderesses who were abused wives, starving mothers, or servants with nowhere to go for help. It is possible, when one looks back to the nineteenth century, to make allowances for extreme behaviour by the oppressed, and perhaps to justify infanticide. It is, I suppose, even possible to accept the killing of murderesses as essential to the social order. It is harder to endorse the class and gender bias that made murder by women a spectator sport.

Appendix:
A Chronology of Murder

The table below identifies the women whose murder cases were among the most sensational of the century in England. Beside the trial date and name are indicated the relationship of the victim (if more than one, the one for which she was convicted is italicized) and the evidence of press and public interest. From mid-century, contemporary murderesses were immortalized in wax by Madame Tussaud's, and, from the early 1870s, depicted in large front-page drawings of the *Illustrated Police News* (IPN). An asterisk after the name indicates that the woman was hanged.

1807	**Martha Alden***	husband	broadside
1809	**Mary Bateman***	elderly woman	pamphlet
1813	**Ann Arnold***	own child	pamphlet
1815	**Eliza Fenning***	employer's family	wide coverage
1816	**Susannah Holroyd***	*husband*, children	broadside
1817	**Elizabeth Warriner***	stepson	broadside
1820	**Ann Heytrey***	employer	broadside
1821	**Ann Barber***	husband	broadside, pamphlet
1822	**Hannah Halley***	own baby	broadside
1827	**Jane Scott***	parents	broadside

1829	**Jane Jamieson***	mother	broadside
	Esther Hibner*	apprentice(s)	wide coverage
1832	**Eliza Ross***	elderly woman (lodger)	broadside, pamphlet, wide coverage
1835	**Mary Ann Burdock***	elderly woman (lodger)	broadside, pamphlet, wide coverage
1836	**Sophia Edney***	husband	broadside
1842	**Elizabeth Eccles***	stepson	pamphlet, broadside
1843	**Sarah Dazely***	husband(s)	broadside
1845	**Martha Brixey**	baby of employer	broadside
	Sarah Freeman*	own family	wide coverage
	Martha Browning*	elderly woman (landlady)	broadside
1847	**Catherine Foster***	husband	broadside, pamphlet
1848	**Harriet Parker***	stepchild(ren)	broadside
	Mary May*	half-brother	broadside
1849	**Sarah Thomas***	employer	wide coverage
	Maria Manning*	lover	wide coverage, Tussaud's
1848–50	**M. Catherine Newton**	mother	wide coverage
1850	**Mary Reeder***	sister	broadside
1851	**Sarah Chesham***	*husband*, sons	broadside
1854	**Mary Ann Brough**	own child(ren)	broadside
1856	**E. Martha Brown***	husband	wide coverage
1862	**Catherine Wilson***	elderly woman (landlady)	broadside
1863	**Alice Holt***	mother	broadside

1865	**Constance Kent**	half-brother	Tussaud's, broadside
	Charlotte Winsor	baby(ies)	Tussaud's, broadside
1870	**Margaret Waters***	baby(ies)	broadside
1872	**Christiana Edmunds**	child	wide coverage, IPN
	Marguerite Diblanc	employer	wide coverage, IPN, Tussaud's
1873	**Mary Ann Cotton***	*stepson*, husbands, own children	wide coverage, IPN, broadside
1879	**Kate Webster***	employer	wide coverage, IPN, Tussaud's
	Hannah Dobbs	employer's lodger	wide coverage, Tussaud's
1884	**Catherine Flannagan***	relatives, friends	wide coverage, Tussaud's
	Margaret Higgins*	*husband*, relatives, friends	wide coverage, Tussaud's
	Eliza Gibbons	husband	wide coverage, Tussaud's
1886	**Adelaide Bartlett**	husband	wide coverage, IPN, pamphlet
1887	**Elizabeth Berry***	*daughter*, mother	wide coverage
1889	**Florence Maybrick**	husband	wide coverage, broadside, IPN, Tussaud's, pamphlet

1890	**Eleanor Mary Pearcey***	lover's wife	wide coverage, broadside, IPN, Tussaud's
1895	**Amy Gregory**	own baby	wide coverage
1896	**Amelia Dyer***	baby(ies)	wide coverage, broadside, Tussaud's
1899	**Louise Masset***	own child	Tussaud's

Notes

CHAPTER 1   The Case of the Vanishing Murderess

1 Patrick Wilson, *Murderess*, 110.
2 Ibid., 53–4.
3 Rachel M. Short, 'Female Criminality 1780–1830,' 142.
4 Ibid., 142–6.
5 Ibid., 156.
6 Martin Daly and Margo Wilson, *Homicide*, chs 6, 7, and 8.
7 Robyn Anderson, 'Criminal Violence in London, 1856–1875,' 172.
8 Short, 'Female Criminality,' 149–50.
9 Mary Beth Wasserlein Emmerichs, 'Trials of Women for Homicide in Nineteenth-Century England,' 103.
10 Short, 'Female Criminality,' 97.
11 Anderson, 'Criminal Violence in London,' 163.
12 These statistics are for the period 1836–70 in England and Wales. See William A. Guy, 'On the Executions for Murder that Have Taken Place in England and Wales during the Last Seventy Years,' 471 n.
13 Short, 'Female Criminality,' 186.
14 Ibid., 202.
15 Ibid., 205.
16 Ibid., 45. Short found that, early in the nineteenth century, married women in London worked as servants, washerwomen, cleaners, and apprentices, while their counterparts in the country worked as agricultural labourers. In 1840 nearly two-fifths of the poor women in Westminster worked outside their homes, largely (though some were street hawkers) in such domestic occupations as washing, cleaning, and needlework. According to Luke Owen Pike, *A History of Crime in England* (London: Smith, Elder 1876),

vol. 1, 529, in 1871 'the great bulk of the grown women in England and Wales were still employed in domestic occupations.'

17 Russell P. Dobash, R. Emerson Dobash, and Sue Gutteridge, *The Imprisonment of Women*, 86.

18 Virginia Morris, *Double Jeopardy: Women Who Kill in Victorian Fiction* (Lexington: University Press of Kentucky, 1990), 7, 103.

19 Guy, 'On the Executions for Murder ...,' 480, 466.

20 The murder rate for women is much lower now. Gerald Falk, in *Murder: An Analysis of Its Forms, Conditions, and Causes* (Jefferson, NC, and London: McFarland 1990), 36, cites a study of 909 cases over forty years in New York State in which males had a homicide rate more than seven times that of females – 799 to 110.

21 'Judicial Statistics [1879],' *Parliamentary Papers* [hereinafter *PP*], vol. 77, xxviii.

22 'Judicial Statistics [1899],' *PP*, vol. 89, 35, 55.

23 Roger Chadwick, *Bureaucratic Mercy*, 291.

24 Mary Hartman, *Victorian Murderesses*, 5.

25 Wilson, *Murderess*, 42.

26 Martin J. Wiener, *Reconstructing the Criminal*, 130.

27 Short, '*Female Criminality*,' 197–8.

28 Anderson, '*Criminal Violence in London*,' 219.

29 Sources: 'Judicial Statistics for England & Wales [1874–1899], *PP*; Guy, 'On Executions for Murder ...'

30 Chadwick, *Bureaucratic Mercy*, 5.

31 Public Record Office, HO144/108/A23081, 19 Dec. 1882. Harcourt was considering whether to recommend a reprieve for Louisa Taylor, who had poisoned an elderly woman but might not have caused her death. Public opinion was decidedly against her, and Harcourt noted on the file, 'Nothing here to warrant commutation.'

CHAPTER 2   The Popular Press

1 Thomas Carlyle, *Past and Present*, Book 1, Chapter 1.

2 Susanna Meredith, *A Book about Criminals* (London: James Nisbet *ca* 1880), 3.

3 *Punch* 17 (1849), 214.

4 Amelia Dyer, Charlotte Winsor, and Ada Chard Williams.

5 Catherine Wilson, Mary Ann Cotton, Catherine Flannagan, and Margaret Higgins.

6 Maria Manning, Constance Kent, Marguerite Diblanc, Kate Webster, Eliza Gibbons, and Louise Masset. Florence Maybrick, who was convicted but never executed, was in the general exhibition until she was pardoned in 1904.

7 Hannah Dobbs.

8 Pauline Chapman, in *Madame Tussaud's Chamber of Horrors* (London: Constable 1984), 100, cites a list in *Lloyd's Newspaper* of 24 Nov. 1890 of the items bought by Tussaud's: piano, ornaments, pictures, carpets, couch, chairs, table, pram, curtains, blinds, and blood-stained garments.

9 *Punch* 17 (1849), 213.

10 Albert Borowitz, *The Woman Who Murdered Black Satin* (Columbus: Ohio State University Press 1981), 155.

11 *Standard*, 31 Aug. 1849, 3; *News of the World*, 1 Apr. 1849, 3.

12 *Annual Register* (London 1849), 429.

13 Borowitz, *The Woman Who Murdered Black Satin*, 280.

14 Charles Hindley, *Curiosities of Street Literature*, 159.

15 Ian A. Bell, *Literature and Crime in Augustan England* (London: Routledge 1991), 50–1.

16 Richard Altick, *Victorian Studies in Scarlet*, 288.

17 Lincoln B. Faller, *Turned to Account: The Forms and Functions of Criminal Biography in Late Seventeenth- and Early Eighteenth-Century England* (Cambridge: Cambridge University Press 1987), 5.

18 Bristol *Mirror*, 21 Apr. 1849, 8.

19 'The Dying Criminal ...,' *Religious Tracts* 61, British Library, 3.

20 Sceptical of this formula, the *Times*, in a leading article on 15 Apr. 1854, p. 7, marvels at how murderers can get a clear passport to eternal happiness without even atoning for their crimes.

21 Rayner Heppenstall, *Reflections on the 'Newgate Calendar'* (London: W.H. Allen 1975), ix.

22 Victor Neuberg, *Popular Literature: A History and Guide from the Beginning of Printing to the Year 1897* (Harmondsworth: Penguin 1977), 165.

23 William Palmer (1856), William Dove (1856), Thomas Smethurst (1859), Catherine Wilson (1862), and Edwin Pritchard (1865).

24 Broadsides: Murders and Executions, John Johnson collection, Bodleian Library.

25 Arthur Appleton, *Mary Ann Cotton*, 148.

26 Susan Tennery, '"The Burglary, Cut-Throat, and Gallows Class of Literature" – Production and Meaning,' unpublished paper presented at the Victorians' Institute conference, Richmond, Virginia, Sep.–Oct. 1994.

27 Sir John Hall, *Trial of Adelaide Bartlett*, 397.

28 H.B. Irving, *Trial of Mrs. Maybrick*, 320–1.

29 *St. James's Gazette*, 16 Aug. 1889, 6–7.

30 Alison Morris, *Women, Crime and Criminal Justice*, 19–27, discusses similarities between *The Moonstone* and the Kent case, pinpointing the disappearance of the nightgown, the aggressive shifting of suspicion from the servant to the daughter of the house, and the solution of the mystery by a gratuitous confession.

31 Margaret Voce, hanged in 1802 for infanticide.

32 Lady Hester Pinney, in *Thomas Hardy and the Birdsmoorgate Murder 1856*, 4, recalls: 'I remember sitting with him [in 1926] over his open fire and hearing him talk about Martha and Tess, whose stories have much in common, just as if they were in the next room. His sympathy for those unhappy women was wonderful.'

33 Morris, *Women, Crime and Criminal Justice*, 132, 164 n. 7.

34 See Michael Millgate, *Thomas Hardy: A Biography* (New York: Random House 1982), 347.

35 R.K. Webb, cited by Geoffrey Best in *Mid-Victorian Britain, 1851–1875* (New York: Schocken 1972), 224.

36 Patricia Anderson, *The Printed Image and the Transformation of Popular Culture, 1790–1860* (Oxford: Clarendon Press 1991), 25, notes that murder and execution broadsides were the best-sellers. As an example she cites the sales figure of 1,166,000 copies of a James Catnach broadside published to mark the execution of William Corder in 1828 for the murder of his pregnant lover. Catnach's was doubtless not the only broadside put out on an occasion momentous enough to warrant a special supplement to the *Observer*.

37 Robert Collison, in *The Story of Street Literature: Forerunner of the Popular Press* (London: Dent 1973), 2, notes that broadsheets have been found under layers of wallpaper in cottages and farm kitchens.

38 Henry Mayhew, *London Labour and the London Poor*, vol. 1, 223.

39 The broadside concerns the execution of Margaret Cunningham, alias Mason. It is in the John Johnson collection (Broadsides: Murders and Executions) of the Bodleian Library.

40 'I get a shilling for a "copy of verses written by the wretched culprit the night previous to his execution,"' one street-ballad singer told Mayhew: *London Labour and the London Poor*, vol. 3, 196.

41 The dramatic impact of the one dated 26 Jan. 1824, headed 'Horrid Murder' and illustrated hopefully with an execution scene, is somewhat

dulled if one has already seen the same story in one dated 28 Aug. 1822. There is another version dated simply May 1826. The earliest one is in the Harding collection of the Bodleian Library; the later ones are at the British Library.

42 Lucy Brown, *Victorian News and Newspapers* (Oxford: Oxford University Press 1985), 52.

43 Ibid., 30–1.

44 Altick, *Victorian Studies in Scarlet*, 66.

45 Mayhew, *London Labour and the London Poor*, vol. 3, 225.

46 Leslie Shepherd, *The History of Street Literature*, 77.

47 Stanley Morison, *The English Newspaper: Some Account of the Physical Development of Journals Printed in London Between 1622 & the Present Day* (Cambridge: Cambridge University Press 1932), 242.

48 Virginia Berridge, 'Popular Sunday Papers and Mid-Victorian Society,' in *Newspaper History from the Seventeenth Century to the Present Day*, ed. George Boyce, James Curran, and Pauline Wingate (London: Constable 1978), 247.

49 Louis James, *Fiction for the Working Man, 1830–1850* (London: Oxford University Press 1963), 35.

50 Neuberg, *Popular Literature*, 171, cites *A Bibliography of the Penny Bloods of Edward Lloyd* (Dundee 1945).

51 Brown, *Victorian News and Newspapers*, 96, 147.

52 James Grant, *The Newspaper Press* (London 1871), vol. 2, 268–70.

53 H.R. Fox Bourne, in *English Newspapers: Chapters in the History of Journalism* (London: Chatto and Windus 1887), vol. 2, 18 n. 1, cites the condemnation by Chief Justice Abbot in 1821 of John Walter, proprietor of the *Times*, for summarizing the evidence given in a trial and drawing conclusions rather than publishing the entire procedure.

54 Robert Hariman, Preface to *Popular Trials: Rhetoric, Mass Media, and the Law*, (Tuscaloosa: University of Alabama Press 1990), vii.

55 Margaret L. Arnot, 'Gender in Focus,' 67, 60.

56 Robert Hariman, 'Performing the Laws: Popular Trials and Social Knowledge,' in *Popular Trials*, 17–30.

57 Morison, *The English Newspaper*, 280–1.

58 R.D. Blumenfeld, *The Press in My Time* (London: Rich and Cowan 1933), 32.

59 Antony Trollope, *An Autobiography*, chapter 12 (London: Oxford World's Classics 1953), 195.

60 *Armadale*, (1866; rep. Chatto and Windus, 1901), 520–1.

61 *Times*, 31 Mar. 1845, 6.

62 Charles Mitchell, *The Newspaper Press Directory*, 3d ed. (London: C. Mitchell 1851), 35.

63 Fox Bourne, *English Newspapers*, vol. 2, 390.

64 Dorset County, *Express and Agricultural Gazette*, 12 Aug. 1856, 4.

CHAPTER 3   Multiple Murder

1 The *Daily News*, 25 Aug. 1849, 3, reprinted from the *Law Magazine* an article on the relation of fluctuations in the economy to crime, analysing trends in the economy, crime statistics, and various official reports.

2 *Daily News*, 10 Aug. 1847, 2.

3 *Times*, 21 Sep. 1846, 4.

4 Ibid., 21 Sep. 1848, 6.

5 *News of the World*, 30 Jul. 1848, 4.

6 Rep. *Times*, 6 Sep. 1849, 5.

7 'A Supplementary Report on the Results of a Special Inquiry into the Practice of Interment in Towns,' *Parliamentary Papers* 1843 (vol. 12).

8 G.K. Behlmer, *Child Abuse and Moral Reform in England, 1870–1908*, makes the point (p. 120), that in Victorian England the convention of conspicuous mourning exerted pressure on the working classes to overspend on funerals.

9 John Johnson street ballads, 578, Bodleian Library.

10 For a full account of the war against burial societies, see Behlmer, *Child Abuse*, 220–35.

11 *Daily News*, 10 Aug. 1847, 1.

12 *Lancet*, 27 Sep. 1862, 336.

13 Dorset *County Chronicle*, 16 Jan. 1845, 4.

14 The term derives from 25th Edward III, chapter 2, which defines 'petty treason' as the murder of an employer by a servant, a husband by his wife, or a prelate by a subordinate.

15 John Johnson collection, Bodleian Library.

16 *Times* 24 Mar. 1828, 5; 25 Mar. 1828, 4; *Morning Herald* 23 Mar., 1828, 4; 24 Mar. 1828, 4; 25 Mar. 1828, 4.

17 Lancaster *Gazette*, 24 Mar. 1828, 3.

18 Published in London in 1843, this pamphlet was held by the British Library but destroyed by bombing.

19 British Library, 1888.c.3.

20 Ibid.

21 Northampton *Herald*, 12 Aug. 1843, 3.

22 Alfred Swaine Taylor, *On Poison, in Relation to Medical Jurisprudence and Medicine* (London: John Churchill 1848), 61–2, says that too much time had elapsed since the deaths of the two older children for the suspicions to be proved, and, in the case of the infant, poisoning was not even suspected.

23 Lincoln, Rutland, and Stanford *Mercury*, 9 Aug. 1844, 3.

24 Letter to the Somerset *County Herald* from Jonathan Toogood, MD, 3 May 1845, 4.

25 A letter from George Davis to the Somerset *County Herald*, 10 May 1845, 4, details Freeman's attempt to get him to drink poisoned ale.

26 Taunton *Courier*, 9 Apr. 1845, 6.

27 Somerset County *Herald*, 26 Apr. 1845, 3.

28 Ibid., 4.

29 Taunton *Courier*, 23 Apr. 1845, 7.

30 *Annual Register* [1845], part 2, 51.

31 Somerset County *Herald*, 26 Apr. 1845, 3.

32 Lincoln, Rutland, and Stanford *Mercury*, 23 Jul. 1847, 2; *Daily News*, 22 Jul. 1847, 4.

33 *Mercury*, 23 Jul. 1847, 2.

34 *Annual Register* [1847], part 2, 101.

35 *Times*, 8 Mar. 1851, 4.

36 Ibid., 21 Sep. 1846, 4.

37 Ibid., 5 Sep. 1846, 7.

38 Essex *Standard*, 28 Aug. 1846, 3.

39 *Times*, 13 Mar. 1847, 8.

40 Chelmsford *Chronicle*, 7 Mar. 1851, 3.

41 Morning *Advertiser*, 7 Mar. 1851, 7.

42 Essex *Standard and General Advertiser*, 18 Aug. 1848, 2.

43 *News of the World*, 30 Jul. 1848, 4.

44 *Lloyd's*, 30 Aug. 1848, 15.

45 *Times*, 21 Sep. 1848, 5; 6 Aug. 1849, 7.

46 *Morning Chronicle*, 15 Aug. 1848, 8.

47 Henry Mayhew, *London Labour and the London Poor*, vol. 1, 282.

48 *Weekly Chronicle*, 9 Mar. 1851, 78.

49 Firth collection 17 (260), Bodleian Library.

50 *Weekly Chronicle*, 30 Mar. 1851, 127.

51 Harding collection, Bodleian Library.

52 *Annual Register for 1849*, 88.

53 *Daily News*, 21 Aug. 1849, 4.

54 *Reynolds's Newspaper*, 16 Mar. 1851, 6.

55 *Poetical Broadsides*, British Library, 88.

56 *Illustrated London News*, 22 Mar. 1851, 236.

57 *Parliamentary Papers* 1850, vol. 45, 447–63.

58 *Times*, 12 Mar. 1851, 8.

59 *Advertiser*, 27 Mar. 1851, 4.

60 *Hansard*, ([13 Mar.] 1851, vol. 14, 1300.

61 Ibid., [7 Apr.] 1851, vol. 15, 422.

62 Ibid., [15 Apr.] 1851, vol. 15, 1117.

63 Letter 48, 5 May 1851, *The Later Letters of John Stuart Mill, 1849–1873*, ed. Francis E. Mineka and Dwight N. Lindley, vols. 14–17 of *The Collected Works of John Stuart Mill* (Toronto: University of Toronto Press, 1967–90), vol. 14, 63–4.

64 *Hansard*, [23 May] 1851, vol. 15, 1328.

65 14 Victoria, c. 13.

66 *Times*, 20 Aug. 1851, 3.

67 Charles Hindley, *Curiosities of Street Literature*, 199.

68 Alfred Swaine Taylor, *The Principles and Practice of Medical Jurisprudence*, 1101.

69 *Annual Register* [1854], part 2, 97.

70 *Times*, 11 Aug. 1854, 6.

71 Roger Smith, *Trial by Medicine*, 159, 160. For a full description of the controversy over whether Brough should have been acquitted, see 157–60.

72 *Lancet*, 18 Oct. 1862, 425.

73 Guildhall Library, Br.5.13.

74 *Annual Register* [1862], part 2, 455.

75 Ibid., 457.

76 Broadsides: Murder and Execution, John Johnson collection, Bodleian Library.

77 *Times*, 21 Oct. 1862, 5.

78 *Daily Telegraph*, 21 Oct. 1862, 3.

79 *Annual Register* [1862], part 2, 454.

80 Vivien Poore, *A Treatise on Medical Jurisprudence*, quoted by John Glaister in *The Power of Poison* (London: Christopher Johnson 1954), 81.

81 Durham County *Advertiser*, 28 Mar. 1873, 5.

82 Firth collection 17 (98), Bodleian Library.

83 Newcaste *Daily Chronicle*, 24 Mar. 1873, 3.

84 Arthur Appleton, *Mary Ann Cotton*, 146.

85 Durham County *Advertiser*, 21 Mar. 1873, 8.

86 Durham *Chronicle*, 4 Oct. 1872, 7.

87 Newcastle *Daily Journal*, 13 Mar. 1873, 2.

88 Appleton, *Mary Ann Cotton*, iii, 67.

89 Chester *Guardian and Record*, 6 Feb. 1878, 3.

90 Ibid., 27 Feb. 1878, 6.

91 Ibid., 26 Jun. 1878, 8.

92 Public Record Office, HO144/126/A33023.

93 Liverpool *Daily Post*, 18 Feb. 1884, 5.

94 Behlmer, *Child Abuse*, 49.

95 *Lancet*, 23 Feb. 1884, 351.

96 Liverpool *Daily Post*, 12 Oct. 1883, 5.

97 *Lloyd's*, 14 Oct. 1883, 7.

98 *Times*, 4 Mar. 1884, 11.

99 Liverpool *Daily Post*, 4 Mar. 1884, 3.

100 Oldham *Daily Standard*, 24 Feb. 1887, 3.

101 Oldham *Chronicle*, 26 Feb. 1887, 5; 5 Mar. 1887, 3; 5 Mar. 1887, 3; 19 Mar. 1887, 3.

102 Ibid., 26 Feb. 1887, 5. Pictures of the girl before and after death appeared in the Oldham *Daily Standard* on 28 Feb. 1887, 3, and in the *Weekly Standard* on 5 Mar., 5.

103 Oldham *Daily Standard*, 28 Feb. 1887, 3.

104 *Lancet*, 23 Feb. 1884, 352.

105 The *Pictorial Times* of 29 Aug. 1846, for example, carried a double-page spread of illustrations of the poor (136–7) and on 10 Oct. 1846 (255) ran an article suggesting that improved sanitation would raise the moral tone of the population 'in districts now reeking with fith, cursed with disease, and sunk into the lowest depth of crime, starvation, and misery.'

106 *Daily News*, 4 Sep. 1849, 6.

CHAPTER 4   Murder of Husbands, Lovers, or Rivals in Love

1 Patrick Wilson, *Murderess*, 94.

2 Ibid., 89–93.

3 Martin Daly and Margo Wilson, *Homicide*, 295.

4 For a discussion of popular concepts of marriage and divorce, see J.M. Golby and A.W. Purdue, *The Civilization of the Crowd*, 47–8.

5 Martin J. Wiener, 'Domestic Homicide in Historical Perspective: Lessons from Nineteenth-Century Britain,' unpublished paper presented at the First European Social Science History Conference, De Leeuwenhorst, Noordwijkerhout, The Netherlands, May 1996.

6 Ruth Harris, *Murders and Madness*, 208.

7 30th George III (1793), chapter 48.

8 *Examiner*, 29 Aug. 1846, 547.

9 *Daily News,* 10 Jul. 1846, 2.

10 Ibid., 28 Aug. 1846, 2.

11 Ibid., 24 Aug. 1846, 3.

12 *Times,* 5 Feb. 1847, 5.

13 *Morning Chronicle,* 29 Mar. 1850, 4.

14 *Echo,* 18 Jan. 1872, 2.

15 *Daily Telegraph,* 23 Jan. 1872, 5.

16 *Saturday Review,* 22 Jun. 1872, 785.

17 Broadsides: Murder and Execution, John Johnson collection, Bodleian Library.

18 *The New Newgate Calendar* 8/1 (12 Dec. 1863), 113–14.

19 Tyne *Mercury,* 23 Aug. 1814, 4. This story also appeared in the *Times,* 26 Aug. 1814, 3.

20 Broadsides: Murder and Execution, John Johnson collection, Bodleian Library.

21 *Times,* 2 Nov. 1818, 3.

22 *Courier,* 12 Nov. 1818, 4.

23 Harding collection, Bodleian Library.

24 Hampshire *Chronicle and Courier,* 2 Nov. 1818, 3.

25 Broadsides: Murder and Execution, John Johnson collection, Bodleian Library.

26 *A Particular Account of the Trial and Execution of Ann Barber ...* (1821), 5.

27 *Times,* 16 Aug. 1821, 3.

28 Taunton *Courier,* 13 Apr. 1836, 7.

29 *Times,* 9 Apr. 1836, 6.

30 *A Voice from the Gaol* (1847), 7.

31 Firth 17 (20), Bodleian Library, an execution broadside, includes a farewell letter to 'Thomas' that expresses her hope of meeting him in the next world.

32 Bury and Norwich *Post,* 21 Apr. 1847, 2.

33 *Bell's Life in London,* 3 Sep. 1848, 3.

34 Essex *Herald,* 13 Mar. 1849, 4.

35 Bell's, 17 Sep. 1848, 3.

36 Ibid., 8 Oct. 1948, 3.

37 *Times,* 8 Aug. 1849, 4.

38 *News of the World,* 19 May 1850, 6.

39 F.M. Evans, 'Murder at Castle Camps ...,' unpublished manuscript, Cambridge Public Library.

40 Cambridgeshire collection, Cambridge Public Library.

41 *News of the World,* 28 Apr. 1850, 3.

42 For a chivalric, but to my mind futile, attempt to rescue Maria Manning's reputation, see Albert Borowitz, *The Woman Who Murdered Black Satin* (Columbus: Ohio State University Press 1981). Borowitz defends her on the ground that the most incriminating evidence against her came from her husband.

43 *Observer*, 24 Aug. 1849, 5.

44 *Morning Post*, 26 Oct. 1849, 5.

45 *Observer*, 26 Aug. 1849, 5. Other papers put forth the same theory, which originated with the police.

46 Ibid., 19 Aug. 1849, 5.

47 *Globe*, 20 Aug. 1849, 4.

48 *Observer*, 26 Aug. 1849, 5.

49 *Standard*, 20 Aug. 1849, 1.

50 Ibid., 13 Nov. 1849, 2.

51 *Times*, 14 Nov. 1849, 4.

52 *Morning Advertiser*, 14 Nov. 1849, 3.

53 *Times*, 14 Nov. 1849, 4.

54 Dorset County *Express*, 15 Jul. 1856, 4.

55 Supplement to the Dorset County *Chronicle*, 31 Jul. 1856, 4.

56 Dorchester County *Express*, 29 Jul. 1856, 4.

57 Lady Hester Pinney, *Thomas Hardy and the Birdsmoorgate Murder 1856*, 5.

58 Dorset County *Express*, 12 Aug. 1856, 4.

59 Pinney, *Thomas Hardy* ..., 6.

60 *Times*, 13 Aug. 1856, 7, letter from H.N. Cox.

61 Ibid., 16 Aug. 1856, 9, letter from Frederick Mallett.

62 Ibid., 26 Feb. 1869, 10; 2 Mar. 1869, 11; 12 Mar. 1869, 11.

63 *Observer*, 21 Dec. 1884, 4.

64 Ibid., 4 Jan. 1885, 5.

65 *Echo*, 10 Jan. 1885, 3.

66 Public Record Office, HO144/38012.

67 Ibid., HO144/A38012.

68 *Times*, 4 Dec. 1890, 4.

69 *Pall Mall Gazette*, 27 Oct. 1890, 5.

70 Though Frank Hogg had been moving furniture all afternoon, an anonymous tipster had told the police that he was not at his home on the night of the murder, and another tipster told of hearing a milkman say that, early on the morning of 25 Oct., he saw Frank come out of the house where the murder was committed. Another man who signed his name but was afraid to give his address claimed to have seen a woman turn over a pram and hurry away from where Phoebe's body was found. 'I am ashamed to tell but

I was starving at the time & took the ring of the woman who was ded,' said the letter. The ring was never found. These clues, which were never publicized but were preserved by the Home Office (Public Record Office, Kew, HO144A52045), add up to his involvement.

71 *Echo*, 1 Nov. 1890, 3.

72 *Lloyd's*, 14 Dec. 1890, 4; 21 Dec. 1890, 4.

73 Ibid., 7 Dec., 4–5; 14 Dec., 4; 21 Dec., 4.

74 Elisabeth Bronfen, *Over Her Dead Body*, 219.

75 *World*, 10 Dec. 1890, 16.

76 'Have not betrayed.'

77 *Daily Telegraph*, 24 Dec. 1890, 2.

78 *Evening Standard*, 4 Dec. 1890, 5.

79 *Pall Mall Gazette*, 4 Dec. 1890, 2.

80 Michael Millgate, *Thomas Hardy: A Biography* (New York: Random House 1982), 347, notes that Hardy arrived in London the day of the verdict and mentioned having seen newspaper accounts everywhere.

81 Bronfen, *Over Her Dead Body*, 234.

82 *Daily Telegraph*, 5 Jul. 1856, 2; 26 Aug. 1856, 2.

83 *Times*, 27 Jul. 1869, 10.

84 Ibid., 6 Aug. 1869, 10.

85 Sir John Hall quotes Paget in *The Trial of Adelaide Bartlett*, 75. Both Kate Clarke, in *The Pimlico Murder: The Strange Case of Adelaide Bartlett* (London: Souvenir 1990), and Yseult Bridges, in *Poison and Adelaide Bartlett* (London: Hutchinson 1962), accuse Adelaide of murder. Clarke believes that she gave him a whiff of chloroform to make him drowsy, and then got him to toast the new year with a glass of chloroform mixed with brandy. This was the prosecution's contention at the trial. Bridges's theory is that she got Edwin to drink the chloroform (with brandy) by first hypnotizing him.

86 The use of chloroform had been given some publicity in Jul. 1885, when the crusading journalist W.T. Stead told in the *Pall Mall Gazette* how easy it had been to purchase a young girl from her mother for prostitution. He had been given a bottle of chloroform to use on a handkerchief for the child to dull the pain of defloration. In discussing it at the trial, the doctor said this method of staving off sexual advances would be familiar to readers of penny novels.

87 *Times*, 17 Apr. 1886, 6.

88 *Evening Standard*, 19 Apr. 1886, 5.

89 Gould Penn, *The Life of the Reverend George Dyson and His Strange Adventures with Mrs. Bartlett* (London: Williams & Co. 1886).

90 *Daily Telegraph*, 20 Apr. 1886, 7.

91 Clarke, *The Pimlico Murder*, 275, 279, 283.

92 The trial was edited by H.B. Irving in the Notable British Trials series, *The Trial of Mrs. Maybrick*. Two modern reconsiderations are 'Poison, Revolvers, and the Double Standard,' in Mary Hartman's *Victorian Murderesses*, and Bernard Ryan's *The Poisoned Life of Mrs. Maybrick.*

93 Letter from Auberon Herbert, quoted by Irving in *The Trial of Mrs. Maybrick*, 19.

94 *Times*, 8 Aug. 1889, 7.

95 *St. James' Gazette*, 8 Aug. 1889, 3.

96 *Evening News & Post*, 8 Aug. 1889, 3.

97 *Star*, 17 Aug. 1889, 2.

98 *Evening News & Post*, 12 Aug. 1889, 4.

99 *Star*, 14 Aug. 1889, 2.

100 Ibid., 17 Aug. 1889, 2.

101 Trevor L. Christie, *Etched in Arsenic* (London: Harrap 1969), 225, cited by Mary Hartman in *Victorian Murderesses*, 433.

102 Alexander MacDougall, *The Maybrick Case: A Treatise* (London: Balliere, Tindall and Cox 1891), 576.

103 Helen Densmore, *The Maybrick Case: English Criminal Law* (London: Swan Sonnenschein 1893), vi.

104 W.T. Stead, 'Ought Mrs. Maybrick to Be Tortured to Death?,' *Review of Reviews*, Oct. 1892, 396.

105 *British Medical Journal*, 29 Sep. 1877, 449.

106 *Lancet*, 29 Sep. 1877, 469.

107 *Medical Times*, 6 Oct. 1877, 392.

108 *Daily Telegraph*, 3 Oct. 1877, 3.

109 *South London Press*, 6 Oct. 1877, 7.

110 Rachel M. Short, 'Female Criminality, 1780–1830,' 193.

111 Carolyn Conley, *The Unwritten Law*, 58–9.

CHAPTER 5   Child Murder

1 Carolyn Conley, *The Unwritten Law*, 107.

2 Robyn Anderson, 'Criminal Violence in London,' 172, 180, 181.

3 G.K. Behlmer, *Child Abuse and Moral Reform*, 9.

4 Margaret L. Arnot, 'Gender in Focus,' 40.

5 *Weekly Times*, 26 Nov. 1848, 525.

6 *Times*, 18 Jan. 1849, 3, attributed to Clay by Behlmer in *Child Abuse and Moral Reform in England*, 124.

7 Stockport *Chronicle*, 6 Nov. 1840, 3.

8 Ibid., 23 Oct. 1840, 3.

9 *News of the World*, 6 Aug. 1846, 6.

10 Bury and Norwich *Post*, 10 Mar. 1813, 2.

11 The *Times* gave it two full columns on 10 Apr. 11.

12 Firth collection 17 (101), Bodleian Library.

13 *Times* letter, 19 Aug. 1856, 9; 23 Aug. 1856, 8.

14 *Annual Register* 1856, part 2, 92.

15 *Daily Telegraph*, 11 Apr. 1856, 3.

16 Roger Smith, *Trial by Medicine*, 154.

17 *Annual Register* 1856, part 2, 92.

18 *Times*, 13 Aug. 1856, 7.

19 *Times*, 19 Dec. 1899, 9.

20 Harding collection, Bodleian Library.

21 Lincoln, Rutland, and Stamford *Mercury*, 1 Aug. 1817, 4.

22 *Courier*, 30 Jul. 1817, 2.

23 The case is referred to in the Lincoln, Rutland, and Stamford *Mercury*, 9 Aug. 1844, 3.

24 *Lloyd's*, 5 Apr. 1868, 7.

25 *Times*, 13 Mar. 1868, 11.

26 According to the *Annual Register*, 1845, part 1, 29, the evidence portrayed Mrs Crosby as 'a woman of most dissolute character, passionate, and greatly addicted to drinking spiritous liquors, and taking laudanum in large quantities.'

27 *Times*, 6 Feb. 1845, 7.

28 Old Bailey Sessions Papers, fourth session, case 641, 47–8.

29 *Lloyd's*, 9 Jan. 1848, 12; *Weekly Chronicle*, 2 Jan. 1848, 1; *Observer*, 9 Jan. 1848, 6.

30 British Library, 1881.d.8./33.

31 Harding collection, Bodleian Library.

32 Her plea was recorded as 'not guilty, by order of Court,' according to Anon., *A Record of One under Sentence of Death* (London n.d.), a church-sponsored pamphlet published about a year after her death, 3.

33 Ibid., 4.

34 *Weekly Chronicle*, 13 Feb. 1848, 5.

35 *A Record ...*, 10.

36 *Daily Telegraph*, 11 Jun. 1874, 2.

37 *Echo*, 29 Jun. 1874, 6.

38 *Times*, 6 Apr. 1824, 6; *Morning Herald*, 5 Apr. 1824, 4.

39 Charles Hindley, *Curiosities of Street Literature*, 227.

40 Brighton *Herald*, 20 Jan. 1872, 3.

41 *Pall Mall Gazette*, 1 Jan. 1872, 4.

42 *Standard*, 16 Jan. 1872, 2; *Times*, 16 Jan. 1872, 11.

43 *Daily Telegraph*, 16 Jan. 1872, 2.

44 Hargrave Adam, *Woman and Crime* (London: T. Werner Lawrie 1912), 67.

45 *Daily News*, 24 Jan. 1872, 5; 17 Jan. 1872, 5.

46 Brighton *Herald*, 20 Jan. 1872, 3.

47 Ibid., 27 Jan. 1872, 3.

48 Reprinted in the *Times*, 29 Jan. 1872, 5.

49 For an overview of the history of psychiatry *vis à vis* the law, see Catherine Crawford, 'Medicine and the Law,' *Companion Encyclopedia of the History of Medicine*, vol. 2, ed. W.F. Bynum and Roy Porter (London: Routledge 1993), 1630–1.

50 *Spectator*, 27 Jan. 1872, 106.

51 Alfred Swaine Taylor, *Principle and Practice*, vol. 2, 1098.

52 The case of Constance Kent is well documented. Mary Hartman revisits the murder and concludes, unaccountably, that Kent was innocent. Bernard Taylor, in *Cruelly Murdered: Constance Kent and the Killing at Road Hill House* (London: Souvenir Press 1979; repr. Grafton Books 1989), dismisses this questionable theory as he describes in detail the complicated story of what must have happened and the motives behind it.

53 A Barrister-at-Law, *The Road Murder: Being a Complete Report and Analysis of the Various Examinations and Opinions of the Press of This Mysterious Tragedy* (London: n.p. 1860), 31.

54 Taylor, *Cruelly Murdered*, 346.

55 *Times*, 26 Apr. 1865, 9.

56 Ibid., 8; 27 Apr. 1865, 10–11; 6 May 1865, 9; 11 May 1865, 11.

57 Hindley, *Curiosities of Street Literature*, 159.

58 Taylor, *Principles and Practice*, vol. 2, 1099–1100.

59 *Morning Post*, 29 Apr. 1865, 4.

60 *Times*, 27 Apr. 1865, 4.

61 Taylor, *Cruelly Murdered*, 346.

62 See Martin Daly and Margo Wilson, *Homicide*, 65–6, for a discussion of the traditional role of plaintiff in homicide cases.

CHAPTER 6 Baby-Farming and Infanticide

1 Broadside on arrest of Ann and Mary Brinkworth for the murder of Ann's infant, British Library, 1880.c.20, vol. 1 (147).

2 I use the term 'infanticide' throughout in its general legal sense of murder of a child under one year.

3 York *Herald and County Advertiser*, 21 Mar. 1810, 2.

4 Referred to by John Scott in *The Fatal Consequences of Licentiousness: A Sermon* (Hull: J. Ferraby 1810), 4 n. 2.

5 York *Herald and County Advertiser*, 31 Mar. 1810, 2; Hull *Packet*, 27 Mar. 1810, 4.

6 Thomas Dikes, *The Tendency of Lewdness to Corrupt the Morals, and Destroy the Happiness of Society, Exposed ...: A Sermon* (Hull: J. Ferraby 1811), 13–14.

7 Martin Daly and Margo Wilson, *Homicide*, 66–7.

8 Derby *Mercury*, 27 Mar. 1822, 3. The *Observer* and the London *Courier* also carried the story.

9 *Star*, 28 Mar. 1827, 4; Lancaster *Gazette*, 31 Mar. 1827, 2; Bodleian Library broadside 2806.c.17 (356).

10 *Star*, 14 Apr. 1828, 3.

11 According to Patrick Wilson, *Murderess*, 74, she was the last woman hanged for the murder of a newborn. Two more women were hanged for the murder of a child under one year, Eliza Joyce in 1844 and Rebecca Smith in 1849, but these were serial killers.

12 J.S. Traile, Robert Christison, and James Syme, *Suggestions for the Medico-legal Examination of Dead Bodies* (Edinburgh: Alex Smellie 1839), 35.

13 *Star*, 26 Mar. 1805, 4; Courier, 25 Mar. 1805, 3; York *Herald and County Advertiser*, 23 Mar. 1805, 3.

14 The first three are in the John Johnson collection (Broadsides: Murders and Executions) at the Bodleian Library, the other two (1888.c.3) at the British Library.

15 British Library, 1880.c.20, vol. 2 (342).

16 Public Record Office, HO45/6955, 28 Nov. 1860.

17 See, for example, the case of Mary Aistrope, reported in the Hull *Packet* of 20 Mar. 1810, 4, in which the judge refused to convict, though the lungs were inflated.

18 See Lionel Rose, *The Massacre of the Innocents*, 71–8, and G.K. Behlmer, *Child Abuse and Moral Reform in England, 1870–1908*, 30–43 for a discussion of the law on infanticide.

19 'The Case of Amy Gregory,' *Spectator*, 6 Apr. 1895, 460.

20 Joel Peter Eigen, *Witnessing Insanity: Madness and Mad-Doctors in the English Court* (New Haven, CT: Yale University Press 1995), 142, 148.

21 *Globe*, 18 Aug. 1849, 6.

22 *Daily News*, 13 Aug. 1849, 6.

23 Devizes and Wiltshire *Gazette*, 23 Aug. 1849, 3; also in *Daily News*, 25 Aug. 1849, 7; *Standard*, 25 Aug. 1849, 3; and Bath *Chronicle*, 30 Aug. 1849, 4.

24 Devizes and Wiltshire *Gazette*, 5 Jul. 1849, 4.

25 Cited by Richard Altick, *Victorian Studies in Scarlet*, 286.

26 Margaret L. Arnot, 'Infant Death, Child Care and the State,' 280.

27 Roger Smith, *Trial by Medicine*, 154.

28 Martin J. Wiener, *Reconstructing the Criminal*, 269.

29 Carolyn Conley, *The Unwritten Law*, 110–11; 117.

30 'Infanticide,' *Saturday Review* 2/41 (9 Aug. 1856), 335–6.

31 Margaret L. Arnot, 'Gender in Focus,' 6.

32 *Annual Register*, 1847, 43–5.

33 *Times*, 2 Aug. 1878, 4.

34 *Star*, 28 Mar. 1895, 1.

35 *Spectator*, 6 Apr. 1895, 459–60.

36 *Pall Mall Gazette*, 10 Aug. 1865, 1.

37 Arnot, 'Infant Death, Child Care and the State,' 272–5; Behlmer, *Child Abuse ...*, 19.

38 Behlmer, *Child Abuse ...*, 33–7.

39 Ibid., 40; Arnot, 'Infant Death, Child Care and the State,' 301 n. 5.

40 'Judicial Statistics [1899],' *PP*, vol. 89, 35. The figures are for 1895–9.

41 Registrar-General's report on vital statistics of London, *Times*, 10 May 1872, 5.

42 *Times*, 29 Apr. 1862, 8, cited by Ann R. Higginbotham, '"Sin of the Age": Infanticide and Illegitimacy in Victorian London,' in *Victorian Scandals*, ed. K.O. Garrigan (Ohio: Ohio University Press 1972), 258.

43 Daly and Wilson, *Homicide*, 68.

44 George Moore, *Esther Waters* (London 1894; rep. Dent Everyman 1936), 136, 137, 143.

45 J. Brandon Curgenven, *On Baby-Farming and the Registration of Nurses* (London 1869), 6, 19.

46 See Lionel Rose, *Masscare of the Innocents*, 108–14, and Behlmer, *Child Abuse ...*, 39–41, on the limitations of the Infant Life Protection Act of 1872.

47 For a description of the cases of baby-farmers Jane Arnold of Wolverton and Mary and George Hayes of Swindon, see Rose, *Massacre of the Innocents*, 113 and 151–2.

48 Cambridge *Advertiser*, 15 Sep. 1847, 3.

49 *Weekly Chronicle*, 18 Sep. 1847, 1.

50 Reprinted in the *Times*, 18 Oct. 1847, 5.

51 Cambridge *Chronicle and Journal*, 16 Oct. 1847, 1.

52 *Daily News*, 12 Aug. 1865, 6.

53 Supplement to the *Western Times*, 21 Mar. 1865, 1.

54 *Western Times*, 4 Aug. 1865, 5.

55 'Execution of Mrs. Winsor,' British Library, X.200.318(5).

56 *Western Times*, 11 Aug., 5.

57 *Pall Mall Gazette*, 10 Aug. 1865, 1.

58 Ibid., 13 Oct. 1870, 1.

59 PRO, HO144/37156/77.

60 Arnot, 'Infant Death, Child Care and the State,' 284.

61 For a detailed descriptions of the campaign, see James Greenwood, 'Baby-Farming,' *The Seven Curses of London* (London 1869), and B.I. Diamond, 'A Precursor of the New Journalism: Frederick Greenwood of the *Pall Mall Gazette*,' *Papers for the Millions: The New Journalism in Britain, 1850s to 1914*, ed. Joel H. Wiener (Westport, CT: Greenwood 1988).

62 The term 'farmer' was used in 1849 by Dickens, among others, to describe Bartholomew Drouet of Tooting, to whom London workhouses had farmed out more than 1,500 pauper children, 155 of whom died in a cholera epidemic. See, for example, *Examiner*, 20 Jan. 1849, 33–4.

63 *Pall Mall Gazette*, 25 Sep. 1867, 1.

64 Ibid., 25 Sep. 1867, 1; 2 Oct. 1867, 1.

65 Ibid., 31 Jan. 1868, 5.

66 *British Medical Journal*, 22 Feb. 1868, 175.

67 Ibid., 8 Feb. 1868, 127.

68 Ibid., 28 Mar. 1868, 301.

69 Ibid., 29 Feb. 1868, 197.

70 Broadside reproduced in Leslie Shepherd, *The History of Street Literature*, 179.

71 Her sister was sentenced to eighteen months for taking money under false pretences.

72 *Pall Mall Gazette*, 13 Oct. 1870, 1.

73 *Daily News*, 12 Oct. 1870, 5.

74 *Times*, 12 Oct. 1870, 9.

75 Arnot, 'Infant Death, Child Care and the State,' 277–8.

76 *Times*, 12 Oct. 1870, 11.

77 *Illustrated Police News*, 15 Oct. 1870, 2.

78 *Pall Mall Gazette*, 13 Oct. 1870, 2.

79 *Observer*, 18 Jan. 1885, 4.

80 *British Medical Journal*, 2 Feb. 1885, 268.

81 *Sun*, 31 Oct. 1895, 2. My attention was drawn to this series by a mention in Rose, *Massacre of the Innocents*, 87.

82 *Sun*, 16 Dec. 1895, 3.

83 *Weekly Dispatch*, 7 Jun. 1896, 1.

84 Public Record Office, HO144/A57858B/20.

85 *Weekly Dispatch*, 21 Jun. 1896, 2.

86 Ibid., 7 Jun. 1896, 1.
87 *Illustrated Police Budget*, 30 May 1896, 8.
88 Berkshire *Chronicle*, 23 May 1896, 5.
89 Ibid., 25 Apr. 1896, 8.
90 *Weekly Dispatch*, 21 Jun., 1896, 2.
91 *Evening News*, 27 Apr. 1896, 3.
92 Reading *Observer*, 13 Jun. 1896, 8.
93 *Evening News*, 27 Apr. 1896, 3.
94 Ibid., 10 Jun. 1896, 2.
95 *Star*, 10 Jun. 1896, 2.
96 Jonathan Goodman, *Bloody Versicles: The Rhymes of Crime* (Kent, OH: Kent State University Press 1993), 108–9.
97 *Times*, 23 May 1896, 11.

CHAPTER 7   Murder of and by Servants

1 Select Committee on Police, P.P. 1816, vol. 5, 261–2, quoted by J.J. Tobias, *Crime and Industrial Society in the 19th Century* (London: Batsford 1967), 168.
2 *Observer*, 2 Apr. 1815, 4.
3 *Morning Chronicle*, 25 Mar. 1815, 3.
4 If, as V.A.C. Gatrell, *The Hanging Tree*, 509, maintains, Silvester was notorious for sexually harassing women who came to him to appeal for mercy, it is quite possible that he thought he had something to gain by harsh treatment of Fenning, and equally possible that such a remedy never occurred to her.
5 *Times*, 12 Apr. 1815, 3.
6 *Examiner*, 16 Apr. 1815, 255.
7 *Times*, 1 Aug. 1815, 3.
8 Ibid.
9 *Examiner*, 27 Aug. 1815, 557.
10 Ibid., 13 Aug. 1815, 524.
11 M.D. Hill, *Suggestions for the Repression of Crime* (London: John W. Parker and Son 1857).
12 C.J.S. Thompson, *Poison Mysteries in History, Romance and Crime* (London: Scientific Press 1923), 272; Edward Hancock, *William Habron's Doom of the Gallows!* (London 1879), 13.
13 'It is like the memorable case of Eliza Fenning,' said the *News of the World* (31 Mar. 1850, 3).
14 Letter to Walter Thornbury, 5 Oct. 1867.
15 *The Modern Newgate Calendar* (London 1868), 304, 306.

16 Edward Hancock, *William Habron's Doom of the Gallows! With the Official Lives and Exploits of Cheshire, Calcraft and Marwood, the Past and Present State Hangmen, and the Horrors of Newgate!* (London 1879), 13.

17 *The New Newgate Calendar* (London 1889), 779.

18 *St. James's Gazette*, 13 Aug. 1889, 5.

19 Ibid., 21 Aug. 1889, 5.

20 Theresa M. McBride, *The Domestic Revolution: The Modernization of Household Service in England and France 1820–1920* (New York: Holmes and Meier 1976), 51, 99.

21 See chapter 3, note 14.

22 *Times*, 20 Apr. 1820, 3.

23 *Star*, 20 Apr. 1820, 4.

24 British Library, 1880.c.20, vol. 2 (341).

25 Disordered menstruation is cited as the cause of Brixey's insanity by Alfred Swaine Taylor in *Principles and Practice*, vol. 2, 1109.

26 For an analysis of this case, see Roger Smith, *Trial by Medicine*, 155–7.

27 Ibid., 155.

28 *Times*, 17 May 1845, 8.

29 Bristol *Mirror and Advertiser*, 21 Apr. 1849, 8.

30 *Weekly Chronicle*, 11 Mar. 1849, 5.

31 Bristol *Mirror and General Advertiser*, 7 Apr. 1849, 6.

32 *Observer*, 9 Apr. 1849, 2.

33 Bristol *Gazette*, 26 Apr. 1849, 5.

34 Ibid.

35 *Saturday Review*, 22 Jun. 1872, 785.

36 *Echo*, 10 Apr. 1872, 1.

37 Reprinted in the *Times*, 12 Apr. 1872, 8.

38 *Echo*, 10 Apr. 1872, 1.

39 *Illustrated Police News*, 20 Apr. 1872, 2.

40 *Times*, 19 Apr. 1872, 10.

41 *Daily Telegraph*, 2 May 1872, 4.

42 Firth 17 (90), Bodleian Library.

43 *Daily Telegraph*, 3 May 1872, 5.

44 *Times*, 2 May 1872, 10.

45 *Daily News*, 15 Jun. 1872, 5.

46 *Daily Telegraph*, 15 Jun. 1872, 5.

47 *Penny Illustrated Paper*, 27 Apr. 1872, 263.

48 *Times*, 15 Jun. 1872, 9.

49 Cf. Constance Kent (p. 143) and Charlotte Winsor (p. 166).

50 *Echo*, 15 Jun. 1872, 1.

51 *Saturday Review*, 22 Jun. 1872, 784–5.

52 *Spectator*, 12 Jul. 1879, 878.

53 *Daily Telegraph*, 30 Jul. 1879, 5.

54 *Illustrated Police News*, 26 Jul. 1879, 4; 2 Aug. 1879, 1.

55 Madame Tussaud's archives record her removal in 1932, but she is listed in a souvenir pamphlet of 1945.

56 McBride, *The Domestic Revolution*, 75, 99.

57 *Morning Post*, 11 Apr. 1829, 1; *Star*, 12 Apr. 1829, 4.

58 *Times*, 13 Apr. 1829, 5; *Observer*, 19 Apr. 1829, 4.

59 *Calcraft's Life and Recollections* (London 1871), 34.

60 *Star*, 13 Apr. 1829, 3.

61 *Times*, 14 Apr. 1829, 4.

62 British Library, 1889.d.3, vol. 1 (38).

63 *Star*, 13 Apr. 1829, 3.

64 *Morning Herald*, 14 Apr. 1829, 4.

65 *Times*, 14 Apr. 1829, 3.

66 *Daily News*, 5 Feb. 1850, 4; *Times*, 2 Feb. 1850, 8.

67 *Weekly Times*, 31 Mar. 1850, 264.

68 *Evening Sun*, 6 Feb. 1861, 2.

69 Firth 17 (105), Bodleian Library.

70 *Morning Advertiser*, 17 Dec. 1850, 2.

71 Firth 17 (106), Bodleian Library.

72 *Weekly Times*, 5 Jan. 1851, 3.

73 *Morning Advertiser*, 9 Dec. 1850, 1.

74 *Weekly Chronicle*, 6 Feb. 1851, 5.

75 Henry Mayhew, *London Labour and the London Poor*, vol. 1, 225–6.

76 *Lloyd's*, 9 Apr. 1865, 6.

CHAPTER 8   Murder of the Elderly

1 Vol. 2, 253–5.

2 *Extraordinary Life and Character of Mary Bateman, the Yorkshire Witch* ... (Leeds: John Davies 1809), 56.

3 *Morning Herald*, 28 Mar. 1809, 4.

4 York *Herald and Country Advertiser*, 25 Mar. 1809, 3.

5 *Extraordinary Life ...*, 24.

6 Firth 17 (265), Bodleian Library.

7 *Times*, 9 Mar. 1829, 6.

8 The latter two broadsides are in the Harding collection, Bodleian Library.

9 *Calcraft's Life and Recollections* (London 1871), 144–50.

10 *The History of the London Burkers* (London: T. Kelly 1832), 347.

11 *Courier*, 9 Jan. 1832, 3.

12 Harding collection, Bodleian Library.

13 *Times*, 4 Nov. 1831, 3.

14 *Courier*, 9 Jan. 1832, 3.

15 *Times*, 10 Jan. 1832, 5.

16 Bristol *Gazette*, 16 Apr. 1835, 1.

17 Ibid., 3.

18 *Times*, 23 Apr. 1835, 5; 13 Apr. 1835, 5; 15 Apr. 1835, 6.

19 *Falmouth Packet and Cornish Herald*, 2 May 1835, 143.

20 There are ten different Burdock broadsides in the British Library, 1880.c.12, and three in 1880.c.20, vol. 2 (366, 367, 368).

21 *Calcraft's Life and Recollections*, 181–9.

22 *Times*, 5 Dec. 1845, 5.

23 'Capital Punishment,' *Miscellaneous Papers* (London: Chapman and Hall 1908), 30. In the same series Dickens insisted that the possibility of mistake and the impossibility of reparation were powerful arguments against capital punishment. Even if there were only one example, the case of Eliza Fenning, he said, that would be enough (45).

24 *Times*, 29 Mar. 1850, 4.

25 *Daily News*, 2 Aug. 1849, 4.

26 *Times*, 28 Mar. 1850, 4.

27 *Daily News*, 29 Dec. 1863, 6.

28 Charles Hindley, *Curiosities of Street Literature*, 223.

29 *Times*, 16 Dec. 1882, 9.

30 *Daily Telegraph*, 16 Dec. 1882, 5.

CHAPTER 9   The Image of the Murderess

1 Gerald Falk, e.g., in *Murder: An Analysis of Its Forms, Conditions, and Causes* (Jefferson, NC, and London: McFarland 1990), 91, says that murder is a power trip – an effort by the killer to compensate for the feeling of powerlessness. Georgina Lloyd, in *One Was Not Enough: True Stories of Multiple Murderers* (London: Robert Hale 1986), 8, says the desire for power over others is an essential part of the multiple-murder syndrome.

2 Terence Morris and Louis Blom-Cooper, *A Calendar of Murder*, 285–6.

3 Mary Carpenter, *Juvenile Delinquents: Their Condition and Treatment* (London: W.F.G. Cash 1853), 86.

4 See an article on the causes of crime, reprinted from *Law Magazine* (*Daily News*, 2 Jul. 1849, 2), arguing that mechanical learning was actually increasing crime.

5 Service and dress-making, usually done at home, were the two largest
  categories of employment, say J.M. Golby and A.W. Purdue in *The Civilization of the Crowd*, 139. 'Only a small minority of women have ever worked in
  factories and a disproportionate amount of attention has been directed
  towards them by historians.' They point out that there was a smaller
  proportion of women in paid employment in the nineteenth century than
  in the eighteenth.

6 Mary Wollstonecraft, *A Vindication of the Rights of Women* (London:
  J. Johnson 1792), 10.

7 Martin Daly and Margo Wilson, *Homicide*, 297.

8 Patrick Wilson, *Murderess*, 45.

9 Florence Maybrick, *Mrs. Maybrick's Own Story*, 122, 75.

10 Russell P. Dobash, R. Emerson Dobash, and Sue Gutteridge, *The Imprisonment of Women*, 61.

11 Ian A. Bell, *Literature and Crime in Augustan England* (London: Routledge
   1991), 99. Bell is here talking about the Augustan period (*ca.* 1660–1760),
   but the tradition was carried over into the nineteenth century.

12 Lucia Zedner, in *Women, Crime, and Custody in Victorian England*, 38,
   calculates that, in the late 1850s and early 1860s, 'women formed a striking
   40 per cent of all those tried for murder.'

13 Cesare Lombroso, *La Femme criminelle et la Prostituée* (trans. 1896), quoted by
   Joelle Guillais in *Crimes of Passion* (New York: Routledge 1991), 186.

14 Leon Radzinowicz, *Ideology and Crime*, 52–3.

15 Martin J. Wiener, *Reconstructing the Criminal*, 328.

16 All are in the HO144 series: Rhodes and Staunton, 26/64091C; Taylor,
   108/A23081; Winsor, 37156/77; Gibbons, 146/A38012; Gregory, 263/
   A56842; Chard Williams, 280/A61654.

17 'Judicial Statistics [1893],' *PP*, vol. 108, 86.

18 William Ferrero, 'Suicide among Women,' *New Review* 11/67 (Dec. 1894),
   646.

19 V.A.C. Gatrell, 'The Decline of Theft and Violence in Victorian and
   Edwardian England,' in *Crime and the Law: The Social History of Crime in
   Western Europe since 1500*, ed. Gatrell et al. (London: Europa 1980), 255.

20 *Weekly Chronicle*, 25 Aug. 1849, 4.

21 Woolf, 'Professions for Women,' *Killing the Angel in the House: Seven Essays*
   (Harmondsworth: Penguin 1995), 3.

CHAPTER 10   The Feminine Perspective

1 Supplement to the *Observer*, 28 and 29 Oct. 1849, 1.

2 Liverpool *Daily Post*, 12 Aug. 1889, 4.

3 Mary Hartman, *Victorian Murderesses*, 336.

4 Florence Maybrick, *Mrs. Maybrick's Own Story*, 57.

5 *Daily News*, 19 Apr. 1886, 5.

6 *Times*, 19 Apr. 1886, 4.

7 *Pall Mall Gazette*, 12 Apr. 1886, 8.

8 *Evening News*, 13 Apr. 1886, 2.

9 *Times*, 19 Apr. 1886, 9.

10 The Contagious Diseases Act was repealed in Apr. 1886.

11 See Lucia Zedner, *Women, Crime, and Custody in Victorian England*, 74.

12 John Glendening, 'The Bartlett Trial Revisited,' 333.

13 Sir John Hall, *Trial of Adelaide Bartlett*, 342.

14 In the fall of 1889, according to Martin Friedland, *The Trials of Israel Lipski* (London: Macmillan 1984), 188, Stephen was ordered to rest for three months, and, in 1890, when he returned to the bench, the press commented on his inability to function adequately. He was later committed to a lunatic asylum.

15 *Evening News & Post*, 6 Jun. 1889, 4.

16 H.B. Irving, *Trial of Mrs. Maybrick*, 110.

17 Quoted by Mary Hartman, *Victorian Murderesses*, 337.

18 *Reynolds's*, 18 Aug. 1889, 8.

19 *Star*, 9 Aug. 1889, 1.

20 Indeed, James was reported by the *Star* (8 Aug. 1889, 2) to be ready to do all he could to have the verdict set aside.

21 *Lloyd's*, 4 Aug. 1889, 3.

22 *Star*, 8 Aug. 1889, 1.

23 *Daily News*, 8 Aug. 1889, 3.

24 See my article, 'She Loves Me, She Loves Me Not: Trends in the Victorian Marriage Market,' *Journal of Communication Inquiry* 18/1 (Winter 1994), 80-94.

25 *Star*, 9 Aug. 1889, 1.

26 *Spectator*, 24 Aug. 1889, quoted by Hartman in *Victorian Murderesses*, 304 n. 131.

27 Quoted in the *St. James's Gazette*, 9 Aug. 1889, 8.

28 William Henderson, ed., *Victorian Street Ballads*, 49.

29 Quoted in the *Pall Mall Gazette*, 8 Aug. 1889, 5.

30 Quoted in ibid.

31 *Truth*, 15 Aug. 1889, 295.

32 *Globe*, 12 Aug. 1889, 1.

33 *St. James's Gazette*, 9 Aug. 1889, 5.

34 *Times*, 23 Aug. 1889, 7. The *Times* believed this consideration to be irrelevant; if there existed no doubt of her guilt, it would urge that she be hanged; but 'suspicion falls short of certainty.'

35 Supplement to *St. Stephen's Review*, 10 Aug. 1889, interleaf 26–7.

36 *Times*, 4 Dec. 1890, 4.

37 *News of the World*, 7 Dec. 1890, 4.

38 *Pall Mall Gazette*, 4 Dec. 1890, 2.

39 *Evening News*, 4 Nov. 1890, 2.

40 *Echo*, 4 Dec. 1890, p. 2.

41 Michael Millgate, *Thomas Hardy: A Biography* (New York: Random House 1982), 347.

42 *Evening News*, 4 Nov. 1890, 2.

43 Ibid., 3 Dec. 1890, 3.

44 *Illustrated Police News*, 15 Nov. 1890, 2.

45 *Evening News and Post*, 27 Oct. 1890, 3.

46 Ibid., 18 Nov. 1890, 3.

47 Ibid., 11 Nov. 1890, 3.

48 Ibid.

CHAPTER 11   The Body of the Murderess

1 Bath *Express*, 29 Apr. 1865, quote by Mary Hartman in *Victorian Murderesses*, 168.

2 Elizabeth Windschuttle, 'Women, Crime and Punishment,' 33.

3 John Binney and Henry Mayhew, *The Criminal Prisons of London and Scenes of Prison Life* (London: Griffin, Bonn 1862), 466, cited in Laura Inman's unpublished paper 'Gender and Victorian Female Crime: The Case of Maria Manning,' presented at the Victorian Mystery Conference of the Dickens Project, University of California at Santa Cruz, August 1993.

4 Helena Michie, *The Flesh Made Word*, 86–7.

5 Rachel M. Short, 'Female Criminality, 1780–1830,' 143.

6 *Standard*, 16 Jan. 1872, 2.

7 *Daily Telegraph*, 16 Jan. 1872, 5.

8 *Times*, 18 Jan. 1872, 5.

9 Elisabeth Bronfen, *Over Her Dead Body*, 182.

10 Ibid., 185.

11 *Daily Telegraph*, 17 Jan. 1872, 2.

12 Mary Poovey, *Uneven Developments: The Ideological Work of Gender in Mid-Victorian England* (Chicago: University of Chicago Press 1988), 25.

13 See Lyn Pykett, *The Improper Feminine: The Women's Sensation Novel and the New Woman Writing* (London: Routledge 1992), 209 and *passim*.

14 Somerset County *Herald*, 26 Apr. 1845, 3.

15 Bristol *Mirror*, 18 Apr. 1835, 3.

16 I am indebted to Laura Inman for a close analysis of the discourse surrounding the trial and execution.

17 *Observer*, 26 Aug. 1849, 5.

18 *Morning Chronicle*, 14 Nov. 1849, 4.

19 *Times*, 14 Nov. 1849, 5.

20 *Morning Chronicle*, 14 Nov. 1849, 4.

21 Ibid.

22 *News of the World*, 2 Sep. 1849, 4.

23 *Daily Herald*, 25 Aug. 1849, 5.

24 Globe, 5 Sep. 1849, 4.

25 *Morning Post*, 26 Oct. 1849, 5.

26 Supplement to the *Observer*, 28 and 29 Oct. 1849, 1, 2.

27 Oldham *Chronicle*, 19 Mar. 1887, 3.

28 Lucia Zedner, *Women, Crime, and Custody in Victorian England*, 86–7, cites Henry Maudsley's *Body and Mind* (1870), which provides a catalogue of mental illnesses to which women were vulnerable on account of their reproductive function.

29 See J.E.D. Esquirol, *Mental Maladies: A Treatise on Insanity*, translated into English in 1845.

30 *Lancet*, 27 Jan. 1872, 124.

31 *Times*, 27 Apr. 1865, 11.

CHAPTER 12   The Murder of the Murderess

1 Randall McGowen, 'The Body and Punishment,' *Journal of Modern History* 59/4 (1987), 561, cited by Thomas Laqueur in 'Crowds, Carnival and the State in English Executions, 1604–1868,' 306.

2 Laqueur, 'Crowds, Carnival and the State,' 308–9.

3 In discussing this linkage, Elisabeth Bronfen, *Over Her Dead Body*, 183, cites Palladas and Merimee; Browning's 'Porphyria's Lover' is another example of the corpse as an object of desire.

4 *Globe*, 15 Sep. 1849, 2.

5 V.A.C. Gatrell, *The Hanging Tree*, 243.

6 Elisabeth Bronfen, *Over Her Dead Body*, 190.

7 I have come upon two reports in broadsides of mistaken executions, though, as these are undated, I have been unable to authenticate them.

The *Times* of 9 Mar. 1827, 4, announces that Daniel Leany, executed the previous summer for murder, had been cleared as a result of the efforts of a surgeon who happened to be in court when what he regarded as inadequate evidence of arsenic poisoning was being given.

8 A report of the trial of Betsey McMullan in the Liverpool *Mercury* of 25 Aug. 1856, 2, quotes the defence counsel, Sergeant Wilkins, who was based in London, as saying he has 'given to this case all the consideration of which I am capable during the last night ...'

9 Florence Maybrick's lawyer had to negotiate permission from the judge for her to make the fatal statement in which she admitted having committed adultery.

10 For a full discussion of the prerogative of mercy, see Roger Chadwick, *Bureaucratic Mercy*, 9–25.

11 Patrick Wilson, *Murderess*, 182.

12 James C. Oldham, 'On Pleading the Belly: A History of the Jury of Matrons,' *Criminal Justice History* 6 (1985), 16.

13 An undated broadside on the execution of Augusta Thornton, Firth 17 (201), Bodleian Library, says that she was 'allowed to live the usual time, one month after her child was born.'

14 See the broadside 'Horrid Murder,' in the Harding collection at the Bodleian library, which describes an 1826 hanging in which the prisoner, Elizabeth Miller, appears at the scaffold 'dressed all in white, with a child suckling at her breast, which was taken from her by the executioner, and her melancholy cries ... [were] shocking for the surrounding multitude to hear.'

15 *Daily Telegraph*, 21 Oct. 1862, 3.

16 Martin J. Wiener, *Reconstructing the Criminal*, 96. While his comments are on the execution of Courvoisier (1840) as described by Thackeray, they apply generally to executions at this time.

17 Laqueur, 'Crowds, Carnival and the State,' 347.

18 Gatrell, *The Hanging Tree*, 264.

19 Lucia Zedner, *Women, Crime, and Custody in Victorian England*, 33.

20 *Morning Chronicle*, 14 Nov. 1849, 5.

21 'Lying Awake at Night,' *Household Words*, 30 Oct. 1852 (no. 136), 145.

22 *Morning Advertiser*, 14 Nov. 1849, 3.

23 *Punch* 17 (Jul.–Dec. 1849), 210.

24 *Times*, 17 Nov. 1849, 4.

25 Ibid., 14 Nov. 1849, 5.

26 Broadsides: Murders and Executions, John Johnson collection, Bodleian Library, italics added.

27 Mary Hartman, *Victorian Murderesses*, 168.

28 *A Voice from the Gaol*, 1–3, italics added.

29 Ibid.

30 Bury and Norwich *Post*, 21 Apr. 1847, 2.

31 Bristol *Mirror*, 21 Apr. 1849, 8.

32 Dorset County *Express*, 12 Aug. 1856, 4, italics added.

33 Letter to Lady Pinney, 20 Jan. 1926. In Hardy, *Selected Letters*, ed. Michael Millgate (Oxford: The Clarendon Press 1990), 404.

34 Dorset County *Express and Agricultural Gazette*, 12 Aug. 1856, 4.

35 Charles Hindley, *Curiosities of Street Literature*, 215.

36 Liverpool *Daily Post*, 4 Mar. 1884, 3.

37 Oldham *Chronicle*, 19 Mar. 1887, 3.

38 Bristol *Mirror*, 18 Apr. 1835, 3.

39 Bath *Chronicle*, 16 Aug. 1849, 2.

40 *Illustrated Police News*, 29 Mar. 1873, 1.

41 Ibid., 3 Jan. 1891, 1.

42 Ibid., 31 Aug. 1889, 1.

43 *Daily Telegraph*, 24 Dec. 1890, 2.

44 *Evening News and Post*, 23 Dec. 1890, 3.

45 *Lloyd's*, 28 Dec. 1890, 3.

Select Bibliography

Altick, Richard. *Deadly Encounters: Two Victorian Sensations.* Philadelphia: University of Pennsylvania Press 1986.
– *Victorian Studies in Scarlet.* New York: Norton 1970.
Anderson, Robyn. 'Criminal Violence in London, 1856–1875.' PhD thesis, University of Toronto, 1990.
Appleton, Arthur. *Mary Ann Cotton: Her Story and Trial.* London: Michael Joseph 1973.
Arnot, Margaret L. 'Gender in Focus: Infanticide in England, 1840–1880.' PhD thesis, University of Essex, 1994.
– 'Infant Death, Child Care and the State: The Baby-Farming Scandal and the First Infant Life Protection Legislation of 1872.' *Continuity and Change* 9/2 (1994), 271–311.
Beattie, John. 'The Criminality of Women in Eighteenth-Century England.' *Journal of Social History* 8 (Summer 1975), 80–116.
Behlmer, G.K. *Child Abuse and Moral Reform in England, 1870–1908.* Stanford, CA: Stanford University Press 1982.
Boyle, Thomas. *Black Swine in the Sewers of Hampstead: Beneath the Surface of Victorian Sensationalism.* New York: Viking 1989.
Bronfen, Elisabeth. *Over Her Dead Body: Death, Femininity, and the Aesthetic.* New York: Routledge 1992.
Butler, Josephine. *Woman's Work and Woman's Culture.* London: Macmillan 1869.
Carlen, Pat, and Anne Worrall. *Gender, Crime and Justice.* Milton Keynes: Open University Press 1987.
Chadwick, Roger. *Bureaucratic Mercy: The Home Office and the Treatment of Capital Cases in Victorian Britain.* New York: Garland, Modern European History Series, 1992.
Chesney, Kellow. *The Victorian Underworld.* New York: Schocken 1972.

Clay, John. *Burial Clubs and Infanticide in England: A Letter to W. Brown, Esq., M.P.* Preston 1854.

Conley, Carolyn. *The Unwritten Law: Criminal Justice in Victorian Kent.* Oxford: Oxford University Press 1991.

Daly, Martin, and Margo Wilson. *Homicide.* New York: Aldine de Gruyter 1988.

Davidoff, Leonore, and Catherine Hall. *Family Fortunes: Men and Women of the English Middle Class, 1780–1850.* London: Hutchinson 1987.

Dobash, Russell, R. Emerson Dobash, and Sue Gutteridge. *The Imprisonment of Women.* Oxford: Basil Blackwell 1986.

Ellis, Havelock. *The Criminal.* London: Walter Scott 1890.

Emmerichs, Mary Beth Wasserlein. 'Trials of Women for Homicide in Nineteenth-Century England.' *Women & Criminal Justice* 5/1 (1993), 99–109.

Emsley, Clive. *Crime and Society in England, 1750–1900.* London and New York: Longman 1987.

Farrell, Michael. *Poisons and Poisoners: An Encyclopedia of Homicidal Poisonings.* London: Robert Hale 1992.

Gatrell, V.A.C. *The Hanging Tree: Execution and the English People, 1770–1868.* Oxford: Oxford University Press 1994.

Glendening, John. 'The Bartlett Trial Revisited: Delicacy, Judicial Bias, and New Women.' *Dalhousie Review* 70/3 (Fall 1990), 309–37.

Golby, J.M., and A.W. Purdue. *The Civilization of the Crowd: Popular Culture in England, 1750–1900.* London: Batsford 1984.

Guy, William A. 'On the Executions for Murder that Have Taken Place in England and Wales during the Last Seventy Years.' *Journal of the Royal Statistical Society* 38 (1875), 463–86.

Hall, Sir John. *Trial of Adelaide Bartlett.* Edinburgh: William Hodge 1927.

Harris, Ruth. *Murders and Madness: Medicine, Law, and Society in the fin de siècle.* Oxford: The Clarendon Press 1989; repr. 1991.

Hartman, Mary. *Victorian Murderesses: A True Story of Thirteen Respectable French and English Women Accused of Unspeakable Crimes.* New York: Schocken 1977.

Hay, Douglas, E.P. Thompson, and Peter Linebaugh, eds. *Albion's Fatal Tree: Crime and Society in Eighteenth-Century England.* New York: Pantheon 1975.

Heidensohn, Frances. *Women and Crime.* London: Macmillan 1985.

Henderson, William, ed. *Victorian Street Ballads: A Selection of Popular Ballads Sold in the Street in the Nineteenth Century.* London: Country Life 1937.

Hindley, Charles. *Curiosities of Street Literature.* London, 1871; repr. Seven Dials Press 1969.

Hoyle, William. *Crime in England and Wales: An Historical and Critical Retrospect.* London: Effingham, Wilson 1876.

Irving, H.B. *Trial of Mrs. Maybrick.* London: Hodge 1912.

James, Louis, ed. *English Popular Literature, 1819–1851.* New York: Columbia University Press 1976.

Jones, Ann. *Women Who Kill.* New York: Fawcett 1981.

Laqueur, Thomas W. 'Crowds, Carnival and the State in English Executions, 1604–1868. In *The First Modern Society: Essays in Honour of Lawrence Stone,* ed. A.L. Beier, David Annadine, and James M. Rosenheim, 305–55. Cambridge: Cambridge University Press 1989.

Lee, Alan J. *The Origins of the Popular Press in England.* London: Croom Helm 1976.

Lombroso, Cesare. *The Criminal.* Trans. Havelock Ellis. London 1890.

– *Man and Woman: A Study of Secondary and Tertiary Sexual Characteristics.* Trans. Havelock Ellis. London 1894; repr. Heinemann, 1934.

Lombroso, Cesare, and William Ferrero. *The Female Offender.* London: Fisher Unwin 1895.

Lustgarden, Edgar. 'Victorian Trumpets.' In *Defender's Triumph,* 9–80. London: Wingate 1951.

Mahon, Paul Augustine Olivier. *An Essay on the Signs of Murder in Newborn Children.* Lancaster 1813.

Maybrick, Florence. *Mrs. Maybrick's Own Story: My Fifteen Lost Years.* New York: Funk & Wagnalls 1905.

Mayhew, Henry. *London Labour and the London Poor,* 4 vols. London 1862; repr., with a new introduction by John D. Rosenberg, New York: Dover 1968.

Michie, Helena. *The Flesh Made Word: Female Figures and Women's Bodies.* Oxford: Oxford University Press 1987.

Morris, Alison. *Women, Crime and Criminal Justice.* Oxford: Basil Blackwell 1987.

Morris, Alison, and Loraine Gelsthorpe, eds. *Women and Crime.* Cambridge: Cropwood Conference Series 1981.

Morris, Terence, and Louis Blom-Cooper. *A Calendar of Murder: Criminal Homicide in England since 1957.* London: Michael Joseph 1964.

Morrison, William D. *Crime and Its Causes.* London: Sonnenschein 1891.

Moscuccii, Ornella. *The Science of Woman.* Cambridge: Cambridge University Press 1990.

Naffine, Ngaire. *Female Crime: The Construction of Women in Criminology.* Sydney: Allen & Unwin 1987.

O'Donnell, Eliot, ed. *Trial of Kate Webster.* Edinburgh: Hodge 1925.

Oldham, James C. 'On Pleading the Belly: A History of the Jury of Matrons.' *Criminal Justice History* 6 (1985), 1–64.

Pelham, Camden. *The Chronicles of Crime, or the New Newgate Calendar.* 2 vols. London, 1886; repr. Croom Helm 1987.

Pinney, Lady Hester. *Thomas Hardy and the Birdsmoorgate Murder 1856.* Monographs of the Life, Times and Works of Thomas Hardy, ed. J. Stevens Cox. Beaminster, Dorset: Toucan 1966.

Plowden, Alison. *The Case of Eliza Armstrong: 'A Child of 13 Bought for £5.'* London: British Broadcasting Corporation 1974.

Pollak, Otto. *The Criminality of Women.* Philadelphia: University of Pennsylvania Press 1950.

Poovey, Mary. *Uneven Developments: The Ideological Work of Gender in Mid-Victorian England.* Chicago: University of Chicago Press 1988.

Pykett, Lyn. *The 'Improper' Feminine: The Women's Sensation Novel and the New Woman Writing.* London: Routledge 1992.

Radzinowicz, Leon. *Ideology and Crime.* London: Heinemann 1966.

Rose, Lionel. *Massacre of the Innocents: Infanticide in Great Britain, 1830–1939.* London: Routledge & Kegan Paul 1986.

Rude, George. *Criminal and Victim: Crime and Society in Early Nineteenth-Century England.* Oxford: Oxford University Press 1985.

Russett, Cynthia Eagle. *Sexual Science: The Victorian Construction of Womanhood.* Cambridge, MA: Harvard University Press 1990.

Ryan, Bernard. *The Poisoned Life of Mrs. Maybrick.* London: Kimber 1977; repr. 1989.

Shepherd, Leslie. *The History of Street Literature.* Newton Abbot, Devon: David & Charles 1973.

Short, Rachel M. 'Female Criminality, 1780–1830.' MLitt thesis, Oxford University, 1989.

Smart, Carol. *Women, Crime and Criminology: A Feminist Critique.* London: Routledge & Kegan Paul 1977.

Smart, Carol, and B. Smart, eds. *Women, Sexuality, and Social Control.* London: Routledge & Kegan Paul 1978.

Smith, Roger. *Trial by Medicine: Insanity and Responsibility in Victorian Trials.* Edinburgh: University of Edinburgh Press 1981.

Taylor, Alfred Swaine. *The Principles and Practice of Medical Jurisprudence,* 2 vols. London 1865.

Thomas, W.T. *The Unadjusted Girl: With Cases and Standpoint for Behavior Analysis.* New York 1923; repr. Harper & Row 1967.

Tobias, J.J. *Nineteenth-Century Crime in England: Prevention and Punishment.* New York: Barnes & Noble 1972.

Tomes, Nancy. 'A "Torrent of Abuse": Crimes of Violence between Working-Class Men and Women in London, 1840–75,' *Journal of Social History* 11 (1978), 328–45.

Trodd, Anthea. *Domestic Crime in the Victorian Novel.* New York: St Martin's 1989.

Vicinus, Martha, ed. *Suffer and Be Still: Women in the Victorian Age.* Bloomington: Indiana University Press 1973.

Walker, Nigel. *Crime and Insanity in England, vol. 1: The Historical Perspective.* Edinburgh: University of Edinburgh Press 1968.

Walkowitz, Judith. *Prostitution and Victorian Society: Women, Class and the State.* Cambridge: Cambridge University Press 1979.

Wiener, Martin J. *Reconstructing the Criminal: Culture, Law, and Policy in England, 1830–1914.* Cambridge: Cambridge University Press 1990.

Wilson, Patrick. *Murderess: A Study of Women Executed in Britain since 1843.* London: Michael Joseph 1971.

Windschuttle, Elizabeth. 'Women, Crime and Punishment.' In *Women and Crime,* ed. S.K. Mukherjee and J.A. Scutt, 31–50. Sydney: Australian Institute of Crime 1981.

Zedner, Lucia. *Women, Crime, and Custody in Victorian England.* Oxford: The Clarendon Press 1991.

Index

abuse: of children, 133; of the
elderly, 207–8, 210, 217–18; of
servants, 199–206; spousal, 85–9
acid, sulphuric, 82
activism, female, 237–8
Adam Bede, 31, 146
Adler, Freda, 270
Advertiser, 36, 104
age of murderesses, 10–11
aggression: against the elderly, 208;
against men, 87
aggression theory, 225–6
Ainsworth, Harrison, 29
Alden, Martha, 89–90, 275
Altick, Richard, 25, 29–30
Anderson, Robyn, 6–7, 9, 16, 123
'angel in the house', 233, 273
Annual Register, 12, 60, 70, 73, 129,
154
antimony, 113
appeal, 260
Armadale, 30, 40
Arnold, Ann, 127–8, 275
Arnold, Matthew, 5
Arnot, Margaret L., 39, 124, 153,
156, 166, 171

arsenic, 53–64, 74–5, 77–9, 93–7,
99–101, 114, 118, 126, 132, 140,
151, 161, 182–4, 186–7, 209, 214,
215, 218, 228, 229; regulation of,
67–8; signs of, 52; tests for, 52, 84,
114
Australia, 143
Aytry, Ann. *See* Heytrey, Ann

baby-farming, 49, 145, 157–80;
advertising for, 167–8; clientele,
159; scandals, 159–60
Baker, Ann, 149
Ball, Mary, 96, 269
ballads, 32, 51, 56, 63, 65–6, 71, 75,
91–2, 101, 112, 128, 134–5, 149,
163–4, 170, 178–9, 194–5, 203–4,
210, 213, 215, 219, 242, 267
Barber, Ann, 93–4, 275
Barnes, Ann, 160–1
Barnes, Catherine, 160, 172
Barnes, John, 172
Barry, Ann, 133
Bartlett, Adelaide, 29, 30, 115–17,
122, 225, 235–8, 244, 270, 277
Bateman, Mary, 208–10, 220, 275